Dear Js,
Although There was no comparison between our towns; the fastest smells & sentiments must have been similar... & finally, the same dichotomies...
You too, once (or twice) "tasted" Colesberg.
Warm wishes
Evan

TIME, Gentlemen!

Evan Kaplan

First published in 2011 by

Osborne Porter Literary Services,

P.O. Box 1957 Westville 3630 South Africa

info@osborne-porter.com

www.osborne-porter.com

ISBN: 978-0-9869919-3-6

Typesetting and Cover Design: Osborne Porter Literary Services

the first spoon of batter into a pan.

Snow dusted the lawn and for some reason or other, I thought about the miracle of chromosomes. Those diagrammatically simple but genetically complicated spirals of invisible life, in which my siblings and I, our children and grandchildren—and hopefully their grandchildren—there will always glow the snuffed sparks of Moisha and Gita Kaplan.

Now the freesias stirred other memories. I would like to tell a story that my grandchildren could read some day, when they are old enough. Not only about my siblings and me, and the family, but also as a reminder that there was a time, in a small country village, when swimming in a river with frogs and algae was probably healthier than many of the lakes and lidos today. A time when two hands could seal a deal; the value of a toy was what it meant to you; finding the first 'Aandblom' was the prize and when the publican called 'Time! Gentlemen,' it meant just that. A sense of permanence and, strange as it may sound, an age of chivalry? It was also a time when three was a family and never a crowd.

'I'll try,' I said, as another flurry of flakes drifted by, 'soon.'

TIME, Gentlemen!

Evan Kaplan

Published by

Osborne Porter
Literary Services

In memory of Miemie, Ann and Natie, who, in their very special ways, *were* the Colesberg Hotel.

For all those loyal men and women, who made it run (albeit, erratically at times).

In fond remembrance of Moisha and Gita Kaplan, my grandparents, who were not given the chance, to enjoy its hospitality.

Acknowledgements

My thanks to Marion Coyne, for redistributing my Platteland punctuation, guiding the grammar and making the story more reader-friendly.

My sincere gratitude to the ever-watchful Patrick 'Crit' Coyne, whose red-pen taught me the value of little words—less, is better than more—and, for being *slightly serious* enough to approach Osborne Porter Literary Services, with them.

My thanks to Ginny Porter and Helen Osborne for their friendly, helpful and efficient service and advice—like Pat, it seems they also never sleep—and for sprucing-up my few battered photographs.

My thanks to the patient Prof John Compton, Department of Geology UCT for "Karoo pangs"; Jan Badenhorst for snippets of "die ou Colesberg" and Stephan & Rina de Wit, for their family tree.

And to Ferdi, who has many times accompanied me to my "past" and more often had to patiently sit beside that long road to Colesberg...with love and unending *muinto obrigada, querida.*

Prologue
86 Temple Fortune Lane, London.
February 2007

Brollies weaved past display windows promising summer wear, and tinselled reindeer were back in musty storerooms. Tyres squelched on Finchley Road, the main thoroughfare through Temple Fortune as it heads north out of London, and conifers hunched under dark skies like hobos in damp overcoats. It had been one of those fortnights.

The trampoline, under a layer of soggy leaves, was a reminder of somersaulting limbs and airborne hair, as I sat beside my granddaughter at the kitchen counter. Mia wanted to draw and so I opted to keep her company, while the rest of the family had risked 'The Heath'. Hampstead Heath is the vast parkland of lawns, ponds and rolling hills that extends beyond Temple Fortune, where my family live, from Hampstead to Highgate. Her pencil outlined a horse with comma-shaped nostrils, a friendly eye and flowing mane, then a sprinkle of daisies. 'He's in a meadow,' she brought me up to date, and finally a hill on the horizon. She sat back to study her work.

Towerberg – Magic Mountain, later baptised Coleskop

The hill, like a healthy inverted muffin, reminded me of a massive flat-topped mountain on the outskirts of Colesberg, the town where we grew up. The old-ones had originally named this landmark Towerberg, the Magic Mountain. I wonder what they might have thought, had they been around when British fifteen-pounders, which had been lugged to its summit, spewed cannon balls at the Boers below. It was baptised 'Coleskop' much later, after the town had been named in honour of Sir Gailbraith Lowry Cole, British Governor of the Cape from 1828 to 1833. Our school emblem had a banner proclaiming *Labor omnia vincet* furled around its base.

It stirred memories of icy winters, flannel sheets and hot water bottles, blazing summers and our intimacy with a variety of pets and animals and everyday exposure to the sprinting courtship of real free-range chickens. Any freer, and they could have ended up in Philippolis or Hanover. Our carefree country life and nature's subtle way of shaping us seemed to beckon at the misted panes.

'That's beautiful, your mountain looks exactly like the one where I came from.'

She looked up. 'Really, grampa? In the country?' I nodded. 'My mom says you are going to tell us all about it,' and she readied a fresh page. 'All about animals and things you used to do...'

I was expecting more, but her pencil drew comforting sounds in the silence left by a pair of magpies, which had taken their squabble elsewhere.

My daughter, Gita, is our ever-watchful pictorial chronicler, with a passion for kith and kin that a stack of hefty albums, miles of video footage and computer slide-shows will confirm. She would like me to put our family background and country upbringing on paper,—'You know, something for the kids one day.'

I was working in Norfolk at the time and my wife and I would visit the family while catching up on London's repertoire. Theatres with curlicues and cupids, where ghosts of the eccentric or famous flit amongst worn drapes… walking the South Bank duffled-and-gloved as barges hauled reflections through oily ripples…and mingling at the British Museum with 'the world and his wife'—from my mother's larder of adages. When snow thickened and queues melted, we finally got to ogle London from the imperceptibly slow orbit of the Big Eye, the 450-foot Millennium Ferris Wheel on the South Bank.

Now this mountain conjured different memories. I plucked and sampled fleeting anecdotes, random places, things we had seen or done growing up in the Colesberg Hotel and some of the people who had helped plait the fabric of our youth. Embracing all this were those endless skies and veld, and the smells, tastes, and textures generated by the changing seasons of the Great Karoo.

'Aah, grampa, you moved!' She leaned forward, pencil scratching the page, confirming her progress by looking up at me, the tip of her tongue peeping between innocent but determined lips.

'You guys would have loved it,' I said, trying not to move, and she asked, 'Did you have ponies?' She is besotted with dogs and horses, all animals, and right now would gladly trade her brothers for our three-legged cat.

'Not ponies'. I pictured the occasional racehorse that came home to rest or roost in the stables down the road from the hotel, skittish and aloof and 'not *exectly* friendly,' as my father would have said. I explained that he did have horses and that got her going with more questions. Did we feed and ride them? How often did we brush them and was I going to tell them all about those days? That allowed me to unfreeze a little and think about her questions.

With DVDs, mind-blowing toys, play-stations and computerised games, I wondered how I could explain the incredible thrill we experienced each autumn, as we set off after school to see who would be the first to find an Aandblom. These were wild freesias, delicate, short-stemmed white trumpets that often grew under bushes or hidden amongst rocks strewn across the low hills. Ysterklip, as it was locally known, was brown-weathered dolerite whose polished black core could throw the sun back at us, and seemed far harder than iron, as the name implied.

Looking back, the thrill, when after hours of fruitless searching we suddenly caught a hint of that subtle perfume, tantalisingly balanced on the still air, had not diminished. In a good season one could collect sizeable bunches, but even if we came home clutching a few flowers, it made us feel like winners of a medal, knowing that for a day or two our flat would be filled with indescribable wonder.

'Our very, very bestest,' I gamely began, tearing myself back from those distant hills, 'was to go looking for tiny white flowers, a special flower with the most amazing smell,' and she countered, 'Couldn't you just buy them?'

'Not that kind, they grew wild.' I tried to find the right weight that would tip the balance of interest. 'You could say they are the great, great, great grandparents of some of the flowers we buy today, and the best part,' I paused for effect, 'was to see who would be the first to find one.' It is fair to say the competitive spirit between these siblings crackles like a plastic comb through mohair. 'Can you draw one for me, grampa?'

I gave it my best shot, while trying to describe the elegant height of a blue crane and the bouncy step of wagtails, a secretary bird's dictatorial stride, the stiff-legged pronk— leaping exhibition—of springbok or the sight of thousands of visiting kestrels effortlessly riding late afternoon thermals, before roosting in the massive blue gum across the road from us.

After she put my bearded fierce-eyed portrait aside, I was pleased to see Aandblomme blooming at the feet of antelope under a sun blazing rays in all directions, and for the first time, seriously began thinking how I could put our simple past—so incredibly rich for us—into meaningful words. Words that hopefully might interest today's children, tomorrow. Now, as she was completely engrossed in capturing this new menagerie I had introduced her to, it gave me a chance to sit back and allow my thoughts to soar...

Chapter One
MERCY FLIGHT ...
Flying to Cape Town—but back, in time, to Colesberg

The roar of the propeller sent a tremor through the Cherokee-6. It bobbed and shook as the wind tugged at its thin skin, tracing every dip or subtle change in pitch somewhere inside me, and I understood how the expression 'flying by the seat of one's pants' originated. Far below, 10,000 feet or more, the Karoo shifted back as the craft pulled 145 knots (260 km/h) from the air, while all around me the horizon remained a static haze in the morning light. Hills and outcrops cast elongated shadows and the N1 unwound like a bleached grey ribbon, sometimes straight as a plank, as cars slid north or south.

Summer had begun and holidaymakers were already getting an early start. I tried to imagine the planning and expectations contained in those minute capsules moving uniformly to their various destinations, but the weight of my immediate problem did not allow me such luxuries.

In the narrow space beside me, where three seats had been removed, my father lay heavily sedated and trussed to a gurney on an emergency flight from Colesberg to Cape Town. I searched his face, trying to find or recognise the man he used to be. The strong nose had become fleshy, splashed with capillaries, and his hooded lids looked bruised and oily. His cheeks, meticulously shaved to a ruddy shine every morning, now rose and fell under a five-day stubble, reminding me of a neglected field, and with each drugged breath, his lips made small popping sounds.

Ian Smith was elected prime minister; Nelson Mandela and seven comrades were sentenced to life imprisonment; Brezhnev took over those enigmatic reins from the jocund, though hot-headed Khrushchev; and both the tail end of 1964 and my fifth

1

year finals lay ahead, when I received news that my father was terribly ill.

I was in medical school at Karl Bremer Hospital, affiliated to Stellenbosch University, and our Professor granted me leave. I set off in my souped-up Anglia well after sundown, zipping through darkened towns tucked away for the night, and petrol attendants blearily went about my pit stops in the early morning hours. In spite of what my mother had told me, my father looked dreadful and Doctor du Plessis, the GP, had been grappling for a diagnosis, as he rapidly deteriorated.

I had had very little sleep the previous night, trying to help or protect him during his bouts of involuntary but frightening lunges. From what seemed like a state of near coma, he would suddenly try to leap out of bed as though another second on his back could be fatal. He had fallen twice on my first watch, when I thought I could doze on the twin bed, so I sat on a chair beside his bed to minimise his frantic efforts.

The next day I phoned one of my part-time senior consultants, trying to sound coherent and professional as I described this hodgepodge of strange movements and behaviour, and other symptoms Dok Dupie had managed to record. He had arranged for a mercy flight and an ambulance to take us to Die Volk's Hospitaal. As the name and era implies, it was the Afrikaner flagship of private hospitals, long before the pandemic of pay-as-you-arrive, don't, if you can't—exorbitant clinics.

The following morning my mother and a driver had left for Cape Town in my car, while we waited for the wings of mercy. The drone of a small plane alerted the townsfolk that something else was in the air and it soon appeared overhead, dipped its wings a couple of times and headed for the airstrip. My father was a tall, well-built man, muscles now gone a bit flabby and a mid-sixties paunch, but Dok Dupie, Kierie, our sturdy Coloured barman-cum-driver, another staff member and I had managed to bundle him into our car as gently as we could.

The plane stood at the far end of the runway, facing into the

2

early morning sun and, judging by the windsock, a limp easterly breeze. A handful of well-wishers and interested onlookers had arrived and stood some distance away. Dok Dupie had already given my father a light sedative and when we got him onto the gurney, which the pilot and male nurse had readied for us, he administered an intramuscular 'knockout cocktail,' prescribed by my consultant.

'The last thing we want is Oom Kappie waking up...' he said, rubbing the site with a cotton wool swab and the way he flicked his brows, up there, gave me palpitations. We helped the crew, as they loaded my father and battened him and the gurney down. With memories of the previous night spooking me, I shook some hands, thanked Kierie and others who had come to comfort me, then finally the good doctor. 'Sterkte en voorspoed, ou maat,' he said, as the pilot closed and latched the door but his wishes of courage and good luck sounded unconvincing in my sleep-deprived state.

The small crowd watched as the engine coughed once or twice and the lean blades sprang to life, shattering the silence. The plane lurched, followed by a few more revs, and then we were bouncing across the uneven strip, the propeller grappling thinner air at this altitude in a blur of sunlight, and then the earth seemed to flip us upwards and we were airborne. The pilot headed into the sun, before banking so steeply, I hoped the fuselage, as it pressed against my left shoulder, would hold and my father not topple onto me. I peered down at the clutch of tiny cars and trucks and grouped figures as we made a wide turn, before heading south.

I suddenly recalled Ou Bolla, a wealthy local businessman with a wicked sense of humour, who had no time to herd sacred cows. Many years before, he had survived a crash in his Piper Cub and had stepped out of the mangled wreckage with only a gash across his eye. The badly-stitched scar always reminded me of the old lace-up leather rugby balls and gave him even more of a swashbuckling appearance. He was a jovial, fun-loving character who had no qualms speaking his mind, and an

3

old prude had commented, 'For some reason, heaven knows why, the Lord must have been in the aircraft with him.'

Now, my biggest fear was that my father would suddenly wake and explode into those frantic heaves. As Miemie would have said: 'My senuwees was gedaan' (my nerves were shredded), because with all my detailed childhood memories, I did not recognise the good driver who took my mother to Cape Town, but he would remind me many years later. And to this day I have no recollection of the names or faces of the pilot and nurse who came to rescue my father. I only remember they both wore droopy, gold-rimmed sunglasses, which were very popular at the time.

He did stir now and again. Once he opened a bleary eye, which he seemed to fix on me, and it triggered a few extra heartbeats, because my father might have been many things, but a flyer he definitely was not. Then the drugs took over again.

The engine found its rhythm, a steady, soothing drone, and I rested my head against the Perspex, a clear curve of nothingness separating me from the stark landscape gently rising or falling away. At times, I could see our shadow cheekily dipping or skipping over dongas and hills as though it had nothing to do with this sombre bird casting it. Occasional white flecks grazing in the monochrome reminded me of a winter when my father had asked me to accompany him on a Springbok hunt. Could it only have been the year before?

Thanks to his National Guard training during the war years, a good eye and steady hand, he was a fine shot with the 'drie-nul-drie,' the old .303 rifle that was every farmer's and many a townsman's friend. That was until his tremor started and confidence began to ebb as Parkinson's disease set in, diagnosed one Saturday afternoon when he finally took time off to visit Dok Dupie.

I had not been keen and told him so. Much as I loved venison and Springbok biltong, I did not have the heart for hunting. Finally, so unlike him, he begged me, and so we went. We joined the brusque camaraderie of the group already

4

enjoying early morning coffee and rusks and exchanging puffs of vapour while reminiscing about previous outings. My father and I were allocated a koppie, those small rocky outcrops first named kopjes, by the Dutch (Boer) settlers, from which we would see buck in either direction. When a small group stopped below us, his shot went wide off the mark. He handed me the gun, and for the first time, I recognised a plea in this stoical man.

The rest was one of the many things I have done that I would rather forget. It sounds so glib to say 'I bagged two buck,' but unfortunately it was not the classical head or heart shots those hunters normally delivered. After the first buck dropped amongst the bushes and the tracker and I ran down, I found it struggling to rise with what I can only describe as a kind of mystical surprise in its trusting eyes. In my own surprise and adrenalin surge, I had left the gun with my father, but what shocked me even more, was how, instinctively, I took my pocket-knife, pulled its head back by a horn and ended the suffering. My second shot looked even more convincing, but turned out to be a repeat performance.

There was much good-natured bantering when the day's kill was laid outside the wool shed. 'Who the hell was the butcher?' someone joked, and I was even more acutely aware of the metallic smell of blood mingling with lanolin and smoke tumbling from the kitchen chimney, where food was being prepared for the hunting party. 'I was,' I said, feeling like a criminal, and they exchanged commiserating looks with Ou Kappie, knowing his earlier steady hand and beady eye would have delivered a head-shot almost every time. 'My shots were a little wild,' I added, in case they thought my father had wounded them.

A downdraught rocked the plane; my father shuddered despite his shackles and moved his lips as if whispering a quick message or prayer, then settled again. I gazed at the old man from Lithuania and wondered what dreams were worrying his troubled sleep. Although we thought him old at the time, when

5

he died three years later, 27th May 1967, he would be sixty-nine.

We have a wedding photo, simply dated 1926. Dark-suited, with a stiff winged-collar and black bow tie, his head held high and arms courteously or uncertainly clasped behind him, he cuts a handsome figure, handsome in an Eastern European sort of way. A sturdy chest, clean-shaven cheeks, high forehead and hair combed straight back cut an image of panache, dashing rather than swagger. He never had the time or inclination to swagger.

The reticent tenor and the innocent flirt.
Ann & Natie, Beaufort West (1926)

6

My mother stands beside him in a below-knee, cut-away lacy dress, the brim of her little white hat almost obscuring her striking dark brows. The veil, thrown back, hangs past her shoulders like a more modern Florence Nightingale. Her left hand, holding a posy, rests on the rounded apex of a polished wooden stand, while her right arm hangs coyly at her side. They are forever captured in sepia. What is it that makes those sepias, irrespective of subject, so evocative?

Being the youngest of the three siblings, I got to know my father when premature aging and insecurities had caught up with him. They were probably kindled by being a very young alien—'in a strange new land,' as Tevyah commiserated in Fiddler on the Roof—and a childhood spent in Lithuania. It was the kind of life that was not always pleasant for Jews. He was physically powerful and unafraid, but his insecurity was a fear of authority, those faceless people in control. In spite of his and my mother's genuine popularity in the town, I think he always felt an outsider, included, but different. My mother was the exact opposite in every way.

I realised how little we knew of his childhood in Zagare, his immediate family or even his early adulthood in South Africa. While one's history and lofty family trees are important, it is the personal things, no matter how small, that make those people real. It would have been wonderful to know what our grandparents or great grandparents were like; if they had talents, idiosyncrasies or eccentricities, as well as something more about other family members and friends. How my father and his siblings got on and what kind of child he was—we know he did not have much time to be one—and what they did on summer afternoons or cold winter evenings. Who were the mischievous ones and who the bookworms? I would have liked him to describe the smell of flour and machinery or the many dusty hiding places in his father's old mill.

My sister once discovered a bundle of letters he wrote to my mother during their courtship, while she was preparing her trousseau at the family home in Beaufort West. He describes, in

7

a letter she could not help reading, how some spring evenings, as a child in Zagare, he would tie a cord to a branch of the lilac tree, and pull it through his bedroom window so he could 'fall asleep with the scent all around me'. Not bad for a pre-bar mitzvah boy. That helped define my father for me, gave a tiny dimension to his past, showed a warmth and the possibility of a—romantic?

Then, circumstances beyond his control shaped or re-shaped that boy into the man he would become. She put the letters back in the linen cupboard, and in time they were either discarded or torn up when my parents moved to Cape Town. There went another small treasure of information we might have gleaned about Nathan Kaplan's youth or aspirations.

As I watched shadows roll across his face, the uncertainty of his future began prodding me. I thought about how little we knew of his past, as well as his mid- and later years, when he had finally bought, renovated and put Colesberg Hotel on the map. I also thought about my siblings and me, and growing up in a humble hotel, in a small country town.

Chapter Two
A SEASONAL WORD...
Time, to introduce customs and a few good people

' Spoil the rod and spare the child'. My mother was easy going and benevolent, and big on spoonerisms, but that did not prevent her serving up a stinging slap or two when pushed beyond the limit of her already limited store of patience. As we were raised in the age of not sparing rods and spoiling children, I cannot be sure if this one was a genuine slip or her jab at society, which she occasionally did, in innocence.

Small towns had their share of customs and protocols. Children and younger folk always referred to anyone older as Oom, Tannie or Antie, Oupa and Ouma, depending on the age-gap, while contemporaries used Ou (old), with the first name, male or female, as a sign of camaraderie and familiarity. Youngsters could refer to an older person as Ou, only if he or she were a colourful character, infamous or eccentric and had earned that prefix of awe.

Addressing someone by their surname could indicate disinterest or bad vibes, and kissing non-family members was a perfunctory touch of the lips, never to linger nor offer a cheek. If a handshake was not bone-crushing, it counted for nought and could be interpreted as your being of weak character or, Ptoei! Ptoei! Ptoei!—an old Yiddish custom to keep the evil eye away—a 'moffie' (gay).

Good manners and an occasional healthy spank were the order of the day. The younger brigade always had to stand up, greet and shake hands, allow elders to enter or leave first, be respectful, i.e. no backchat, and never interrupt a conversation. Unless it was something dire: 'Dad! Sorry to interrupt, but the old bull in the far paddock has just serviced the prize milk Friesian that Uncle Piet's stud was going to cover!' 'Please,' 'no thank you' and 'excuse me' were drummed in from an early age, and were heavily frowned on if omitted. It was also still

9

the age of children being seen and not heard, and although there were the odd goody-two-shoes, country kids were, generally speaking, well-balanced and mannered.

On the flip side of that same coin were the narrow-minded and bigoted, and a sprinkle of perversions that were knowingly or sometimes innocently swept under the carpet of 'eccentricities'. There was usually a standard opening for those. 'Ag, don't worry about Tannie Sarah, she's just terribly fond of girls...' or 'Ou Jan is really quite a good chap, he's just mad about children.'

If you were in the presence of a fine raconteur or someone spinning a good yarn, you took part by regular nods of encouragement and the occasional exclamation of riveted enjoyment: 'Ja, wragtig!'(really!) or 'Kêrel! Kêrel!' (good one, old chap). Later, you could tell your mates old so-and-so spoke a lot of rubbish, but during a good story, everyone played along. If, on the other hand, you felt inclined for a bit of verbal wrestling, an interjection of doubt or disbelief at the right (wrong) moment could really get the party going.

There were parents and teachers who overstepped the boundaries, which is not the sole right of small towns, but our respect for them and authority was part of the country code. If rules did seem a bit stringent or repressive, we found our expression in the freedom of being independent, creative in play and adventurous in our quests. We scaled cliffs for hawk nests, tobogganed down sandstone gullies, swung from embankments, played Tarzan or balanced in treetops, searching for nestlings and bird eggs along the 'sloot,' a stream that (usually) meandered sluggishly through town.

No matter their age, Black and Coloured servants were referred to as 'boy' or 'girl'. Thus in the hotel there were 'bar boys,' 'yard boys,' garage boys,' shop boys,' stable boys' (for my father's horses) and 'room girls,' 'kitchen girls' or 'flat girls'. Sometimes they were very young men and women, but mostly they were loyal, trusted old-timers.

There was also the usual clutter of naughty or rebellious

kids, who pushed their parents and neighbours' patience to the limits, but we generally knew when to behave hordentlik (properly), and when we could spread our wings and fly.

*

All these years later, I vividly remember the bevelled glass and mahogany swing doors and their soft sigh, as visitors entered or left the hotel lobby. 'Foi yee,' as my mother referred to our humble entrance. They had no locks and were only closed against the cold or dust-laden winds.

My father, Nathan Kaplan, usually stood at his post by the till, in the White Bar, quietly watching how the new barman was going about his duties and Kierie, our Coloured barman, in the Coloured Bar next door. He was Natie to family members, Oom Kappie to the younger brigade and Ou Kappie to his mates. He was polite, well mannered and reserved, shy, one can say, and 'not a very talkative chappie,' as my mother would have put it.

The Bottle Store was at the far end of this corridor connecting the two bars, and that was generally my mother's post, seated on an old bentwood behind the counter. Family and friends called her Ann or Annie and she was Antie/ Tannie Annie to the townsfolk. Her spectacles were either perched at the end of her nose or slung by a cord from her neck. The lenses or catchment area, as we referred to them, were under a fine patina of biscuit crumbs, a smear of tea or the odd grain of rice. During quiet spells, she would snatch a page or two from Miller, Mailer or Maugham, or any new book she could have laid her hands on. She was much more gregarious and friendlier than Natie, 'like chalk 'n cheese,' to use one of her maxims.

The front door to our flat separated the hotel from the General Dealer, as town shops were known, and that was where Maria Francina de Wit would be found, when she was not attending to other chores. She was Miemie, to friends and the

11

family, Tannie Miems to younger folk and Mejuffrou de Wit in the formal business world. She ran the hotel, one could say, and was in charge of the shop, kitchen and housekeeping, until we got Anna to take over the latter duty and assist in the shop.

She was also our second mother, and many a time my siblings and I turned to Miemie, rather than Ann, for solace. Her post was behind the shop counter, on the padded high stool, bringing her books up to date. She could only do that if she was not showing rolls of starched African Print called shwe-shwe to women who carefully fingered each flap of material to assess durability and texture, and whether they could afford it. Their hard-earned money, wrapped in the folds of a doek or headscarf, was carefully removed only when they were completely satisfied with the purchase. Ever formal and reserved, Miemie had patience in abundance, and, over the years, customers had learned to appreciate her expert and genuine advice, as she did not give or take soft-sell.

The door to our private quarters or flat—sorely in need of a fresh coat of varnish—opened on a long passage before reaching the living area. We normally only slept there: all our other activities were elsewhere.

My brother Boris, or Bo, ten years my senior, was a big shot at school. He was a side drummer in the cadet band, a fearless gymnast and played for the first rugby team. He started off as a bit of a bully, but fortunately outgrew the habit, although I occasionally enjoyed a bit of his roughhousing if I knew help was close at hand.

Beryl, or Bee, (not to be confused with our cook, who was affectionately known as Antie Bee), arrived halfway between Bo and me. A stunning, dark-haired beauty, and bright, she was also a voracious reader, like Ann, and popular with the staff and tourists, who, as my mother would say, 'took an instant shine' to her.

The Plaatjies were an extended family who lived in a tiny house, shaded by giant pepper trees, across the dirt road that ran behind the hotel. Boris was friendly with Martin, one of the

12

older boys and Bee's best friend was Martie, one of the daughters. Koerie, who was a good few months older than me, and his brother Ziems, some months younger, were my closest friends and until I went to boarding school, age eleven, the three of us would be inseparable.

I can see Koerie, in his neatly patched shorts, scrubbed shirt, and barefoot, lugging a bucket of water from the outside tap to their kitchen. Ziems, doing his homework at the voorhuis table (entrance utility room), while I impatiently wait for him to finish. I would learn more in that simple home, where day-to-day living must have been more of a battle than I realised at the time, or even in my early adulthood.

Chapter Three
TIME OUT OF MIND... A CHALLENGE FOR GENESIS...

'Die aarde is so vas en stewig soos 'n rots, en niks sal dit beweeg nie!' (The earth is as immovable and solid as a rock and nothing will disturb it.)

That's what Miemie used to say.

Geography was one of my favourite subjects and on vacation from boarding school, I happened to mention that not only was the earth round, like a netball, but it spun, just like a top, while whizzing around the sun. We were sitting in the kitchen after lunch one day, before the shops re-opened for the afternoon stretch. She fixed me with her good left and slightly lazy right eye, and then shook her head. 'No, my child,' she patiently corrected me, 'the Bible says the earth, as God created it, is as solid and immovable as a rock. I don't know where you get these funny stories from.'

Young and headstrong, I persisted, until finally she got up, clomped across the floor in her no-nonsense shoes, which did not differ much from her church-shoes, and headed for the backdoor. It was one of those idyllic days. She pointed a finger, knobbed with arthritis, beyond the gauze-screen where the sun hung motionless in a cloudless sky, burnishing the rocks, and not a blade of grass or leaf stirred. 'If everything is now supposed to be spinning so,' she asked with genuine interest, 'why then is nothing moving out there?' She allowed the tiniest bite of sarcasm to line her question, permissible on this occasion, I imagine, because she was defending the Lord's Word.

But we were all blissfully unaware, as we leaped up and down our familiar koppies, trudged across the veld or explored dongas and dry riverbanks, what this land had gone through, before finally donning the cloak of the Great Karoo. We had no idea of the weird and wonderful plants and animals that once

14

thrived, where scraggy Karoobossies and springbok now eked out their existence. They were the days of general innocence or ignorance and, misinformation. It was safer to say 'moer'—a pithy oath that guaranteed a belting—than 'ewolusie'. We were familiar with copulating cats and comfortable with the birth of puppies, but we were unaware of the heaves and earth-shattering labour pangs of 'The Old Ancestor,' as some folk still occasionally referred to the Karoo.

I try to imagine how some of our burghers would have reacted, if anyone had told us this land once lay beneath an inland sea, rimmed by rich marshes and fertile deltas. 'Ek wil nie snaaks wees nie, maar nou praat u sommer twak!' That is what Tant Marie from Doringvlei, might have told them, in her soft, kindly voice—I am not trying to be funny, but now you are really talking twaddle.

If they went on to tell us that frightening creatures like Gorgonopsians went about ripping placid old Patranomodons to shreds, a retort from someone like Ou Labbes, the jovial stationmaster, would have been a defiant: 'Nou praat jy wragtig kak, ou maat!' which is a tad more forceful than bullshit! old chap.

That a desert once stretched way into central Africa, turning that lush Eden to sand and snuffing all those living organisms, might have made more sense. But thick sheets of intolerant ice, slowly planing or piling up and leaving scars like linear acne...? 'Nee wat kêrel, jy moenie alles glo wat jy lees nie!' (Don't believe everything you read...) That's what Oupa Ben, in charge of the power station, would say about most things he did not understand or agree with, in his toothless lisp. That, by a man who read even less than I did.

Even more alarming would have been a notion that massive continents could drift around, like Coot nests on a farm dam, and that this giant crossword puzzle had first come together as Pangaea. 'Pan-wat'se ding?' I can hear someone like Bertus Grobbelaar ask, spluttering on his Mellowood and coke. And, that the whole caboodle would split up and drift apart, to come

15

together again in the Southern Hemisphere as Gondwana Land. 'Gondwana Land!—is that something from a Grimm's fairy tale?' I can imagine old Mr Perkins muttering, seated on his stool at the far end of the bar.

If that were not enough, 182 million years ago, give or take a few years on either side, this landmass broke up once more. What would one day be South America, Africa and Madagascar, Antarctica, India and Australia—giving the Brits a large piece of real estate upon which to start a new colony for wayward souls someday—would slowly drift to their present temporary moorings.

I remember our teacher, Mrs Van, who gallantly juggled all the English Medium grades in one classroom. The large drop-map would be unrolled and hung over the blackboard during geography classes, and I see her identifying cities, countries and continents with the shaft of a featherless duster. Although she struck us as someone with an open mind, I wonder what her comments would have been about all that drifting.

Our typical flat-topped hills and koppies—that seem to glow as late afternoon sun slants across the veld—are the result of mantle plumes that gushed lava all over the place. They give some dimension to the vast flatness of the Karoo. On a train to Windhoek many years later, one old gent in our compartment, when he heard where I was heading, told me it was so flat, 'that even if you lay on your stomach, you could still see two weeks ahead of you!'

Another type of volcanic rock delivered Kimberlite, with its stash that would become a girl's best friend and in the process, man's blood diamonds. The next time you see even a teensy carat, do not scoff; that little shiner could be anywhere up to 1,600 million years old! Unlike us, they are possibly one of the only things that become brighter with age.

Clocking in at a piffling 2.6 million years, hominids, more modern man-like creatures, have combed our beaches, taken shelter in mountain caves and traipsed the open savannas. Later, Stone Age forebears, about 40,000 years ago, were

16

among the early humans who roamed the Karoo. Very much later, as Boer trekkers and hunters, as well as British missionaries and soldiers from both camps, moved north during the early 1800s, bivouacs and mission stations sprang up along the way to quell and reform or to decimate. Between the Boers and other (black) tribes, they managed to annihilate thousands of San, who were no threat, but going about their day-to-day activities with the Old Ancestor they had learned to live with and revere. (That also seems to have been an Australian and New Zealand pastime, which possibly led to the Tri-Nations?)

One could say those late hunter-gatherers would be some of the first inhabitants of hamlets, villages and small towns dotting the hinterland. Colesberg was no exception and even in my day, judging purely on physical characteristics, there were many San amongst the aged. Allegedly, their mitochondrial DNA suggests they are the most ancient, genetically-modern people on earth. 'Wat? 'n Donnerse Boesman?' is the kind of thing someone like Luiperd Le Roux would have growled. Yet he was rather fond of them…especially the women.

My first introduction to the history or culture of the San, or 'Bushmen' as they were referred to, was watching my brother sort and store artefacts from middens he had discovered in the surrounding hills. My first glimpse of the San, as a real people, so to speak, was much later in the Cape Town Museum. I was immediately captivated by the nostalgia of a lost moment in time, when 'those funny little people,' as an older cousin explained, 'actually lived there.' I was spellbound by the dioramas, where these slight folk gazed out from their high cave entrance, at an unchanging vista towards the distant hills. It reminded me of the many late afternoons when we sat on Kiep-Kiep, a massive koppie rising above the Coloured Location, not far from the hotel; when even as kids, we somehow fell silent and just listened to the silence.

*

I was astounded, too, by the realistic settings, their meagre but practical belongings and the splendid backdrops. But the thrill of adventure and their inherent sense of child-like humour, was noticeably absent from their eyes.

*

I thought I would add that bit of 'inconsequential history'—as someone once referred to archaeology and palaeontology—because of the standard replies whenever we were asked where we hailed from. 'Hell, it's bloody cold!' or 'Geez! That place gets fuckin' hot!' There was a third quip: 'I blinked and next second the town was fading in our rear-view mirror!'

That was the sum of this beautifully stark, seemingly transparent yet spiritually rich and mysterious land, where folk were generally warm and unpretentious. One can see that a lot more faded in their rear view mirrors than they might have imagined, including some wonderful memories.

Chapter Four
TIME AND AGAIN...
Of winter greens and summer trots...early
recollections in a country inn

My three earliest memories were at a very young age and possibly explain the quirks of being raised in a country inn. It is early evening, the hotel in full swing, I must have had a rash of sorts between the buttocks and my mother asked the nanny to spread some Vaseline over the affected quarters. All our modern medicines and 'Old Dutch' remedies were kept in an ornate wooden chest, well out of reach on our bedroom wall and it permanently exuded a mixed aroma of camphorated spirits, out-of-date sulphas, and boracic powder.

I remember her laying me across the bed, taking off my pants and hoisting my legs with one hand, while reaching for the salve with the other. Even at that tender age, I recall it being a little too businesslike for my liking, and, as it turned out, 'twas not Vaseline, but a tub of Methyl Salicylate she had accidentally taken. Tender is the operative word. Anyone who remembers the pungent smell and sting of Wintergreen will know what I mean. For those unfamiliar with that old cure-all for painful joints or stiff muscles, let me say that when applied to that particular region, missiles could be launched with less combustible fuel.

Next. I could have been just over three and had probably gorged myself on early summer fruits, probably unripe apricots, when I got a sudden urge to trot to the loo. I recall my long trousers had criss-cross straps that fastened at the back and I began running hell-for-leather up the long passage connecting our flat with the hotel frontage, yelping for someone to come to the rescue. Everyone must have been busy and the inevitable happened. Down my legs it gushed, into my shoes and left an embarrassing trail along the wooden floor, polished to a brilliant glare once a week. The ignominy of having shat in my troozers was bad enough, but the warm, scratchy feeling as they clung to my legs, felt like being trapped in a cesspit from the hips down.

While on that slant, here is another quick anecdote that describes the times. The hotels and most homes had flush toilets, but those were very much the days of long-drops and cesspits or sewage tanks in the back yard. Every week or two the old night wagon—'die kakwa,' as locals christened it—a tanker truck painted a suitable drab green and equipped with a thick suction hose, did its nocturnal slurps, with a jocular crew on board. One could pinpoint its whereabouts not only by clanking buckets, but the rich aroma that followed it. Awakened one night by loud laughter and even louder cursing, we stumbled out of the back door. There stood Shortie—five feet would be a very generous offer—dripping ooze in the dull glow of a streetlight, while his helpmates formed a wide raucous circle around him.

My third memory is the nanny trying to give me castor oil. I cannot recall why I had to have it, but this elixir was given for anything from tummy ache ('boych vaytik,' as they say in Yiddish) to constipation and from headache or bad appetite, to overeating, feeling out of sorts ('tsukrochen'), fever ('kadoches') or insomnia. Occasionally the bottle would be removed from the cabinet as a fail-safe threat to blackmail. On that occasion, I was not being very cooperative, and she finally had to call in the reserves; my mother and Miemie.

From the brisk frustration in their step and the black dress with scratchy sequins—when my mother finally clutched me to her bosom, pinched my nostrils and Miemie ladled it in—I gathered there must have been a dinner party or some other fancy occasion in progress. They had scarcely started to cheer when the oily yuck plus din-dins erupted onto my mother's smart evening dress, and I remember her trading me a smarter smack or two in the transaction.

Much as it would be in vogue to join the Oliver Twists and Nicholas Nicklebys by saying we had a dreadful Dickensian upbringing, truth is, it was anything but. It was an incredible childhood, free to do things most city children could not or would never have been allowed to do. My sister calls it 'our period of benign neglect,' which sums up our past. The three of us grew up amongst hotel staff and nannies, not to mention access to a shop, the kitchen and bar, but we were extremely independent from a very young age. We had to be; everyone was usually busy getting on with his or her duties.

While these early memories are fresh on the page, I include the following anecdote because not only does it seem to fit the earlier theme, but to illustrate how history has a strange way of repeating itself. The French had uncovered (yet another) plot to assassinate de Gaulle, the Americans had been successful with Kennedy and the Cape sweltered that summer of 1963. My little Anglia was cramped and hot as I whizzed home on varsity vacation to help man the fort during the busy season. I could not be blamed for thinking that a touch of discomfort in the region of my jocks, was merely a case of heat rash. A day later, when I thought I was either going to scratch or dance myself to death, I had a sneaky suspicion everything was 'nisht kosher,' and in the lull between lunch and the evening onslaught, I decided to consult Dok Dupie.

He happened to be on two weeks' leave and had found a newly qualified young *locum tenens*. After a brief and nonchalant examination—while I stared equally nonchalantly at a row of antique medicinal jars arranged along a shelf above the cabinets—he confirmed my suspicions. While sowing the oats, I had been blessed with a fine crop of 'Papillion de Amour,' as the textbooks referred to these non-edible 'crustaceans', who seemed to have no qualms about devouring me. What a misnomer. The little buggers are nothing like butterflies and I think 'love' seldom makes an appearance during those passing trysts.

It must have been celestial retribution. The posh lass I had only recently met implored me to accompany her to a 'smashing twenty-first at K.G.' (Kelvin Grove). Those days the club was still very much... (*sotto voce*) ...not favourable towards Jews, (unwritten regulation…?) and I had politely declined previous invitations in my boycott of solidarity. I capitulated on this occasion, and for that, the Lord smote me with posh crabs, which I have to admit, turned out to be no better than strains from more humble vendors.

When I first heard about this unwritten code—in my naivety I could not believe such things still existed circa nineteen-sixties—a friend and I independently enquired about joining the club, using unmistakably Jewish surnames. He was a 'Mr Lipschitz' and I, 'Mr Cohen'. Alas, no one came back to us 'in due course,' and I can now safely report, neither over the past forty-five years. These days, I believe it is open house.

Back to the *locum*. He scrabbled through some cupboards and handed me a tub of ointment with the comforting words: 'This will kill the little bliksems.' Little did I know that could have applied to me. After my father and I had finally cashed up and locked the pub that evening, I couldn't wait to anoint myself. Thank heavens my mother was on her annual vacation in Cape Town, nowhere near the bizarre spectacle about to unfold.

In my bedroom I ripped off my pants, yanked down my undies and with grand sweeps and pats thoroughly daubed myself with what should have been cool, soothing Blue Butter; a preparation designed to smother and destroy any non-paying residents. It all happened so fast and in such frenzy that too late, I caught the whiff of…Wintergreen. Within seconds, it felt as if my entire genetic stowage department was on fire (again) and I instinctively acted as most people would. One of my parents' greater joys, at the end of a long, trying day, would be to sit on the toilet lid, lean over the washbasin and enjoy whatever fruit was available or in season. My father's best was farm peaches and my mother had a crush on juicy mangos, not always available that far inland. So there Natie sat, slicing fresh Alberta peaches with his Joseph Rodgers penknife, when I came hobbling down the passage, underpants still caught around my ankles. Without any explanation, I bunged in the plug, turned

22

on the coldwater tap full blast, went on tiptoe and submerged said department. (I was expecting a loud hiss or billow of steam, at least.)

In spite of my agony, I will never forget his face. Incredulous is too tame; gob-smacked would probably be closest. 'Vot are you doing, kakker?' (his term of endearment), but I was beyond caring. No matter what I did, the ointment is meant to cling and in spite of repeated douches—and at one point fanning myself with a piece of cardboard—I finally fell asleep in the early morning hours, exhausted and burnt-out 'oysgebrendt,' as they say.

When I bumped into the locum a day or two later, stepping out of the surgery on his way to a house call, I learned he was not only a son of the Oranje Vrystaat, but far less circumspect than me. After apologising with the empathy one usually reserves for accidentally jostling someone on a crowded sidewalk, he did make up for it by adding: 'Jesus fellow, but your balls must surely have been on fire?' I could see right away his blend of dispassionate empathy and colloquial patter would make him a fine clinician; one who would not get too emotionally involved with his patients and allow him to lead a well-balanced practitioner's-cum-family life.

I can hear Miemie's admonishings when we were naughty or difficult. 'The Lord will still punish you...' was her way of guidance, rather than any heavenly retribution wished upon us. I could not even begin to think what her thoughts would have been concerning that little pantomime.

Chapter Five
THERE'S NO TIME LIKE THE PAST...
A flat, by any other name, will still smell as sweetly

Colesberg lies roughly halfway between Johannesburg and Cape Town, but our home, was more than a half-way house; it was a half-and-half mixture. There was the relative tranquillity of the flat and Sturm und Drang of the hotel. We grew up in a period between antiquity (coal stoves and paraffin heaters) and modernity (hot and cold running water in bedrooms and flush toilets). Our world was steeped in Yiddishkeit (Lithuania, a hint of pogroms and no pork) on the one hand, and Afrikaans, (Platteland, 'baasmanskap,' Nationalist era, melktert and Boerebeskuit) on the other. We went with our parents to the Synagogue on High Holy days and occasionally with Miemie to the Dutch Reformed Church on a Sunday morning. My friends were predominantly Black and Coloured kids until I went to school, age six, and then I met White friends, and our flat was always open to both.

I find smell, the most evocative of our senses, and, more than a halfway house, our flat was a poignant collection of smells. (Unfortunately, I also use it like an animal, much to my wife's displeasure, as I have no qualms sniffing a dish in a restaurant or meat in a supermarket, if an alarm sensor twitches somewhere.) It has blended a collection of crisp or nostalgically blurred images that breathe life into the people, places and incidents that filled my childhood, and it can instantly whisk or subtly lure me into the past.

My siblings and I often discuss how Colesberg comes to life in a mosaic of aroma-memories, each depicting characters we knew or places we had been familiar with: a certain period, incidents or simply the passing of seasons. Smells, which I might not have sensed for years, ferry me to the exact time and place when those molecules first wafted onto the nerve endings, before scuttling along the olfactory tracts and settling—nice and

24

comfy—in the anterior temporal lobes of the brain. But as the Bard said: 'A rose, by any other name....'

My earliest memories of our flat—three bedrooms, a bathroom and tiny lounge, sandwiched between the hotel, shop, and storerooms at the back—are defined and textured by its odours.

From the same medicine chest in our bedroom, drifted Vicks chest rub—staying home from school; Friar's Balsam—bad cuts or scrapes and antiphlogistine paste—the anxious odour of illness. In the flu epidemic of 1943, my brother suffered double pneumonia and pleurisy. Doctor Cooper, the GP who delivered the three of us—and hundreds of other kids—did not think he would make it and sat with my parents at his bedside during the crisis, expecting the worst. A combination of good doctoring, good fortune and the boy's natural immunity and physical strength, got him through.

He told us years later, while discussing our resistance and immunity we developed 'growing up off the floor and sand,' as he likes to say, he was so ill that he couldn't speak or lift a hand. I was too young to have an image of him and his illness, but I distinctly remember the smell, associated with tense, silent activity in the bedroom as my mother and a nurse buttered large plasters with the heated paste and applied those hot poultices to his back and chest. Two of his school friends in the hostel and one or two townsfolk were not as lucky, so maybe the plasters did do something after all.

Those smells remind me of our bedroom. Bright floral curtains, fly-screens at the window, a brommer (bluebottle) banging the panes in summer and winter sun throwing bright rhomboids across the Linoleum floor and our beds. A padded poof with hinged lid stood before my sister's dressing table, in which the three of us, in turn, hid our treasures. A stained-glass door enclosed a few bookshelves and a linen cupboard next to it, smelling of fresh sheets and eiderdowns, had a large recess above them, where we could clamber up and play, until we outgrew the space.

Talcum powder, naphthalene and the pleasant musty smell of furs, when they thought pelts looked better on people, remind me of my mother's wardrobe. Amongst other things, that is where she kept our piggybanks; my (small) Eno's Fruit Salts tickey-bottle and my sister's (large) Eno's sixpence-bottle. Although her cupboard was locked, the key remained in the door. When I grew taller and crafty enough I would raid it for my tickeys and on a good day find a piece of Cadburys or Nestle, real chocolate, not the el-cheapo lines we sold in the store.

The smell of starched collars, leather shoes and pipe-tobacco leaked from my father's wardrobe when the door was open and now allows me to peer into their bedroom. It is another hot afternoon. My mother has come in to rest and lies on their twin-beds, propped on an elbow, engrossed in a book she could have loaned from the library—when new stock came in—or borrowed from a friend. Bessie Gordon, Bill Cooper, the GP and my mother were a spontaneous book club that sprang to life through their craving for new authors. They did not necessarily meet once a month, but a steady flow, a three-way-exchange of 'manna from heaven'—Doc Cooper's view of literature's nourishing powers—was continually in motion between them.

Now there is the tireless buzzing of a fly and drone of voices filtering through from the Bottle Store and Coloured Bar, our Karoo mantra. Soon those words of intrigue, love, deception, detection, murder or biographical delights begin to blur. She places the book on her bedside pedestal and drops off for a nap.

Her dressing table had a round mirror, large as a dining table, with two arched side mirrors and shelf space between drawers set on either side. The only time she sat before it was when she prepared for a function or one of our High Holy days. Annie, as everyone knew my mother, was definitely not a titivator, a word that often crept into her conversation. A splash of rouge, a dab of powder, a reckless swish of lipstick—all too often not quite following the given contours—and a mole on her chin, 'my beauty spot,' did the rest.

26

Ingram shaving sticks, a block of immortal Lifebuoy soap and a smaller medicine cabinet, smelling of Dettol and rusty Minora razor blades, bring to life our little bathroom, in spite of a tube of Kolynos or Ipana squashed and curled up in agony on the already cluttered windowsill. I see my father, striped flannel pyjama top hanging upside-down from the trouser cord, as he lathers his face in the steaming tilt-mirror, set in a circular chrome frame above the basin. It was probably from their original Art Nouveau set of furniture and fittings when they moved into the flat. The opening, where a bulb once lit up the show, has been a black hole as long as I can remember. He rolls his tongue inside his cheeks or uses his left hand to pull at the dewlaps, and I am mesmerised by the loud scraping sounds that I'm sure must be painful. Then he washes his face in scorching water with loud snorts and splutters as fingers briskly clear excess foam from nose and ear holes.

A fluted cup, minus an ear, with little red flowers painted around the top, remained on the windowsill long after my maternal grandfather, Isaac Traub, returned to the Cape. When he had done shaving, he would half fill it with warm water, add a teaspoon of salt, also stowed on the sill, give it a thorough stir and do his morning death-rattle routine. The noises, especially when the old chap's breath was running out and the brine ebbed near 'the little tongue'; were bloodcurdling to this three or four-year old. I was always relieved to see him emerge pink-cheeked and blue-eyed and looking remarkably normal.

Some time after my grandmother Eva died, Isaac came to stay with us, where he lent a hand in the shop and Bottle Store while he still could, but he was too old and impatient and set in his ways to be a publican. He was given the back room in our flat, since it was closest to the bathroom and furthest from our racketing or squabbling, where the three of us shared the room for a while. After the old man left, his room became my brother's den and later Beryl inherited it, when Bo, needing his independence and privacy, managed to talk my father into giving him a room in the hotel. If the little I saw of it was a revelation, the mind boggles to think of what we did not see. When Beryl matriculated from Eunice High School in Bloemfontein and went to Cape Town, I inherited the tiny principality.

It had no particular smell, other than the synthetic leopard-skin cloth I slung across the opening of a low storage cupboard I built, and then was too lazy to fit a door. It gave off a strange smell in summer, which did not blend well with occasional spilt Monis Moscato or Jerepigo, when pouring myself a nightcap. I smuggled a bottle or two from the Bottle Store on my first varsity vac and exponentially increased stocks the following year, when I was forced to come home and make up for squandering what had otherwise been a magnificent year at Rhodes.

This room shared a flat roof with two storerooms at the rear of the building. The smaller of the two was for our trunks and private belongings, while the large one housed spirits, the kind that come in bottles, but couldn't grant favours, like genies. Crates and boxes of whiskey, gin, vodka, brandy, French cognac, cane and a colourful collection of local and imported liqueurs were stacked to the ceiling.

The corrugated zinc roofing over my bedroom was particularly old and rusty and there were at least half a dozen leaks. When farmers prayed for rain, I was torn between their plight and mine. It took some practice arranging enamel and porcelain chamber-pots, as well as a collection of buckets and large cans, to coincide with leaks, and then to gauge the changing tones as they filled, so as to empty them in time. For many years, the smell of sweet wine reminded me of hot summer nights; the whine of mosquitoes, lying on my divan sipping a bottle of Monis Moscato, while Ella Fitzgerald gamely tried to lend some atmosphere, accompanied by the contrapuntal plinks and plonks in a much friskier range of keys.

Unaired carpets—in spite of their weekly thrashing—furniture polish and Cobra floor wax bring to mind our lounge, at the end of the passage connecting the front door with the rest

28

of our flat. The window opened into an overhang and sunlight never touched or warmed the tiny room. Even the globes in their Nouveau shades could hardly dispel the gloom. That was where my father found some kind of solace on Saturday afternoons, if the European bar was quiet. (The Coloured bar and Bottle Store closed at 1 pm.) He would sit with his ear to the Philco as the broadcaster's nasal tone—accompanied by static blips and squeaks—filtered through the screened veneer arches. I found it miraculous—(still do)—that meetings at Kenilworth, Turffontein or Durban came right into our little lounge in Colesberg, while my father sat glued to the wireless, its emerald eye reflecting off his high forehead.

Chapter Six
A LEDGER IN HER OWN TIME...
'Van horen zeggen liegt men veel' *(From hearsay, many lies are told)* - one of Miemie's favourite sayings

A month after Lautrec immortalised Jane Avril's flamboyant debut on canvas at the Jardin de Paris—in that heady era of gas-lit salons, top hats and canes; bonnets, fans and crinolines—Maria Francina de Wit was born on 22nd May 1893. Baptised 2nd July the same year, little is known about her early life, other than that she grew up on her parents' farm near the hamlet of Anysberg, west of Ladismith in the Little Karoo.

A robust family tree has its uppermost branches tangling into the late sixteen hundreds, when her great, great, great, great grandfather, Christoffel de Wit, was born in 1695 at De Elbe, in Germany. He came to South Africa in 1713, where he did not waste much time and married a Judith Stevens, (born 1698, at Druten, Holland) on the 25th September 1717, in Paarl.

Her father, Stephanus Petrus, Oupa Faan to us kids, had already been an aged widower when we first began visiting the farm, having outlived two wives who each bore him six children. Miemie was the second oldest child from his first wife, Petronella Hermina, and was nine years old when her mother died, at the age of thirty-one, a year after the youngest child, Christoffel (Stoffeltjie), was born.

A surviving anecdote points to Miemie's instinctive lateral thinking, considering the times. Stoffeltjie was a sickly child, having developed what may have been a type of lactose intolerance. Miemie told us how they tried everything; sheep and goat milk, powders and medicines from the doctor or chemist in Ladismith, but the child was rapidly getting weaker and more emaciated by the day.

A donkey foal suckling at the mare gave her an idea and ass's milk did the trick. Superstitious predictions proved groundless and Stoffeltjie grew into an astute young businessman. He bought a General Dealer store, at a small cross-roads called Winkelplaas, on the road between Anysberg and Ladismith, which he and his wife Miems ran for many years.

Miemie was many things, but in a walnut shell, she was a reassuring, reliable and fearless presence. We knew we were safe with her and that all was secure. She was a steady, familiar voice that soothed or scolded, someone who taught by example, never faltered and remained an unobtrusive adviser, arbitrator and leak-proof confidante. She was our second mother, though their roles were always interchangeable, and we turned to her, especially when we thought our parents were being unnecessarily strict. She would never undermine their authority but came to our rescue at opportune moments.

Honest, straightforward, doggedly loyal, indefatigable and unpretentious as a landscape, she was an amazing blend of opposites that came together like a fine piece of marquetry. Soft as dough but tough as leather; someone who could change with the times but knew when not to bend; quiet and non-aggressive, but who would fearlessly step into the breach and give as good as she got when the occasion arose. Miemie would rather say nothing if she had nothing to add, which on the face of it seems a cliché, but in the 'passing trade,' we came across windbags, who, on a good day, made Hara-kiri seem attractive.

'Uh.' The three of us came to know that flat, faintly condescending sound from the back of her nose that meant neither agreement nor disagreement. It did not signal comprehension or misunderstanding and was not a maybe, or a sign of interest or disinterest. While she always tried to advise, caution, promote or confirm when she thought something warranted an answer, we soon learned that 'uh,' meant end of story and any further begging or whinging could be dangerous. It was like negotiating traffic lights when we wheedled or begged. A definite 'Nee!' was the green light—scram, while

31

the going is good; 'uh' was the orange light—I heard you the first time—and as we learned the road rules, with a few minor or major collisions with her 'natlap,' we didn't wait for the red light. 'Hou nou op met grens of ek klits jou boude vuurwarm,' was a warning she sometimes gave—she would warm our backsides with a good walloping if we didn't stop whingeing.

On vacation with my mother and Boris in Cape Town, she once brought traffic to a halt on a bustling Saturday morning. She put down her parcels in the middle of Adderley Street, securely racked him across her thigh and gave him a well deserved spanking for throwing a couple of 'tantra' and nearly pulling her off her feet. Drivers apparently leaned from their windows and gave her a resounding ovation. I saw her once fly into the hefty scullery maid, Lena, a morose, unanimated woman and squat as a new cake of Lifebuoy, who in one of her more sullen moods had given Miemie lip. Her attack, with nothing but a wet dishcloth, was so sudden and determined that she drove poor Lena out of the kitchen door and down the back steps. I felt the sting of her cloth many a time on my bare legs but I also witnessed her quiet empathy and benevolence towards the aged or needy.

I think what everyone admired—friend and adversary alike, (including pushy politicians) was her absolute fearlessness. She would only stand back 'Vir my God.' Also thunder and lightning, although I have a feeling she saw them as biblical or celestial messages from the Big Man in person.

The only times I ever saw her fearful and silent were during thunderstorms. She would take shelter in the darkened dining room, seated well away from the windows, clutching me to her chest until the storm had passed. That was the closest Miemie came to 'kvetching'. Nothing held more terror for us than the second or two after seeing a warning twinkle of light between the gaudy curtains, and that ear-splitting crack of thunder, an explosion that seemed to rip the ysterklip koppies apart. We could always find solace, loosely clasped on her lap—as opposed to Ann's demonstrative 'kvetches' (bear like hugs)—

while at other times all three of us felt the sting of a natlap when jumping a late orange light.

Miemie did not gossip and would lend a silent, if unwilling ear in its presence, but never minced her words if someone deserved it. She had a few picturesque, self-explanatory sayings. If we happened to relate a weird or fanciful story that someone else might have impressed or promised us with, she would tell us 'Van horen zeggen liegt men veel.' That was without doubt her favourite, from a Dutch maxim meaning: don't believe everything you hear. She had a stiff Afrikaans 'Church Bible,' with gold-edged pages, and a soft, leather-bound, much-fingered pink-edged bedroom edition, in 'Hoog Hollands'. Though she lived by her Bible, she was never messianic or better than the next.

We were told to use 'dapper en stapper' if we enquired how we were going to get somewhere. The right foot was 'the brave one,' the left was 'the walker,' and those two trusty appendages got her everywhere, until, in her late sixties, she decided to buy a small second hand motorcar and take driving lessons. She was a gutsy lady and learned to drive when most folk were getting ready to retire. 'If my car did not just suddenly jump off the road with me,' she told us, she would have continued driving much longer. She was on her way to visit her sister-in-law Miems, at Winkelplaas, when due to bad corrugations or mistiming the turnoff, her car slewed down the steep shoulder and that put 'dapper en stapper' back in commission again.

Another of her pithy sayings, directed at a small handful of pretentious folk who thought they were better than the rest, was that they were no better than ''n Drol op 'n dreskas!' A turd on a tea trolley comes close enough. 'You can shit on my head, but don't rub it in,' was another beauty and the peak of her expletives, when defining the limits of her benevolence. If we mixed in the wrong circles or got involved where we ought not to, there would be a warning and a choice. 'They will shit on you so heavily that the sea could not cleanse you,' or 'Cover yourself with bran (slops) and the pigs will devour you.' In

33

Yiddish, the saying goes 'Az mi shloft mit hint shtayt men uf mit flay': if you sleep with dogs, you get up with fleas.

As a child, I used to think all the nice people were 'Sappe' and abrupt or nasty folk were 'Natte'. I asked Miemie about it one day. 'No, my child,' she said, looking at me as though I could have been right, 'most Nats are good people, it is just that they believe badly.' Those were the days of the 'Nationalist Party' and 'South African Party,' the 'Natte' and 'Sappe'. Miemie was a loyal Sap and made no bones about it in a town that might have been nine-tenths Nationalist. In earlier days, when elections were in the offing and local or visiting bigwigs from the Nat camp came to canvass—'koek en koffie' sessions—she would look them in the eye: 'Nee dankie, ek is 'n Sap gebore en 'n Sap sal ek sterwe!' I was born a Sap and shall die a Sap. Epic words from an epic woman, who kept her promise.

My sister once wrote a beautiful short story called: 'His Right-Hand Man'. It was based on Miemie and my father and that, she most certainly was.

For many years, she ran the kitchen, housekeeping department and shop as efficiently and meticulously as the whims of wholesale suppliers; the pitfalls of alcohol or domestic home abuse amongst staff members, and occasional 'acts of God' would allow. When pressure became too great and age began creeping up on her, they took on Anna, as a sturdy assistant.

During quiet spells, Miemie would sit on the high stool behind the shop counter, bringing journals, cashbooks and the old ledger up to date, her style of writing in keeping with the period. She used a dip-pen for many years and it took a few more before she grudgingly took up the ballpoint. 'Die verdomde goed mors meer as hulle skryf!' (the damned things mess more than they write.) For someone who never went beyond Standard Three or Four in a small farm school, her writing, arithmetic abilities, natural aptitude for business, decisive decision-making, and a gift, which she shared with my

34

father, to instinctively spot character flaws, were remarkable.

Fortunately, price increases were rare, as Miemie would sit on her stool painstakingly calculating length or weight increases from the Government Gazette, her lips and fingers silently doing the sums but always keeping the poor in mind. Sometimes my father would be leaning up against the counter, waiting for her bulletin and might wince at the new prices, but she would put his mind at ease, telling him, 'It is actually not as bad as we had thought it would be.'

Other times, she found increases rather steep, and knew, that for the next few weeks there would have to be patient explanations, to folk who found it hard to fathom these seemingly random jumps and had learned to budget to the last farthing.

Miemie was captain of the kitchen and our cook, the gutsy Antie Bee, her first mate. On the long treks between Johannesburg and Cape Town, most visitors opted for early starts to get as much tar behind them during the cooler hours and breakfasts were usually a breeze compared with dinners. She and the room-girls, Miena and Daisy, would use this lull before the shop opened, to set out fresh linen and toiletries in preparation for the next onslaught.

They would also take stock of any items that may have inadvertently gone on holiday with the occupants. Not that it was crippling, but there was a modest amount of, shall we call it, souvenir collecting, which was not added on or tax-deductible in country inns. Certainly not Natie's.

I remember when her osteoarthritis first set in, how she would uncomplainingly knead her fingers. Even though she was never one for taking pills or 'midisyne,' Dispirin or Aspirin didn't seem to bring relief, and there was not much else for her to try those days. Then she heard about boiling a 'tea' from guava leaves. Cold weather was the worst and our winters were bitter. After dinner was done, she would sit with her elbows on the kitchen table, sipping the hot brew, her hands clasped around the mug, wistfully staring over the brim, while I had my coffee and rusks.

'Sjoe! But my joints are really sore tonight,' was all she ever said. Then she put our mugs in the sink and filled her hot water bottle from the blackened cauldron that always stood over the day's embers.

Up to the age of five or so, my biggest treat, very rarely, was to sleep behind Miemie's back on her high cast-iron katel. It had four, brass-capped posts and was unusually high, compared with our slightly more modern ones. I would ask her why I could not do it more often and her reply would invariably be, 'Want jy kriewel soos 'n risper die hele nag!' I could never understand why squirming like a caterpillar should have been such a deterrent between loved ones and it would be nearly sixty years before I discovered the answer. If my wriggling was anything even remotely close to my granddaughter's nocturnal acrobatics, those indiscriminate—but somehow amazingly accurate—flailing of arms and legs, then I offer sincere posthumous apologies to the ever-patient Miemie.

Beds were built to accommodate a chamber pot; 'po,' as the English demurely referred to them and 'pispot' in Afrikaans. Potties, as we called them, came in ceramic or enamelled tin, plain, brightly decorated or often fluted and each one had its distinctive ring-tone as it filled. Because of her distance from a bathroom, Miemie had a tall, white enamelled bucket, with a doughnut-shaped lid and brilliant acoustics. Its merry tune was another reassuring presence for me, on those lonesome nights before the rest of the family came to bed.

I have two photographs taken by Bee when she and her kids visited Miemie in Ladismith. They are dated 1978—five years before her death in 1983—and define the essence of this amazing woman. It is winter and they are taken moments apart as she prepares one of her typical lunches.

In the first picture, she stands at her kitchen table, left hand steadying one of her farmhouse loaves, thick as a Yellowwood beam, while the other holds a bread knife, her knotty fingers clearly caught by the flash. Beyond the loaf peeps the top of a 'Balls' canned fruit jar filled with preserved green figs in syrup. She wears her favourite hand-knitted bottle green cardigan with wide lapels, over a paler green jersey. A small scarf knotted around her throat keeps her kuiltjie, the sensitive hollow at the base of the throat, from the cold air. The apron, simple blue flowers on a white background, was part of Miemie's dress and the only time it came off was when she went to church.

A loaf of bread, a bottle of figs and Miemie.
Ladismith (1978)

Her hairstyle has not changed in all the years we have known her and as she looks up at the camera, almost shyly, the same fold of grey hair sweeps up and back over her head, into the large bolla hidden from view. By this time of day, fine wisps have come adrift, wafting past her ears and a stranger could miss her lazy right eye, but the faint, straight-lipped smile puckering her cheeks, is unmistakable.

In the other picture, she sits at the table and now her right eye has involuntarily closed as she laughs at something my sister may have said. She is handing a dish of veggies around, her own plate is empty, waiting for everyone to help themselves. In the foreground, a large porcelain server is laden with braised potatoes and delectably browned lamb-neck. There would have been veggies, including her decadent 'soetpatatas,' pickled beetroot, boiled baby onions in homemade egg-mayonnaise or stewed dry peaches, which complemented lamb like horseradish does 'gefilter-fish'. All harvested from her garden. Occasionally she served koring (whole-wheat kernels) or gort (barley), which we mixed with dark lamb gravy.

The tracings of age and endurance are visible across her brow, lichenous as an ancient rock. She died on May 5th 1983, a few weeks before her 90th birthday, from complications following a second, severe bout of pneumonia. She always had a weak chest, possibly due to a bad infection in her youth and over the years; she had a few nasty bouts of 'bromkaaikies,' as she called it. As long as we knew her, she had a kuggie, a habitual little cough or clearing of the throat.

Her bedroom was next to ours, but detached from our flat. Many a night, after the nanny or my sister had put me to bed, my parents busy in the hotel and a slither of ghost stories had been doing the rounds—when every shadow, coat or cupboard looked sinister in the dark—her occasional cough next door was enough to reassure me.

Chapter Seven
HOW TIME FLIES...
Life with the innocent flirt: never dull, but
sometimes... embarrassing

We often heard my mother use that one. 'My, my, how time flies'. It took time, nearly half a century, to grasp the meaning. She was the oldest of Isaac and Eva Traub's four children, born 9th May 1902. We know nothing about my maternal grandparents' early days in Eastern Europe and the scraps of information we have are typically conflicting.

The striking and the strict. Our maternal
grandparents Eva & Isaac Traub (Date?)

In my grandfather's South African Naturalization papers—granted 13th February 1905—his place of birth is written as 'Kadane Russia,' while in my mother's passport it is 'Kadan Lithuania'. My mother told us she was one-year-old when they emigrated to South Africa, but according to his papers, applied

39

for in 1903, it states, 'Isaac Traub has resided in the Colony for two years and 3 months.' In one of the applications, signed in 1903, it states he will be '29 years at next birthday,' suggesting a birth date round about 1874. Eva was born in 1879.

Once upon a time... The bubbly Ann, caught in a moment of repose (Date?)

Ann was born a day after Mont Pelée's eruption. Martinique may have lain on the other side of the world, but could seismic stirrings and spectacular sunsets have played a role in shaping her? She often used the word 'vivacious,' as applied to others, and I think that would describe her. A bubbly, fun-loving, jaunty girl, who became caring and empathetic, in love with people and the beauty of nature. And sometimes, just a little too (embarrassingly) spontaneous for her children, though everyone adored her for it.

My grandfather emigrated to South Africa and once he was settled in Beaufort West, he sent for my grandmother and Ann. He bought a small shop and they went on to raise three more boys, Eli, Israel (Issy) and Philip (Pip), the youngest. When the children had gone their separate ways, they sold up and moved to a flat in Queen's Road, Sea Point, Cape Town. It was a two-minute walk from Queen's Beach, where they lived until my grandmother died. Everyone who knew Eva, spoke of her loving and kind nature and her close relationship with her four children, especially my mother. She died suddenly, 16th March 1935, possibly from a heart attack, in the arms of Philip, who was on leave in Cape Town at the time. My mother, also on holiday, had gone shopping that morning and came home with an armful of flowers, knowing how much Eva adored them. Boris, four or five at the time, came skipping down the steps to meet her, 'Granny died...granny died...' he sang to the innocent tune of infancy. 'Ah bitterer gelechter,' as we say in Yiddish, bitter laughter indeed. She was only fifty-six.

Eli and Issy both did law and were in partnership for a few years in Vryburg. After marrying Jane Geffen, Eli went on to establish a practice in Worcester—where he served terms as mayor. They had two children, Bernice and Colin.

Issy gave up the bar for the brush not long after qualifying and, untutored; he chose the life of a painter. His portraits and landscapes were exceptionally good. On a painting vacation in Arniston, near Hermanus, he met Rhoda Lazarus, a fine sculptor from Johannesburg. She was doing watercolours—her other

41

forte—on the rocks early one morning, and it was love at first light. They emigrated to Israel after their marriage, where, amongst other commissions, she would later do the large pieces for the Rothschild Gardens. They had no children.

Philip initially became a pharmacist and he and Issy served in the Second World War. In Durban to board HMS Amra, he accidentally left his sunglasses in a cab taking him to the harbour. Back in Durban more than a year later, he caught a cab into town and in passing, related the incident to the cabby, who nonchalantly opened the cubbyhole and handed him his glasses. It is a simple anecdote, but one which qualifies those times.

After demobilization, he returned to Wits to do medicine. I remember his mid-year holidays in Colesberg and I was impressed by the size and 'fatness' of his textbooks. He studied mostly in his bedroom, but would sometimes sit by the heater in the bar or on one of the empty paraffin drums in the garden, comfortably warmed by the sun. Soon after graduation, he set sail for Britain, where he joined a GP practice in London (Fulham), which he finally took over. He married Pauline Taylor and they had a son, Nicholas.

We knew Oupa Traub as 'intelligent and well-read,' but he was also a tough disciplinarian, with very little patience and stubborn as a rusty lock. In their late teens, my mother and uncles were still under his tight reins, and that was Beaufort West, a mere village those days. He must have taken a liking to my father when he first met Ann, and after an unknown period of courtship and letter writing, they married in 1926.

On the back of another sepia photo, my mother has written, in her lackadaisical longhand, 'July 1926,' and across, what must have been a crisp blue sky at the top of the picture: 'Still on honeymoon!' The pair are seated on the rear trunk of a boxy little roadster—could it be his first Ford?—with square canvas top and separate canvas windows clipped into place. The paleness of the tyres and fingerprints on the narrow mudguards show a healthy coating of dust.

The coy honeymooners, Ann & Nathan (1926)

Despite being 'on honeymoon,' he wears a dark suit, neatly knotted tie and a hanky peeps from the breast pocket. His pomaded hair looks slightly dishevelled, as he leans against his new bride, right arm draped around her neck and the way she daintily holds his hand, could either be a sign of endearment or modesty, by its proximity to her boobs. The sun glints off their hair—his has grown quite a bit since the wedding photo, maybe the honeymoon was delayed due to pressures at the hotel?—and they both peer rather shyly at the camera.

We still try to fathom 'where' Ann came from. She was outgoing and chatty, sometimes frivolous and often had us squirming with her down-to-earth spontaneity. Although we sometimes referred to her as a bit of a 'luft mensch,' scatterbrain, she was extremely caring, generous to a fault and empathetic. She was not one for self-praise or self-seeking and dressed very plainly, often throwing on the closest items at hand. 'I've never liked being oysgeputst,' (dolled up), she would say. (I must have inherited that trait, because I once received a birthday card that read: 'Don't drink and dress!') She was also not a gossip, but unlike Miemie and Natie, she did enjoy a bit of pithy news.

Like her mother, she was besotted about flowers, fruit and

43

salad veggies. It could be awkward in Colesberg, but more so after they came to live in Cape Town, when she would pick flowers, or worst of all, snap cuttings from private gardens and hedges. We did not risk taking her into our National Parks for fear of being arrested. It was bad enough picking fruit dangling over walls, but she would occasionally amble onto a property to filch bigger or better specimens. 'You people are forever picking on one, it's only fruit, for God's sake!' She probably perceived all things natural as being universal and I am sure if we still had a proper garden in Colesberg, she would have been equally generous in her sentiments.

Other than the village kids, she and Ou Labbes, the stationmaster, were Colesberg's most avid filmgoers. In winter, they went well fortified against the cold, plus a good supply of their favourite nibbles. Anne had quite a sweet tooth. My father did not, although he occasionally enjoyed 'Caramels'. Whoever went to the 'bioscope,' as they referred to the cinema those days, would pop across to the Palace Café during the interval to buy him a packet. By the time we got home, he would be in bed reading the papers, his dentures dozing in a glass of Steradent on his bedside table, cheek-by-jowl with a packet of Rennies. He would suck his Caramels with great gusto, 'geshmak,' and tell us 'si tsugayt in moyl,' they melt in the mouth.

Ann and I would walk to the cinema, a good distance up town, and the fun would begin on our way home, when a stealthy striptease began. First, undoing her bra, then unbuttoning a few jersey or blouse buttons, ever so sneakily; not in the interest of public concern but to try and fool whoever accompanied her. At some point, she would undo the skirt catch and a few of the upper corset stays, and nearer home, release one or two suspender toggles. By the time we reached the hotel, she resembled a tornado survivor, as one sees them on TV. One hand clutched near her groin held stockings and skirt; the other ditto for blouse and upper garments. She had honed it to a fine art and as she stepped into our flat, she simultaneously stepped out of her clothing. When I got my driving licence, it made the street-part of our trip less of an ordeal, but when dropping her in front of the hotel, before garaging the car, her skirt sometimes fell to her ankles as she ever so genteelly tried manoeuvring her way out.

She was always involved with the community and a big supporter of various 'bazaars' and activities for White, Coloured and Black schools. An old Dutch Reformed Church, originally built in what would one day become the Non-White location, served as a Black school, but as far as I can recall, I am not aware of any concerts or other public activities. The hospital was up on 'Vaalbank,' the plateau at the southern end of town that divided it into an upper and lower section. She would get one of the drivers to take her when visiting patients, irrespective of colour, and invariably took 'just a little something' for them.

Ann could be forgetful or 'sketter-brained,' as my father sometimes referred to her, which could have been a combination of personality and her early medical history. Putting bits and pieces together, she suffered many years from what could have been malignant hypertension. I remember her having to rest, almost daily, in their darkened bedroom because of tiredness and excruciating headaches. There would be a cool damp cloth pressed to her forehead, brows puckered with pain, and we were forbidden to play in or anywhere near the flat. Anti-hypertensive drugs were in the embryonic stage and she was a candidate for a stroke, acute heart failure or a heart attack. In retrospect, her mother may have died from the same disease.

As a last resort, Doc Cooper advised a new and somewhat untried operation. He knew an excellent surgeon at Wits, Mr Lee McGregor, who was pioneering the Smithwick Technique in South Africa. Two long chains of intricate nerves on either side of the spine (sympathetic nerves), are surgically severed in an attempt to lower severe, uncontrollable high blood pressure. Although she was the right candidate, it did not come without risk. I seem to recall she was only the second patient to have it in South Africa, and they were not holding out much hope. She had bad complications after the first operation, and they nearly lost her after the second. The surgeon phoned my father and told him Ann was at death's door, so he caught a train to Johannesburg. He found her semi-conscious, doctors, nurses and technicians fussing around the bed. The rebound effect of this operation is that blood pressure suddenly plummets from those unbelievable heights to near fatal rock-bottom—playing havoc with the other organs—and few of the sophisticated counter-medications were available those days.

She was away for ages, possibly a few months—like dogs and cats, young children have no real time frame of measure—and when she returned, pale and thin, she seemed like a stranger. Our initial days or weeks of pining had faded into indifference, and Miemie had been there throughout. We were given strict instructions not to hug or squeeze her too tightly and I remember those two dark 'herring-bones,' as my sister described the massive scars cascading down her back. All the years of (morbid) hypertension and those periods of hypotension, must have taken their toll, affecting her short-term memory and possibly tinting some of her eccentricities. It did however give her almost thirty years of reasonably healthy life.

'Nonsense! I'm just a grootbek,' my mother would scoff when friends jokingly called her a flirt. Having spent most of her life in the hotel trade, surrounded predominantly by men, Ann was not so much a flirt as someone who enjoyed the attentions and compliments given her by locals and passers-by.

'He can park his gum under my instep any day,' we often heard her and her Cape Town cronies say, indicating someone was handsome or a 'chap' (hard 'g'): a catch. She said that about James Mason and Clark Gable, when they appeared in the papers and once about Peter Cheyney. I'm not sure whether she meant the author or Lemmy Caution and Slim Callaghan, his larger than life fictitious characters. She was friendly and chatty and I imagine men found her cuddlesome, but she was only tactile or 'kvetzy' with her children; dispensing smothering

46

hugs and embraces that sometimes left us breathless. 'Out of the mouths of babes and drunks you hear the truth,' was another favourite, and she must have heard enough of that to last her a lifetime.

With all her *joie de vivre* and chattiness came a good dollop of undisguised impatience and restlessness. There was always the drumming of fingernails or a tapping foot, lips pulled askew and arched brows demanding: So? When are we going, already?

'Go put on a cardigan, I'm freezing!' she would tell us, or 'Bring me your nose, it's running.' I was in my late teens when I discovered 'blessed' wasn't a curse, after hearing rebukes like 'I told you to put your shoes on, you blessed idiot,' or 'I'm tired of telling you blessed children not to make a noise when I'm resting.' We should have put her spoonerisms and malapropisms to paper. 'Have you seen Peter Panther in the Pink Sellers?' She overheard me telling Boris that one of my varsity mates, Warwick, had married. 'What! Warrick marrick?' she blurted excitedly. And when she went to the UK in '53 to visit her brother, Philip, she told Boris that after watching the Queen's procession to collect her crown, she had done a little shopping at 'Tom and Jerry's,' (Derry and Toms).

Ann and her fly swatter went hand-in-hand. We loathed the bloody thing. She had no compunction—as she dutifully sat listening to us—to swat, with the speed and skill of a chameleon, a fly that may have perched on us. Not only did we get a hell of a fright, but when we complained, she would flick off the remains with an offish, 'It's only a damned fly, for God's sake!'

She loved shows, music and dancing and had a wonderful sense of humour. Bottle all that up and send it to Colesberg, far from the maddeningly exciting city life, and it must have been difficult for her to adapt to those surroundings. Although Beaufort West was not Las Vegas, it was much larger than our dorpie and had a bigger Jewish community where she had a wide circle of friends.

She never learned to drive and was dependent on drivers, especially when she began tiring in later years. I remember my brother driving us back from the station one day, which was a few miles out of town, and on a whim, she asked him to teach her. It was hilarious. After the third time she nearly took the fence down—within a distance of fifty metres—she lost her nerve, he lost his patience and I nearly lost control of my bladder. She never bothered again. They say family members should never teach each other to drive and I learned why, the hard way. I asked Bo to teach me once and my left arm was tattooed black and blue. 'Clutch!'—zap! 'Brake!'—zap! 'Second, God damn it!'—zap! It would take Kierie and his timeless patience to finally get me through.

Ann was a good sport, but not the sporty type, although she did play golf at one stage. There were no greens but miles of sand, stones and dry scrub; the holes were set in compacted earth and scraped with a collapsible T-frame before putting. My brother caddied for her once and he says that put him off golf for good. (What with Gary Player farming in the district, I believe they now have a very nice golf course.) In her younger days, she pedalled her lady's bike to the post office, but if a lift was not readily available, she had no qualms getting around on foot.

Reading and the movies were her escape from the trying and tiring hotel routine. 'I loved the classics at school,' she would tell us, but soon realised she would need more gutsy stimulation when she settled in Colesberg. She devoured anything reasonably literate, from Cheney to Bellow, Chase to Steinbeck and O'Hara to Du Maurier, as well as a posse of other novelists, poets and playwrights, who sprang to the rescue each night and allowed her to soar above the dark hills and starlit veld.

Her baize card table—like an elderly matron who retains a hint of her former beauty—had taken the brunt of loyal service in its stride. It would be unfolded, its spindly legs locked into place, matching green fold-out chairs dusted, and Ann and her mates spent a couple of hours doing some heavy gambling in our tiny flat lounge. Never an expletive was heard during their games of rummy. Although 'that was a loverly kitty' (Auntie Bessie, ex UK) could hardly buy a small slab of Cadburys, the oohing and aahing when someone 'blitzed'—unexpectedly laid the hand down in one foul swoop—would sound like a lotto winner.

Ann's mornings started at six a.m. or earlier in summer. She always woke long before that, did a bit of reading, bathed and was ready for action on the hour. Her day began overseeing the 'tapmanne,' a motley crew of dedicated freelancing wine-bottlers, who did part-time shifts according to demand. There were also a handful of apprentices, the up-and-coming brigade champing at the bit, who could be called on in an emergency. They became less and less enthusiastic to fill the shoes of their mentors when my mother, back in the nineteen-fifties, decided to change the age-old 'dop-system' to groceries: sugar, dried beans, mealie-meal or samp from the shop. The 'dop-system,' a throwback from colonial days, was a fairly common practice, especially amongst the farming communities, whereby labourers would receive a ration of raspy wine, in lieu of a salary. It was officially abolished in 1961, but is probably still being practiced in certain areas. She was not so much a freethinker, as a free spirit and unwittingly bucked the system in different ways.

When the destructive force of water turning to ice burst pipes, when ponds froze and hoarfrost sparkled in the mornings, my mother later handed the tapkamer reins to Kierie, our Coloured barman, or one of us if we were home. Ann would use this free time going over correspondence or outstanding accounts, or perusing her Reservations Book. This hefty volume was not only the bane of her life, but ours, the only difference being that as difficult as it was for her to decipher, it was impossible for us. In addition to her illegible scrawl, she had developed her own shorthand over the years, which like fashion, was in continual flux.

When she took annual leave, it would be up to my father or

us, to play Champollion to this Rosetta stone. He at least benefited from symbols that remained unchanged for centuries, whereas our clues altered with the seasons and the whims of our mum. It is pure good fortune that more botched-bookings did not occur, as the stress associated with one or two nail-biting incidents I witnessed, was draining.

At seven a.m., Alfred and Moses, the bar-boys, dusted, swept and polished the bar and Bottle Store floors, and then fridges and shelves would be replenished. Bottles of sherry (cheap red wine) were carried in large wicker baskets, which required keen perusal by those in charge at either end. Only after the first man had packed his eighteen bottles and been given time to reach the bar, could the second begin. These lads were sharp, and by one slowing while the other speeded up, they would soon be on each other's heels, and one or two extra bottles could be packed and stashed in a toilet, en route. On one occasion, realising a 'sting' was in progress, I pre-empted Moses, and the look on his face, as he scurried into the cloakroom clutching an extra bottle in each hand, was vintage Three Stooges stuff. My paltry attempt at ticking him off was unnecessary, but I did warn him, 'Next time it will be between you and the Old Master.' I was known as a softie and when in need, a soft touch, but the old master was another story.

In the period between completing the bars and opening time at ten, the driver would take Ann to the post office to collect or send mail and do one or two rounds about town. It could also include a quick visit to the hospital, if she knew someone had been admitted. Even strangers, who may have fallen victim to those soporific Karoo highways.

She generally worked in the Bottle Store. Unless the shop was extraordinarily busy—and we happened to have a full complement of barmen—there was a 'gentle ladies' agreement that Ann did not do shop duty, as Miemie found her a little too impatient. Even in the Bottle Store, where customers usually knew exactly what they wanted, her fingers would drum the counter if they dithered a bit. Ann was never demanding or

50

assertive and with all her glowing attributes, even 'luft ladies' had their limitations.

Every year, the weeks leading up to the festive season slowly brewed a barely controlled mania, when it seemed money was endless and time not; when shops and bars hummed and bristled like a cornered porcupine and sometimes threatened to erupt. Hotel life could bring out the best and worst in us, and she always had a good chuckle when recalling an incident, when shoving and shouting had become impossible.

On this particular occasion, the store was packed and none of my mother's calls-to-order made the slightest difference. A nasty brawl was in the making, as the minute hand on the clock neared 5 p.m. She reached for the 'sjambok'—a long plaited leather whip hanging on the wall behind her—hoisted her dress, climbed onto the chair, then up onto the counter, and gave a few indiscriminate lashes about some heads and shoulders. The crowd instantly fell back and in that moment of stunned silence, a voice rang out: 'Pas op! Hier kom medim Pagel!' Two circuses used to do the country rounds: 'Boswell's' and 'Pagel's.' Amongst Mrs Pagel's many talents, was an exciting 'Madam Pagel's lion-taming act'. 'I had to get down and turn my back on the lions for a moment,' Ann told us, 'and have a quiet giggle to myself.'

Our holidays with her in Cape Town, were like being on the lam. On buses, off buses, catching trains or trams, 'schlepping' up or down steep roads or stairs or cramming into sluggish cage-lifts. Not to mention hitching—commandeering—lifts, as she stuffed more into a day than most people I knew could do in a fortnight. Her nonchalance and lack of inhibitions made her a colourful character and when family members or friends spoke about her 'charm,' we reminded them 'If you're not related to her'.

After the old Bordeaux Hotel was sold, she would stay at the Arthur's Seat Hotel, when on vacation. She invited me and two of my varsity mates for dinner once, and later, we sat in the crowded lounge, the holiday season in full swing, enjoying coffee, cheese and biscuits. She excused herself, 'I'm just going for a pee'. Instantly on guard, I watched the ladies' door. The evening had gone remarkably well, but as the door opened and she stepped out, I saw impatience had reared its 'dread', and the entire back section of her dress was caught up in her broeks (knickers). I desperately tried catching her eye as she began the long cat-walk back, but she was far too busy eyeing the gentle folk around her and returning, what she thought was their friendly smiles. 'Ma!' I hissed through clenched teeth when she was near enough, trying to indicate as subtly as I could, and she gave me one of her classic, what's-wrong-now pissed-off looks.

'Oh, this?' she said, casually flipping out her dress with the snap of a spinnaker swallowing the breeze, dropped into her chair and ticked me off, for always picking on her. My friends, who had got to know her over the years, adored her.

On another occasion, also at the Arthur's Seat, she had found the entrance steps too much for her and would walk down the ramp into the basement parking area to get the elevator. On this occasion, four young men dashed in as the doors were sliding shut, their long hair fashionably dishevelled. I could see from the way she was eyeing the quartet that she was going to say something embarrassing, but I was helpless to stop her, and could possibly have caused further complications by trying. Almost at the lobby, I was handing her a mental pat on the back for good behaviour, when she shook her head. 'You chappies must damma really have a haircut,' she said, in the maternally familiar tone she used on us. With that the doors opened, they gave her a quizzical smile and politely stood aside as she strode out. I caught up with her and asked if she knew who they were? 'No,' she said, 'but they do need haircuts'. 'Those are the Shadows!' She didn't look impressed. I explained they were Cliff Richard's band—(performing at the Alhambra Theatre at the time)—and that got her interest. She was fond of his music and seemed quite chuffed with this bit of information, but standing at reception, drumming her fingers while waiting (fifteen seconds) for her room key, she clucked her tongue, 'I still think they would look better with a bit of a haircut.'

She would think nothing of cadging a lift into town if buses were full or running late. If she had had a rough day, she would hitch her dress and sit on the kerb until a bus or potential lift appeared. Natie would sooner have eaten 'trayf,' (ham on a buttered sandwich) than hitch a lift with a stranger.

Years later, while visiting my brother in Israel, she chose to stay in the city and he had booked her into a small, well-known hotel on Ben Yehuda Street in Tel Aviv. It was in a good area and more 'lebedik,' lively, as in those years his home was still completely surrounded by orange orchards. Up early for breakfast, she noticed 'quite a gallant chappie sitting at the next table, who looked familiar.' After she was done, she strolled over...he invited her to sit down and 'I had a very nice chat with Moshe Dyan this morning,' she told Bo when he came to fetch her.

The earlier years of hypertension had taken their toll and weakened her heart, which now required treatment for low-grade failure. In nineteen seventy-two she suffered a series of strokes and the running of her flat and needs fell on Beryl, who lived in the apartment next door. 'You're so precious,' she used to say, almost grinding her teeth with love and delectable wonderment when bathing the grandchildren, 'granny can just eat your little tootsies all up' and she would playfully nibble their podgy pink feet, beaming her infectious smile.

On 29th September 1973, aged seventy, another stroke ended her last 'vegetoid' months, when she no longer seemed to recognise her grandchildren or us and had to be fed and constantly supervised by day and night nurses. While some stroke patients may not be able to speak or communicate, it does not always mean they cannot hear or understand. I hope this was not the case with her, as she was much too passionate about life and laughter, which she took in or gave by the armful, to have been trapped within her mind.

Chapter Eight
A MATTER OF TIME...
'A Vanished World'...life, as it was, in Zagare

That is the title of a book by Roman Vishniac. For posterity, it timeously records his black and white memories (photographs)—'many taken with hidden cameras'—the lives of Jews in shtetls, towns and cities across Central and Eastern Europe, before theirs became 'A Vanished World'.

'It is a vanished but not vanquished world...,' Vishniac writes in a short dedication, and, in the foreword, Elie Wiesel writes: 'A supreme witness, Vishniac evokes with sorrow and with love this picturesque and fascinating Jewish world he has seen engulfed by fire and darkness.'

A survivor herself, my cousin, Eva (Kolska) Horwitz, gave it to me as a birthday present, and in the flyleaf, she wrote: '...and who cares to keep the vanished world kindled.' That meant even more to me. She came from an extremely close, cultured and talented family in Poland. They spent two and a half years in the Tomashov (Thomaszów Mazowiecka) main ghetto, under abysmal conditions, until 31st October 1943, when her entire family and 12,000 other Jews were sent to Treblinka, where they were all murdered. She and a friend went to live in a smaller ghetto for six months and were then transferred to Majdanek and later to Auschwitz. They were then sent to Bergen Belsen, where they were liberated at the end of the war.

Her passage to womanhood was though unspeakable devastation. Although she could never bring herself to talk or write about it, she introduced me to some of the survival authors. I had always thought of those books as taboo, after accidentally coming across 'The Scourge of the Swastika' on my mother's bookshelf, and she had been very upset by her (supposed) negligence, which I will touch on, later. Like all the other survivors, Eva could not forgive herself for having managed that. She died of cancer, but like many others who

54

came through, it was compounded, no doubt, by an irrevocably broken heart.

I have very dear memories of Eva. I was a season ticket holder with the CTSO (Cape Town Symphony Orchestra) and for many years I took her to the Thursday evening concerts. On the way home—depending on how the music had touched her...how close it came to 'the vanished world' and what memories or emotions it stirred—there would either be silence or we would chat about the evening's fare. Occasionally our discussions touched on those who deny that the Holocaust ever took place, that it was a Jewish myth or 'another' of our fiendish schemes to get sympathy and financial reparations, or, people that say it's time the Jews stop brooding and whingeing about the Holocaust. Later, we would talk about those eminent figures and countries who compare Israel with Hitler and Nazi Germany. Germany was such a civilized and cultured country, she once said; how could he (Hitler) have done that to us?

She had large expressive blue eyes, that silently expressed the horrors and inhumanity they had witnessed, passing through not one, but three death camps. And she laughed a lot, no doubt to hide the ever present pain of having lost her parents, siblings and other family members; through the barbarous maws of Hitler's relentless 'final solution'.

I wonder, if those deny-ists of the Holocaust have ever seen the irretrievable loss, the sadness and the slow trickle of a tear, on the face of a 'survivor' during the poignant movements of Beethoven's Pastoral or Dvorak's New World?

*

For the Holocaust deny-ists, allow me to state a few brief facts.

My paternal grandparents were murdered by Hitler and/or his Gestapo and/or his Nazi Regime. There were regular letters from our grandmother, in Yiddish. They spoke about whispered, then suspected, and finally, corroborated German atrocities. None survived, probably thrown out with all the unnecessary hotel mail every few days, BUT; there are millions of other archival letters and documents, should the deny-ists bother to read them.

Sometime between 1940 and 1941, the flow of letters suddenly ran dry. The early German brutalities were supposedly hearsay, falling on the deaf ears of many Western leaders. But the 'slaves,' lucky enough to have escaped Hitler's determined tightening of the net—does the word jewfish come to mind?—had alerted others, and by now my parents expected the worst. Although Hitler's 'Final Solution' only became 'official policy,' following the Swannsee Conference in Berlin, on January 20th 1942—four days before my second birthday—where they Rationalised Mass Extinction of the Jews et al...history would later confirm that on the 2nd October 1941, Hitler's murderers caught up with the Jews of Zagare. 633 Men, 1017 women and 496 children were herded to various centres out of town to receive their fateful benediction. Massacred and dumped in mass graves!

If that was not heinous enough, history also reminds us that 'benches were provided for spectators'. That kind of etiquette is no doubt doubled, when audience participation is the order of the day. (From Sir Martin Gilbert: 'The Second World War.' A complete history.) 'Not a feather in their cap,' as my mother would have referred to the Zagare residents who turned out to watch this macabre execution.

One wonders how many deny-ists have bothered to visit the rash of labour / death camps dotting Germany and Eastern Europe? Idyllic places with lilting names like: Buchenwald, Treblinka, Auschwitz, Birkinau, Dachau, Chelmno, Sobibor, Belzek, Theresienstadt...to name but a few. All, no doubt, figments or schemes of the Jewish mind...

*

One of our biggest regrets is that we never took the trouble to

56

extract or tap more of Natie's past. Those rich but not always pleasant memories of his Zagare childhood in Lithuania and his often harsh and varied experiences during his early years in Ladismith and the Little Karoo, on first coming to South Africa. Partially in our defence is that hotel life did not often pander to such luxuries of intimacy, and Nathan was anything but a talkative man, especially about his turbulent youth.

How much more fulfilling it would have been, to have known about his childhood, intimacies and anecdotes about his parents, their home, his siblings and other family members who remained in Lithuania and Russia. What his school and the town were like, friends he may have had, the games they played and how the boy had perceived life in Lithuania. Fortunately, he managed to get his younger brother, Percy, to South Africa in 1925.

We only have a sprinkling of dates, names and places. What we do know is that my paternal grandmother Gita, nee Daniller, was one of six children: Max, Koppel, Heina Reisa, Sarah and Rochel, born to Boruch Hillel Daniller and Sheina Leah— surname unknown—our paternal great-grandparents.

Gita married Moisha Chaim Kaplan, a young miller, and they had seven children. We cannot be sure, but it seems my father, born 1898, and his younger brother Percy or Pinchas, born 1st May 1905, may have been the youngest, though one or two of the sisters could have arrived between them. The other siblings were Leah, Dinah, Chilla, Zelda and an older brother Leizer. Unable to remember his birth date, Natie chose July 10th , the day my brother was born.

My grandmother's younger brother Max (Daniller), emigrated to South Africa some years earlier and like so many others, sought his future in the hinterland, where he began doing business in the Ladismith (Cape) area. With the First World War looming, he must have arranged with my grandparents to send my father, and, after his 13th birthday, post-bar mitzvah, circa 1911, Nathan joined his uncle in Ladismith.

After some years, he set out on his own and it was only after

57

he settled in Colesberg, in the mid nineteen-twenties, that he sent for Percy. It is not known how he or my father made their way from Lithuania to England, but as the records show, 'Pinkuss' (sic) Kaplan departed Southampton aboard the Grantully Castle, of the Union Castle Line, third class on January 27th 1925 and arrived in Cape Town on February 21st 1925.

An archival photocopy of the 'Particulars of Immigration'—with vertical columns ruled in pencil for 'date of arrival,' 'No. of Pass'(engers,) 'Sex,' 'Age'—shows name upon name flowing down those long-forgotten pages in the classic light-up, bold-down longhand. Carefully recorded with a dipping pen, Jews arriving from Seda, Riga, Vilna, Poneviz, Majeska, Rokiska, Bialystok, Ostrovno…spilled from the Grantully Castle. They must have looked up in awe at Table Mountain, so different from the Steppes of their youth. The South-Easter could have spread a white tablecloth to welcome them; the abundance of fruit and flowers in the city was probably overwhelming and may have helped ease their insecurities and fears.

Finally the name appears: 'Kaplan, Pincas'—M—19—'Zagara'— and on the opposite page, headed: 'Proceeding To,' and more ruled columns of names, addresses and relationship of those who had motivated the journey: 'Nathan Kaplan'—'Ladismith' 'C.Town'—'bro.'(ther). Lists and figures cannot describe—and I can now only surmise—the reaction when the two brothers finally came face-to-face amidst the cacophony and bustle of strange looking people, noises, smells and a barrage of foreign languages, while gulls wheeled and screeched above.

From the little I saw of my uncle, he too seemed a quiet, introspective man. He was shorter than my father and not as robust, but both had the characteristic Daniller features. He was six or seven when his thirteen-year-old brother left home, but each in their own way must have been emotional, filled with feelings they needed to express and happiness at being together again. My father finally being able to embrace his baby brother, the younger brother overjoyed and relieved that the long journey was over.

Sometime during the First World War, Jews, who had never been warmly welcome in Europe and especially Eastern Europe, were expelled from Zagare. 'Life was being made difficult,' as one of my grandmother's letters intimated and the family fled to Moscow. Chilla, (who could have been sickly?) died en route and Percy, in his pre-teens, must have witnessed her death, and who knows what other horrors he had to face in Russia and back in Zagare again, after the war.

Neither the whereabouts nor their length of stay in Moscow was recorded, but Leizer and Zelda both married and remained after the rest of the family returned to Lithuania. Nothing more is known about Leizer nor the names of Zelda's husband, son and daughter. Back in Zagare, 'Leah married a Kremer...' (the above facts are from some of my grandmother's letters), his first name and their daughter's are also not known. Dinah never married and lived with her parents.

Moisha Chaim, as Natie told Ann, was an observant and religious man, who knew the books of the Pentateuch very well. 'Moshe Kaplan, owner of mill paid Tax; 1913,' is the terse entry from an archival document; the sum total of his pedigree and only official documentation of their lives in Zagare. My grandmother Gita was warm and caring, involved with her family and neighbours, and early every Friday morning, she baked breads and kitkes to give to the poor in their neighbourhood. We got these snippets from my father and ex-Zagare acquaintances my parents came across during the immediate post war years. Had we all been more aware, we might have caught a better glimpse of what life was like for them, their trek to Moscow and back to Zagare.

In his London days, late 'fifties early 'sixties, my brother met many interesting people, including the daughter of Sir Barnett Janner, who would become Baron Janner in 1970. She invited him for a Friday evening 'Shabbes' meal and it transpired her father was also from Zagare and knew Moisha Kaplan and the family, who owned the mill. He had seemed genuinely interested to continue this conversation, but it may have been the timing of the occasion or possibly, as Wilde bemoaned, Youth being wasted on the young, and the input from what could have been a very reliable first-hand witness, was unfortunately squandered.

My father occasionally mentioned that his sisters were very clever girls and could have done well... Although there is not a single grave to mark their place of rest, his sentiments would later bring to mind Thomas Gray (1716—1771) and his Elegy, written in a country church yard:

> Perhaps in this neglected spot is laid
> Some heart once pregnant with celestial fire,
> Hands, that the rod of empires might have swayed,
> Or waked to ecstasy the living lyre.

All we have is a tiny snapshot of Gita and Moisha, which modern technology has touched-up and enlarged for us, and was possibly taken after their return from Moscow. She has a friendly round face and by the set of her lips and the way she watches the camera, there is a hint of humour or mischief in her eyes.

A Vanished World: Our paternal grandparents
Moisha & Gita Kaplan, circa 1930

She wears a traditional 'shaytl' (wig), and a small simple clasp decorously keeps her throat covered.

Everyone who has seen this picture comments on the slant of Moisha's penetrating, almost hypnotic, almond-shaped eyes; his prominent cheekbones, a handsome chiselled nose and clear forehead. They are nothing like the caricatures daubed or pasted on walls and shop windows at the height of the scourge and Kristallnacht. (We find his origins interesting, as his ancestors may have come from much further north and east than we imagined.) His salt-and-pepper beard, shaped to a point, and the cap he wears, are in keeping with the period. That little picture is the sum total of their existence.

The photograph hangs amongst a collection of their grand, great and great-great grandchildren, who they were never granted the opportunity of meeting. I often try to fathom what, or how bad, 'the Jewish problem' could have been. A 'problem' that necessitated stuffing millions of decent, law-abiding men, women and babes in arms into cattle trucks—during stifling summers and freezing winters—and railing them hundreds of miles to 'resettlement' or 'labour' camps, with less care than cattle. A dead cow fetched no kopeks at the market, but another dead Jew simplified the mathematics.

There, they were overworked, underfed, beaten, experimented upon, shot, gassed and incinerated. As history and archival film footage tells us, many died of malnutrition, typhus and exhaustion. Corpses were often left to lie in full view of their fellow slaves, or buried—not always dead—in mass graves.

It is so patently obvious that the erudite men and women who claim the Holocaust was bogus and those who compare Israel with Nazi Germany, have not read or bothered to peruse the sizeable documents, thousands of photographs and reels of film, which not only the Allies, but the Nazis themselves, so arrogantly, but meticulously documented and filmed for posterity. No doubt, to have been screened every year, on

61

'Führer Tag,' and into the 1000 Year Reich.

When I think of my grandparents; the kind and loving Gita and the pious, observant miller, Moisha Kaplan—no different than the 'oupas' and 'oumas' I knew in Colesberg—being force-marched through once familiar, now ridiculing streets and into the forests, where, unlike sheep and cattle, they knew what awaited them… then the demented minds of the Holocaust deny-ists must surely be no different to those of the perpetrators.

Chapter Nine
IN LESS THAN NO TIME...
The reticent tenor, who could have been so much more

My father was not so much insecure, as that he thought the world around him never felt secure. Growing up in Zagare and leaving home at a young age he viewed authority, badges and uniforms with first-hand distrust. Miemie would reprimand him for his suspicious nature whenever official-looking mail arrived, and he would rather pay a little more than look for tax breaks or the possibility 'of a trap' lurking in that foolish world of wheeling-and-dealing. With Natie, everything had to be up-front, 'All your Ts dotted and Is crossed,' as Ann once said.

During and after the depression of '29, farmers were desperately trying to sell their land. Miemie urged him to buy, but he countered, 'People will think I'm a greedy Jew,' capitalising on the plight of others. She admired his giving commodities to those who were really struggling and could not afford everyday necessities, but she was not always comfortable with his financial assistance to certain folk or those that borrowed from him to buy these farms. 'There are people that sign loans with invisible ink,' his myopic old accountant, Mr van Rooyen, who scrutinised documents at nose-length, once told him.

Both he and Miemie recognised the pitfalls; too astute not to distinguish the sincere from the 'shlenters' (nogoodniks), or 'ganeyvim' (thieves), from the honest. Whereas Miemie was secure enough to know when or how to say no, my father was trapped between 'rachmones' (pity) and not wanting to be the stingy Jew (stigma).

As things began to turn ugly in Zagare, Natie sent for Percy, who joined him in the hotel. There he met Rebecca ('Rivkah'), only child of Benjamin and Hettie Kaufman, who owned the store across the road. They married 10th July 1932 and later moved to Johannesburg, with their daughter, Beulah.

My father was the exact opposite to Ann. Reserved, not tactile, undemonstrative —unless something made him 'die moer in'—and taciturn, although I think that is probably a bit too severe. He had a wry sense of humour and he would occasionally respond to a joke with a good chuckle, but generally, it would only be the slight twitching of his shoulders and a crinkling of the eyes that reflected mirth. It was as though the serious business of living did not permit a hearty guffaw. Like Miemie, he was a better listener and reserved comment for only when asked. He was formal, correct and considerate, but not a big entertainer or ready mixer, preferring not to get too involved with the patrons. He seldom took leave, but when he did, when he allowed himself to get away from the pressures and deadlines of the business, he was a different person. Totally relaxed and humorous, and never allowed any of his friends to pay. Everything was on him.

I was a Standard Four lad at boarding school, when he and his friends came to Port Elizabeth for a big meet at Arlington. They picked me up in Grahamstown on the way and booked into the old Palmerston Hotel, where the two of us shared a room. After his bath next morning, he politely turned his back on me, bent forward to put on his baggy old 'ghatkes'— 'They're worse than bloomers,' my mother used to tease him— when he sneezed. A wee 'turdlet,' no larger than a child's pinkie, dropped to the plush carpet and proudly stood between his feet.

There was a moment's silence and then his face slowly appeared round his naked thigh, so full of mischievous innocence that I started to laugh. Slowly his shoulders began shaking as he joined in and finally he wiped away tears of mirth with the back of his hand. 'Nu! Kakker, get some toilet paper and take it avay!' he said, still bent and laughing with his shoulders.

Our bar was the hub of raucous, smoke-veiled camaraderie

64

that had witnessed the odd fight or altercation over the years. I was a toddler when, as I was coming into the hotel entrance one afternoon, he was rushing out of the bar and told one of the wine stewards to immediately take me to Miemie in the shop. An inebriated young man had apparently drawn and waved his handgun in the pub, punctuated with some nasty threats, and then bolted when my father told him to put it away or he would call the police. Natie had followed him to the back yard, where he persuaded the fellow to hand it over and by the time the police arrived, to some good-natured ribbing from the crowd, the excitement was over.

He became an avid horseman, which was not bad for an ex-Litvak. As he had promised himself during those smousing years on a donkey cart, he did purchase two smart carriage horses and felt much more respectable and respected, when he trotted by on his trap. But there are horses and then there are horses, and his penchant would be race horses. I think he enjoyed the thrill of backing, taking the proverbial 'flutter or two' every Saturday, and especially when it came to the annual Metropolitan and Durban July. Being the local Tattersalls man, all bets went through him and if his punters lost, payback could be weeks or months and occasionally, never. Betting debts were a gentleman's agreement and occasionally some of those gentlemen took advantage of that little codicil. My brother happened to be in Colesberg at the time my parents were selling the hotel and packing up to move to Cape Town. Natie looked a little embarrassed when Bo opened a small box he found in his built-in-cupboard, full of old IOUs, signed and dated, for racing bets, sale of horses and monies owed by trainers, all written on old bits of racing sheets and cards cut from cigarette cartons. 'I couldn't believe it, thousands of Rands!' he told me.

Every Wednesday a tight roll of pink 'Tattersalls Racing Forms' arrived in the mail and that always put a purpose in his stride, when he collected it in the shop, and marched to the bar. Carefully slitting it open with a pocketknife, he would roll the papers in the opposite direction to get the curl out and then feast his eyes on trainers, jockeys, sires, dams, and those taunting damn odds. He couldn't wait for Saturday afternoons, to listen to the races. Now and again, he would come back to the pub and we knew his patter so well, we could pre-empt him.

'Mind you,' a pause as he adjusted his heavy framed glasses in the doorway, 'I had a feeling so-and-so would come in,' and we would commiserate with him, knowing he had backed the wrong horse. He would use this opportunity to cast a professional eye around to make sure we were not neglecting our duty. For a racing-man, he was not a big punter—much too aware of where he had come from and the long, unknown road ahead—but enjoyed the excitement of going through those pink racing forms and 'choosing a vienner.'

If he could not make up his mind toward week's end, especially a big meeting coming up like the 'Met' or 'July,' he would ask anyone of us, Miemie, Ann, staff members or a customer in the Coloured or White bar. Miemie would occasionally humour him with a choice, but usually told him 'I am busy, Neitin, I don't have time for such nonsense.' Ann would fit her food-speckled glasses to her nose and choose a romantic or exotic-sounding name, to which he invariably muttered: 'Oi Vey! Vos far ah ferd is dat, Annie?' In desperation times, an innocent passer-by from the location (yesteryear's township) would be hailed: 'Hierjy!' he would call, and then instruct the bemused person to 'Kom, pick a naam, point met die finger'. He would watch them trying to make head or tail of the forms and finally guide them where to press a work worn finger. 'Mind you, dat could be a vienner,' he would say, if they happened to choose a favourite, and that was about as eccentric as my father would be.

During busy times, if he was not serving in the bar or attending to tourists, he would be at his post, where the solid mahogany bar began. Darkened with age, it could still clearly reflect every bottle and glass after a good wipe and polish. The upright till was in front of him, the office immediately to his right and the corridor connecting the bars and Bottle Store, led

66

to his left. It was a strategic command point, Natie's very own flying bridge.

I have no recollection of him ever reading a book but he relished any newspaper he could lay his hands on, carefully perusing anything interesting or newsworthy and leaving the racing pages for 'shtoch,' the titbit for the very end. He and Ann would also devour the 'Zionist Record,' for any glimmer of good news. (In his early Ladismith days, he did attend a farm school for a while.) If we kids were home, he would send one of us, late Sunday afternoons, to see if we could cadge him a paper from a passing car pulling into Hennie's garage across the road, for a pit-stop. He had no special predilection: a Cape or Weekend Argus from Cape Town, The Star from Johannesburg, The Friend from Bloemfontein and Port Elizabeth's Eastern Province Herald. We dreaded having to approach complete strangers, something he would never do, and if we were not home, the unfortunate wine steward on duty would become the newsboy.

Home from boarding school once and now more aware of our dad's Lithuanian accent, I asked him one day why he never pronounced the 'th'. We were standing at his command centre and I remember him giving his lips a preparatory lick, steadily looked me in the eye and concentrating like mad, he began, 'I always say th-is, th-at, th-em, th-ose, so dere you are!' 'In less than no time,' was the only cliché or English phrase that grabbed him, and he would use it to highlight his conversation. 'In less than no time the horse was running at Kenilworth...' or 'in less than no time, they had skinned the buck.'

Every season he bagged a supply of springbok for the hotel. Antie Bee would make delicious fall-off-the-bone braised venison—with a tang of naëltjies (cloves)—which tourists went crazy about, while Miemie made a fresh supply of biltong from fillets marinated in vinegar, then salted, dusted with freshly crushed coriander and hung to dry on wires strung across the pantry. There was always a supply of fresh or dry 'Boere-jerky,' which hung in old flour bags between the gauzed pantry windows. I have never tasted better since.

Natie had a natural ear for music. On rare occasions—which we relished in disbelief—we watched him working over a tune on the piano in the main lounge, until he got a reasonable rendition going. At one stage, we had a young boarder, Thinus, who would bring down his fiddle and draw plaintive or perky tunes from the old instrument if a spontaneous party ignited in one of the lounges. My father asked if he could have a try and after some painful screeches while getting a feel of the strings, he managed to stroke a recognisable tune or two, which any violinist will tell you, takes some doing. Who knows, with a bit of tutoring at the right time, he could have been another Yehudi Menuhin and we might have had to deal with concert tours, rather than concerned tourists.

My brother remembers an occasion when two hikers came into the pub, one with a guitar slung across his shoulder. My father asked if he could strum it and to humour the old chap, it seemed, he handed it over. Natie did a few practice chords and runs, then played and sang one of his two all-time favourites, Shostakovich's 1920s 'Anniversary Waltz'.

Aaronson and Webster's adaptation of the old Spanish song, *Sobre los olas* (Over the waves), for Mario Lanza's 1951 film, 'The Great Caruso,' became the smash hit: 'Loveliest night of the year,' and the second song in Natie's two-song repertoire. They, like his lilac story back in Zagare and the love letters my sister found, are what made my father a real person for us. He was not one who sought centre stage. He had a good voice and if in the right mood or after a few 'schnappses' and friends egging him on, he enjoyed singing these old favourites. He would take up a convincing 'Caruso' pose, one hand to his bosom, the other reaching out in professional supplication, and deliver a heartfelt recital. Modest and unassuming, he seemed to enjoy the applause in his reticent way and sadly, they may have been some of the few times he received genuine recognition.

One of my other regrets is that I never thought of keeping his

68

doodles or the spontaneous sketches he scribbled in spare moments. He had a natural, free-flowing way of drawing on scraps of paper or the pink racing forms. Sometimes it would be a passer-by, at other times he simply followed the fancy that took him at that moment. With a pencil or ballpoint, he constructed his drawings with quick, repetitive outlines until the shape of a man's face, a woman with a fancy hat, my dog, Doxie or a galloping horse, slowly took shape. He did amazing caricatures of 'B.C.'—who boarded with us for many years— that beautifully captured the sometimes-grumpy old gent. Looking back now, his whirly sketches, not unlike those of Ronald Searle, which would grace Punch Magazine many years later, could have been a wonderful memento.

There are no recorded memories of that period when he and Miemie were, so to speak, in the wilderness. There were only snatches mentioned here and there over the years but nothing about their personal relationship. He must have found Ann a bright young woman, with a great sense of humour, and she in turn, although besotted with her mum, was probably ready to shuck the confining reins of her father and gallop off with this handsome chappie.

When we kids were not supposed to understand, my parents spoke Yiddish, and English or Afrikaans for the rest. Their relationship, like others of that period, was not one where love or inseparable adoration were flourished like a flag, but solid in understanding and respect, honesty and trust, in a professionally difficult partnership. In the early days, Ann and Natie took my brother and sister on rare family holidays but by the time I came along, the hotel was far too busy. In the absence of his self-imposed 'no managers' policy, the hotel trade took over and regulated their—our—lives.

Sundays, (not always), allowed a quick snatch at personal and family ties. He would lie in even later than usual perusing the papers, while Ann might read one of her books. Considering their opposing personalities and the nature of the trade, they got on reasonably well. Natie was never aggressive or violent, but if Ann happened to have forgotten an outstanding bill, made a double payment or, catastrophe of catastrophes, a miss-booking; he would send for her and let her have it in a flurry of 'Eng-Yid-aans'. Instead of being contrite when recognising the seriousness of her omission, she would swagger in even more overtly, flashing her peeved, what's wrong now? look. He would be angry, frustrated and at wits' end because he was always aware of doing the right things in business, never offending the large wholesale companies and staying on the right side of the law and customers.

I am sure in his own way he loved Ann and needed and appreciated her multifaceted, if erratic, input and I'm sure he missed aspects of her when she went on holiday. But I know he absolutely dreaded the very thought of Miemie's vacation looming each year, because there lay the solid, dependable and unwavering strength of his business. As Bee once wrote, 'she was his right-hand-man'.

Ann was his partner in marriage; Miemie was his partner in business. Ann made all our socio-domestic decisions; she might have had to work on Natie for days or weeks or months—like the rest of us when we needed something—slowly grinding him down, and the good man would finally capitulate. Miemie confirmed or suggested business deals, changes and staff problems, when Natie sought her advice.

Barring his chronic heartburn—always a packet of Rennies on his bedside table, one in the shop and another in the bar—he enjoyed a healthy, fairly robust life into his mid-sixties, when he was diagnosed with Parkinson's Disease. Then he had the nasty setback necessitating the emergency flight to Cape Town and, after he recovered, they sold the hotel in 1964.

They retired to Sea Point, where they rented a comfortable old flat in Gloucester Court on the Beach Road. His health steadily deteriorated, and in spite of Ann taking care of him with the help of day and night nurses, it became too difficult and he was placed in Highlands House, where he died on 27th May, 1967; a run short of the Biblical Innings.

70

Chapter Ten
BEHIND THE TIMES...
Into the hinterland, where Billy Goat Gruff met his match

I have no dates as to my Uncle Max's arrival in South Africa from Lithuania. He chose Ladismith, where he began by trading or 'smousing' like so many other immigrant Jews. Finally, he was able to purchase a farm and from there his business steadily blossomed. With some of his land under vines, he was one of those who first joined KWV (Koöperatiewe Wijnbouwers Vereniging van Zuid Afrika), established in 1918, and played a role in the establishment of the original Ladismith Cheese Factory.

With threats of what would turn out to be the Great War darkening the horizon, he persuaded my grandparents, his sister, to send my father. Natie must have arrived in South Africa between 1911 and 1912, with all those hundreds of other immigrants heading for places like Doornkraal, Klaver, Garries, Carnarvon, Prieska or Pofadder. The Archives list occupations ranging from general dealers to dental mechanics, shoemakers to salesmen, not to mention dairymen, jewellers, tailors and speculators, as well as feather-buyers and cigarette-makers. Over the centuries, often barred from gymnasia, colleges and universities, they had learned to be multi-taskers and often, Jacobs of all trades.

My father went to work for his uncle and after a year or two tried to join the South African army, but he was too young and he returned to his guardian. After another few years, with a sketchy understanding of Afrikaans and a smidgen of pidgin English, he decided the time had come to branch out on his own. He realised he would need an assistant-cum-interpreter and luck was with him. By word of mouth, he was directed to a farmer in the Anysberg area and that is how he ended up with Oom Stephanus de Wit. The old man introduced him to his

71

daughter, Miemie, who not only knew the district but was familiar with Ladismith, where other family members lived. She was five years older than Natie.

Once again, we have no detailed information about that period of their lives, when the intrepid pair set out into the hinterland, and we could only rely on sketchy anecdotes relating to the type of work and how they coped. The ramshackle corrugated iron huts they put up, were 'fiery hot' in summer and 'like an ice chest' in winter, but there was no hint or mention of any personal…dealings.

My father was granted concessions to open stores where dams, roads or railway lines were being built, cut or laid— which sounds like the introduction to a financial tycoon's biography—but conditions were tough and business slow. Assisted by foremen and labourers, they knocked up temporary shacks, where the most basic essentials were stocked. They initially kept chickens for eggs and meat, but the abundance of small predators and large hungry labourers soon closed off the chicken run.

Natie was a deceptively powerful man. Miemie told the story of buying fresh produce at a farm one day, when a rambunctious Billy goat, 'a solid brute with scruffy beard, a fine set of horns and kwaai (malevolent) eyes,' repeatedly butted my father's thigh. In a rare fit of anger, he took out his pocketknife and, grabbing it by a horn, extended its neck over a parapet and slit the creature's throat. The farmer, impressed by this Tarzanian stunt, initially refused reimbursement but Natie paid him for the carcass and off they went. (That may have been a subliminal thought, so many years later, when for different reasons I slit the Springbok's throat.)

Miemie had already learned to skin and dress small livestock on their farm and so fresh goat and mutton became part of their trade. Our meat at the hotel was always exceptionally good, because butchers realised that she knew more about cuts or quality and the difference between young and old stock, than they did. When a new butchery opened on the block and she did not like the block-man's fare, it was sent back right away. If there were any further ado, she would stride up the street and tell him how her meat should be cut and what type best suited her needs. Boerewors was so fresh and spicy, my siblings and I nipped off chunks and ate it raw, having to dodge Antie Bee's wet cloth, in the absence of Miemie's.

We gathered from some of the Colesberg locals that in his day, Natie was an arm-wrestling and 'finger-pulling' champion, probably honed by those years of rough work. Old-timers or passers-by, especially fortified with a few drinks, were always keen to prove themselves and, while finger-pulling may sound a little flimsy, there was quite an art to it. In my youth, I witnessed two victims with broken fingers. Not only is the pain excruciating, but one of them, the unfortunate David Gordon's—snapped with an audible 'crack'.

I would think of that incident years later. After my parents had settled in Cape Town, I occasionally took them on Sunday drives and Ann got me to pull over at a fruit and veggie cart near Seekoeivlei once. She inspected the carrots—, which, I will admit, did look a little road weary—and told the young hawker, with her friendly candour, that they were foos! (wilted). His retort was equally friendly. 'Nei merrem, dei so fress, dei creck like bones!' he said, trying to snap one, which could easier have been tied in a bow.

As projects were completed, Miemie and Nathan—'Neitin,' as she called him—would pack their meagre goods and belongings onto a donkey cart and set off for the next job. That was when he decided, he told my sister once, that if he had some cash to spare one day, he would splurge on a pair of smart carriage horses. While they were working near Prince Albert, he occasionally accompanied an engineer, who drove them over the Swartberg Pass to enjoy a few drinks in Oudtshoorn, returning to base camp well after dark. Bacchus must have blessed them; it was a formidable road by day, at night it must have been suicidal.

When they worked south of Oudtshoorn for a while, a friend

73

would drive him to Knysna, probably along the 'Passes' Pass. Not always having the time or wherewithal for dental hygiene, he had to go there on one occasion for multiple extractions. On the dentist's advice, he got 'nicely shickered' on Guinness Stout (plus a bucket of oysters) and the 'tson dokter' did the rest, while his equally 'shickered' friend looked on.

Then, another bit of luck. On a train clacking along moonlit rails, the first seeds of Colesberg were sown in the dining saloon. He and Miemie had finished an assignment and were going to move to new roadworks near Mossel Bay, when on the way to Beaufort West, (possibly for one of the Jewish High-Holy days), he happened to meet a bank manager from Colesberg. The fellow mentioned that a small hotel was coming up for sale and that it might be a proposition for the young man to consider.

In Beaufort West he met Ann, daughter of Isaac and Eva Traub, with whom he fell in love. First, he had to return to Anysberg to put the bank manager's proposal—(and possibly this new romantic development)—to Miemie. She obviously gave the green light to the former and knowing the kind of person she was, I am sure she readily accepted the latter. 'Sy (my mother) was 'n goeie vrou en jou pa was glo verlief op haar,' she told me when I raised the subject many years later— your mother was a good woman and I believe he was in love with her. The word 'glo' can mean believe, as in alleged, trust or credit, but I'm sure she used it without innuendo.

The exact dates around these interesting times are not known, but it could have been sometime during 1925 that they moved to Colesberg, because he first bought the hotel, and then married Ann in July 1926. And then there were three! As far as we were concerned, three was never a crowd, three was a family.

They did minor alterations and the name was changed to 'Colesberg Hotel'. In the early nineteen-forties he did major alterations, upgrading existing bedrooms, adding new ones and enlarging the dining room to accommodate the larger volume of guests. Miemie was at their side through all those years—and long after—until ill-health would overtake Natie and he sold up.

Ann & Percy, Nathan's younger brother, in front of the original Colesberg Hotel (late 1920s)

N. Kaplan Cash Store, as it originally was.
(late 1920s)

As Boris, Beryl and then I made our five-yearly appearances, we automatically took Miemie as an interchangeable mother. I think she and my mother accepted each other as family members, although Miemie was a strict adherer to protocol. While Natie was Ann's husband, Miemie always saw and respected him as her 'baas'.

In later years, the three of us were intrigued by how she had really felt about my father, and him about her. They had been two young adults who spent many years in the middle of nowhere, through many cold winters, and we often fantasised. It would be many years later that I finally plucked up the courage to ask her.

Chapter Eleven
ALL IN GOOD TIMES...
Of shards and plants and silkworm eggs, and many other things...

Growing up in a small country town, we probably learned more from our older siblings and certain friends, than from anyone else. I could call our early years: 'Unrivalled sibliary'—that is not one of Ann's slips, though they often sounded similar—but being five years apart, other than some roughhousing I mentioned, I can't recall any significant rivalry. We had our respective friends, plenty of space and the world was our roister.

A low koppie stood across the street between the old Kaufman shop on the corner and the petrol station a little further up. Large boulders had tumbled down; either at the time of those erupting plumes or over millennia, and now lay scattered around its base, some abutting on the kerb of the main street. There was nothing strange about that. In a town dotted with hills, our hotel must have been the only one that could boast in its promotional blurb—if it ever aspired to such vanity—of having a koppie immediately opposite and a cemetery, dating back to the early 1800s, diagonally across the road.

This koppie had been our first playground, where we ferreted amongst 'bloubos,' wild chrysanthemums (like miniature sunflowers), thistle, prickly pear (generously providing delicious fruits each year), 'melkbos' (one of the euphorbia family), succulents and a collection of birds, field mice, dassies, spiders and scorpions. We carved roads and garages into the lower sandy ridges, where we played for hours; climbed along narrow paths between gigantic rocks—a warren of dark nooks and crannies giving shelter to 'cowboys and crooks' as well as snakes—up to the summit, where we sat and viewed the town or gazed out to the distant hills.

In another snapshot, a beautiful eight-year-old girl and a

chubby-cheeked three-year-old boy sit on one of those large dolerite rocks beside the kerb, their faces close together and her left arm protectively clasped around his shoulders. Her dark poncho-like long-sleeved dress and his cardigan and woolly trousers suggest a winter's day; the sun touches their black hair and reflects off the rocks. One could literally fry eggs on them in summer, but they also retained the winter sun's energy, which slowly seeped from them until well after dark. An abrasion peeps between the fingers of her right hand, casually splayed over a knee and the tips of her dusty buckle shoes barely touch the ground. Receding into the background are more rocks, then whitewashed cottages, eucalyptus and acacia trees, and finally a range of larger hills serrate the horizon. It is my sister and I, nineteen-forty-three.

The beautiful and the 'expletivist', Beryl and Evan on the dolerite boulders (1943)

Following the birth of Boris, who was a fair, tubby child, my mother evidently prayed for a dark-haired daughter. Her wish was granted, when Beryl joined the family in March 1934. There was apparently very little brow between eyes and hairline; she had a small pinched face and was dark as a coffee bean. The story goes that Doc Cooper took one look at the mite and told my mother, 'You obviously prayed too hard, Ann, God sent you a little monkey instead!'

My sister has two interesting anecdotes of her youth. Sir Ernest Oppenheimer and his wife (number two?) stayed over one weekend, as the good lady wanted to visit the English War Cemetery, where a family member had been buried. It was a half-hour stroll out of town and my sister gladly agreed to play guide. His wife left a sum of money with my father, to have someone take care of the grave until their next visit. On one of the rare occasions for an evening chat, my mother asked Beryl what it was like and she excitedly described the outing, 'En die oomie kon darem lekker poep!' she added.

On another occasion, Professor Raymond Dart and a colleague stayed at the hotel on a work-related trip. It was Dart, who named the 'Taung Child' in 1925 and coined the term Australopithecus africanus, which was thought to be the missing link. (Had he searched a bit harder, he might have found one or two in Colesberg).

While chatting to my mother on the front veranda one morning, my sister happened to wander by and he asked her who the child was. Both he and his colleague insisted that it was impossible or something to that effect, for Beryl to be her daughter. She was too young to remember the exact details, but in retrospect it may have been her very prominent 'epicanthic folds' and a green naevus—which adorns her botty. The inner aspect of the Caucasian upper eyelid makes a clean angle with the lower lid, while the Oriental upper lid, folds over the lower. Both this fold and a green tinged mole or birthmark, as opposed to our common brown moles, are characteristics of Mongolian origin. So who knows, somewhere in my paternal background, a fiery Tartar may have ravished (or hopefully, revered) a young Jewish damsel, which reflects on Moisha Kaplan's extraordinary features and origins?

Shortly into her teens, circa 1946, she went down with a kidney disease, acute glomerulo nephritis, diagnosed the same day that my father had to leave for Johannesburg. Renal treatment was skimpy at best and in the absence of my parents, and Miemie having to double up; Doc Cooper got her into his Packard and drove her to their home, where he and his wife Haydee could keep an eye on her. Patients with renal disease have to have their protein and fluid intake carefully monitored. He kept her nearly two weeks, until the worst was over and then she spent a further couple of weeks in bed at home. She made an uncomplicated recovery.

A year later she went to boarding school, Eunice, in Bloemfontein, and sometimes brought a friend on vacation, whom I invariably honoured with a reticent crush. I could be a real pain in the arse, but they were reasonably tolerant of my 'nudniking' (nagging). Fired with ideals generated at a boarding school for young ladies, she heard via the hotel grapevine that I had called one of the staff members a 'poephol'. Arsehole is derogatory in any language and coming from a seven-year-old was unacceptable, so she decided to take matters into her own hands, invited me to the bedroom and ordered me to 'Bend down!'

Dumbstruck, I refused, this coming from my adoring sister. She played her trump card. 'In that case I will have to tell Mom'. I decided to take my chances with Bee, bent down and got two whacks with a flimsy ruler. Many years later, at the receiving end of more zealous teachers and a particular woodwork master, with a fetish for a length of Oregon Pine— and always with a gap-toothed smile—I would gladly have swapped two dozen of hers, for one of theirs.

She recalls another anecdote, after the '49 Springboks played the All Blacks in Bloemfontein. She spent the weekend with a friend whose older brother had arranged a party that Saturday night. Some of the Boks, including Okie Geffen and Cecil Moss, were invited and one of them, handing her an autographed photo, told her what a stunning girl she was. Then he discovered she was only fourteen and suggested he had 'better look you up when you're older,' and there went my potential season tickets to the tests.

She was another voracious reader, devouring certain authors in her early teens that were usually sampled much later. Although I was aware of Ann's love of books, it was Beryl who first brought books, and what was inside them, to my attention. I remember her reading me passages from (Rabelais') 'Gargantua and Pantagruel,' and I was spellbound by their appetites, as well as one of the illustrations showing Gargantua holding, what looks like a toy cow in one hand. She would later read me passages from 'The Last of the Just,' before I was motivated enough to read it myself.

I was spellbound by her poetry reading. My best was Chesterton's Battle of Lepanto, which she knew off by heart and the following lines had me riveted.

Strong gongs groaning as the guns boom far,
Don Juan of Austria is going to the war,
Stiff flags straining in the night blasts cold,
In the gloom black-purple, in the glint old gold,
Torchlight crimson on the copper kettle-drums,
Then the tuckets, then the trumpets, *then the cannon...and he comes!*

Those are my italics and exclamation mark. I remember springing a flock of geese bumps every time she leant forward, made her voice husky, and enunciated those last words. Although they took a long time to germinate, it was her input that planted my first seeds of reading.

Having matriculated too young for university, she attended art school for a few semesters before going into modelling. She took up judo and when her picture appeared in 'Die Beeld,'

'Throwing a man much heavier than her,' as the caption read, the boys used to badger her for a throw every time she stepped onto Clifton Beach. Possibly one of Clifton's first 'bikini girls,' she started a trend by cutting the feet off black school-stockings and turning them into tights. Long before it became fashionable, she spent Tuesday nights teaching Black men and women to read and write at the old Social Centre, in Tramway Road, while completing a secretarial course at college.

Then it was off to France and her 'crazy' years in Paris, where she learned French while teaching English. She should have written about her experiences. The people she met and jobs that ranged from au pairing to teaching at a school for underprivileged children. On a flight to Johannesburg once, a man boarded in Khartoum and they got chatting. He told her she must be from Paris and as she was congratulating herself on her fine Parisian accent, he popped her bubble. 'I see you are smoh-king Golwahz' (Gauloises).

She met interesting people. The daughter-in-law of one of the 'champagne families,' in the process of divorce, who became a good friend and introduced her to sipping 'bubbly' at any hour of the day. There was a never ending supply of cases stacked to the ceiling in her apartment, in lieu of alimony. Amazing tramps and entrepreneurs…A scoop of journalists and photographers from 'Life' and 'Magnum' magazines, which got her into one or two exciting, if hair-raising situations at the time of the French-Algerian shenanigans.

After a few years, she opted for the quiet life and went to teach English at a school in Toucy, a small village smothered in lilacs blooming amongst quaint little cottages, and later to Lyon, where she met her future husband, who was studying medicine.

On vacation in Colesberg, her 'stovies' made quite a stir. Natie, always a stickler for protocol, told her to change into something decent, when she offered to drive them to a farm one Sunday afternoon, in skin-tight blue jeans. 'The boys' once invited her to join them for a game of poker in the writing room.

82

They were a spirited bunch of regulars, who were often joined by one of the commercial travellers, when they were in town. She told them, tongue in cheek, that she did not want to clean them out and they good-naturedly humoured her. By the end of the evening, she had miraculously done just that and 'straight-faced-gambler!' was added to her list of attributes.

*

And then there were five, Natie, Ann, Bo, Bee and Evan (1942)

There is another photograph, possibly taken within the same period as the other, which shows a tubby boy in his early teens, wearing a leather lumber jacket, khaki shorts and rumpled socks, levelling a slightly aloof challenge at the camera. He leans against a late nineteen-thirties Dodge, arms tucked behind his back, a large scab on his knee, and a Brylcreemed coif barely reaches the runnel above the doors. The same eight-year-old girl, now in a lighter-coloured winter dress, stands in front of him, her hands on the shoulders of the three-year-old boy, who seems to be wearing…yet the same jersey and woollen trousers! (I have a sneaky suspicion they may have been the same pair I wore at the time of my enteric emergency.) The car, our dress, scuffed shoes and abrasions, nostalgically define the era.

'Tintin,' 'Popeye,' 'Oscar' and Boris were all born in 1929. The first Academy Awards were held on May 16th at the Roosevelt Hotel in Hollywood, but there was not enough time for Ann, the film lover, to get there. He was chubby until well after puberty, when the grub turned into a fine scarab, and he became a good-looking, athletic young man.

'Not just a fatty, but English speaking and Jewish, in a small town…' he once reminisced, 'you know, I just had to show the Boertjies and Rooinekke (the red-necked English) a thing or two.' This roly-poly literally threw himself into gymnastics with such passion, that the PT master would get him to demonstrate any new vaults, jumps, dives or somersaults. Later he became a side-drummer in the band, played first team rugby and was chosen for the town team while still in matric. He was quite a rake in the 'Volkspele,' (Afrikaans folk dancing) and a hit amongst the netball 'poppies'.

My mother once allowed him to bath the new baby. No sooner had he got the hang of cradling the head and neck in his left hand, when he lost the soap and in his frenzy to find it, began scrabbling around with both hands. Ann fortunately arrived in time to cuff the back of his head and lift mine from the sudsy water, while a few bubbles still gamely rose to the surface. The hairbreadth between comedy and tragedy is sometimes frightening. On a much later occasion, having to wash my hair one evening—nanny and parents busy—he noticed me wince each time he touched a certain spot. Carefully parting my hair, he found a half-inch splinter from a broken twig, embedded in my scalp.

Some of his more benign shenanigans (which I unfortunately mimicked) were dropping water bombs from the upstairs balcony or dangling life-like spiders they made, onto unsuspecting folk below. They fashioned equally realistic snakes from bicycle inner tubes and dragged them across the road with black cotton, after sunset. This caused blasphemous curses and it was thanks to the low level of heart disease and a high level of patience (acceptance?) that no heart attacks were recorded and that Bo and his mates were not given a good walloping.

Our flat soon cramped his adventurous spirit and Ann must have persuaded Natie to allow the young man to move into Room 5, on the first floor, where he and his chums could freely express themselves. Chemistry and Meccano sets were popular; the latter were at least bystander friendly. He brewed a range of foul-smelling concoctions that not only made the occasional dead mouse or rotten egg smell good, but set off explosions that could have removed an eye or any other balls in close proximity. It was finally confiscated and with the absence of foul fart-like smells, guests no longer had to eye each other with suspicion when walking down the long corridor.

He used to roughhouse my sister or me until our shrieks and complaints reached zero-tolerance level and my mother or Miemie would step in with a few well aimed smacks or dire reprimands. That spoiled the fun for us and we would taunt him until he started messing us around again. 'What's wrong with you blessed children?' Ann would demand, shaking her head in frustration.

Emerging from his mischievous youth, and having discovered the old Museum on the dusty square at the far end of Murray Street, he began taking a keen interest in the town's historical background, much to everyone's surprise. On his outings, scouring cliffs and overhangs, he discovered campsites and middens of the hunter-gatherers, who roamed those hills and plains eons before White or Black men came to spoil the

85

party. In his collection were pottery shards, some displaying the reticular patterns of the artist; ostrich shell beads and fragments; needles and arrowheads carved from antelope bone and once, the withered remains of a small leather pouch.

He discovered traces left by the Anglo Boer War. Rusted cartridge casings and bullets from old Henri-Martinis, possibly dropped in a moment of crisis; tunic buttons, the leather sole of a boot, horseshoes, tin fragments for making casings, shell shrapnel and magazines. He combed the veld for petrified trees and old bones, not realising at the time just how deep we were in fossil territory.

He tells a wonderful anecdote about the Royal Visit in 1947. The White Train, with its 'eight ivory saloons'—like the sun-bleached shells of giant millipedes ('isongololos') we used to find in the veld—snaked its way across the Karoo and was to stop at Graaff Reinet, allowing the Royal Family to take a quick cuppa in Te Water Huis. The old school bus had been polished and he borrowed, what he calls, a 'concertina' camera; bought two spools at Neville's Chemist and thus armed, he and the small crowd awaited the royal train. Overeager as it neared the station, 'I began snapping furiously from all angles.' The Royal Four stepped onto the red carpet, were led up onto an elevated wooden viewing platform and he clambered up the scaffolding, 'no one stopped me, and so I literally came face-to-face with the Queen. She never had good teeth, did you know that?'

Chock-a-block with 'chutzpah' (nerve), he was the only one who followed the Rolls that drove them to their venue and he waited in the shade of one of the ancient Oaks for the tea party to end. King George VI, the Queen and the two Princesses finally emerged and he realised he had come to the end of his first spool. While trying to insert the next one, a plastic cap from the spindle fell into a furrow, along which water happened to be flowing to the garden, and as he ran after it, losing precious seconds, he kept looking over his shoulder. 'You know something, I just knew the King was holding the driver back, to give me a chance, and the Princesses were giggling as I

86

kept bending, in my short khaki pants, bum in the air, until I scooped it out, dried it on my shirt and began snapping again.'

It has a rather Roald Dahl-ish ending. The next day he rushed back to Neville's Chemist, handed in his two 'fillums' and impatiently waited the week or two for them to come back from Bloemfontein. When they did, he sat on the chemist steps, tore open the packet 'and there were three shots of the White Train, miles away, and twenty-one bloody blanks!' When he lived in London during the late 1950s, he wrote a letter to Buckingham Palace, mentioning this incident and received a royal billet-doux, regretting Her Majesty has no recollection of wayward boys or bums in the air...

On our porch—no larger than an average toilet—he cultivated succulents and other plants in a collection of tin drums and small pots, while coaxing geraniums to clamber along string-and-nail trellises right up into the trap under the ceiling. 'The boy has green fingers,' old timers used to tell my parents, 'he should farm.' It would turn out to be quite an accurate suggestion, in the end, although it wouldn't be farming, 'exectly,' and not in Colesberg. The double porch doors had stained-glass panes and for me, one of my 'spring memories,' is a swathe of colour splashed across the linoleum floor and the smell of the would-be farmer's pelargonium oils, rising to the new season.

With all the brashness of youth, he was the one who sparked my interest in antiquity, fossils, plants and not just nature, but the functions and magic of nature. While I was on duty in the bar one afternoon, a fellow who worked on the town council popped in for a drink. He unwrapped a yellowed skull they had found in a shallow grave amongst the hills, while digging holes for new telephone posts and he was taking it to the office. When he saw how eagerly I ran my fingers across the prominent cheekbones and sutures, of what probably could have been a young adult, he intimated that 'a little something' could make it mine. I thought of Boris and what a thrill that would have been for him. Such was our stupidity or naivety, that for a half-jack

87

of gin, I inherited young Yorick (or Ophelia), who would later help me and some of my friends in our anatomy studies.

After matriculating in Colesberg—things were too cosy to even consider the boarding school my parents had in mind for him—my brother left for Cape Town, where he put a wide range of potential occupations and professions to the test. A cool dancer with natural rhythm, he would try teaching my sister the latest moves if they were both on vacation. His frustration showed in the cranking of the old gramophone or the needle screeching across the grooves of 'Parlophone' and 'His Master's Voice' records. 'Remember the bloody steps and move naturally!' he shouted. 'Not like that! Watch me; one, two, cha-cha-cha...!' until Bee could take no more and stormed out in a huff.

We both adored her, but I think he simply could not understand or accept the fact that such a bright, beautiful and talented girl, with a stunning figure, was not capable of a titillating Tango or sensual Samba. I was too young to be involved in those 'Arthur Murray' moments, but would stand at the door and watch him put her through the paces, intrigued and a little nervous that dancing could be so heated and belligerent, when it all seemed rather carefree and happily-tipsy during parties in the lounges.

My brother was not really into gambling, but had an incredible windfall...or a quintet of windfalls. Of all my father's horses, Pugmill came closest to Pegasus, but alas and alack, his wings were prematurely clipped. Young Pugmill romped home five Saturdays in a row with his nose well ahead of the field. On the sixth he came in third and then...'The bloody trainer raced him off his feet,' the moguls mourned, 'he should've had time to breathe.' I never thought my father superstitious, but his one 'meshugas' (craziness/eccentricity), as they say in Yiddish, was that he never backed his own horses. Boris, on the other hand, didn't believe in like father, like son and made enough 'latkes' for some serious socialising and acquisitions.

When the lure of London grew stronger, he signed up on the 'Caernarfon Castle'—where my sister had booked her berth—and while those mighty screws bore them over the water, he crewed his way to Southampton and a new life.

He could also write a book about his years in Swinging London and the people he met, dated or worked with at the popular Corillo Coffee Bar in Earl's Court, and a few other venues that sampled his talents. He once went to a premiere with Gloria Swanson, Maureen's sister, in a borrowed evening suit, 'a good few sizes too big for me,' and everyone thought he was Norman Wisdom as he fumbled his way out of the cab and nearly tripped, at Leicester Square.

'I wonder what happened to...' his reminisces often begin, and names like June Ritchie, Michael Gogh, Ivan King, June Shaw, John Le Mesurier, Johnny Dankworth, Nancy Kwan, Cleo Lane or Tsai Chin sometimes pop into our conversations. 'Did I tell you Adelaide Hall used to drop in at the Corillo, for my special coffee? I could perform miracles with those espresso and coffee machines and knew every regular's personal taste.' She would tell him about her early days in America and the woes of being a 'Black' artist, and how she ended up with Duke Ellington and his orchestra; 'Bojangles,' Grapelli, her night club in Paris and other performers she worked with...like Josephine Baker, Louis Armstrong, Lena Horne... 'I used to get so carried away listening to her, my boss, Ma Stanley, who was very fond of me, used to kak on me for ignoring the other customers.'

Then there was a saucy story about 'Kay,' a dancer he met at the Windmill. He had become friendly with a fruit and veggie barrow-boy, a real Cockney character and this fellow was dating a dancer at the club. He invited Bo to a show one evening and that was when he met 'Kay'. As chance would have it, they discovered they lived, not only in the same complex in Earl's Court, but the same building.

'Our affair was unfortunately short-lived.' Under, uhm, awkward circumstances, a car hooted one night and she scrambled to the window. It was a fellow named Stephen Ward, of the John Profumo affair, 1963, who was also dating her. (Natie would have 'chaapen ah chalossis' (thrown a fit), but I think Ann might have enjoyed the anecdote.) A white convertible E-Type Jaguar stood purring below the window. 'It was great while it lasted, but I didn't stand a chance in hell,' he said, with his usual candour.

He worked for Helena Rubinstein—first in London and later in Israel, when she opened in Tel Aviv—who took a liking to the young South African, but life in the cosmetic world was much too taxing and volatile for him. In Tel Aviv, he had to accompany her when she showed Marc Chagall around her new premises.

Then there was the woman at John Lewis (Oxford Street). She had put Terence Conran, one of the leading furniture and interior designers on the map. She was very impressed with drawings Bo showed her and put one of the smaller pieces he made on display. (He had briefly studied art with Maurice van Esche, while still in Cape Town.) She wanted him to find someone who could construct his larger designs, but the logistics involved overrode his enthusiasm. Life was much too good, who needed all that 'kop dreyenes' (problems), and, what might have been a golden opportunity, slipped away.

When the 'green-fingered' rascal (finally) married and settled in Israel, he built his own hothouses and grew amazing chrysanthemums; a hobby that turned into a living. So sought after were the magnificent 'heads' and 'bunches' that florists, who usually had growers delivering to their doorstep, would personally fetch their flowers from his smallholding. 'The rolling stone who gathers no moss,' as Ann sometimes described him, had finally come to rest, in a mossy bed.

Chapter Twelve
TIME CAN BE A GREAT STEALER...
Hatched, patched and gullible as hell... childhood friends

W atching someone relish the crisped head and eyes of a kabeljou, at a barbeque recently, it brought on a rush of almost forgotten pleasures. It not only conjured images of grilled fish heads, but sheep and cow heads, skaapkop and beeskop in Afrikaans or 'intloko yegusha' and 'intloko yenkomo' in Xhosa. After every morsel of meat had been eaten or scraped from the bone, skulls were cracked open with an axe and the brain, 'ingqondo,' was a great delicacy. These memories stirred the pot of tastes and smells of other delights, such as dry mealie-meal porridge—stywepap or 'umphokoqo,' and sheep's stomach and intestines—pens en derms or 'upenisi' and 'amathumbu'.

I remembered the earthy taste of samp and bean stew, 'umgqusho,' and if it had been a good month in those poor homes, a little stewing lamb. There was also delicious roosterkoek, 'irhostile onkanye iikuku'. Many years later, our domestic help from Transkei—the infamous 'Homelands'— would prepare these two dishes for us, and my children still enjoy them. My all time favourite was 'Skaapkop, pens en pootjies,' 'Sheep's head, stomach and trotters,' as Miemie or Ann would type on the DINNER menu. The natural sauce, peppery and slightly gelatinous, from the trotters, was a treat on its own.

In my later youth, I had these dishes in the homes of our Xhosa staff members, who lived in the higgledy-piggledy streets of Die Draai, in the Black location; but my earliest recollections were in the home of the Plaatjies family. Like everything else in our youth, it seemed the Plaatjies were just another extension of our surroundings, though in retrospect, I think they helped shape me (and possibly my siblings) more positively than I realised.

As far back as I can remember, the large extended family lived in a small cottage behind the hotel. The house and property belonged to my father and the women did our personal laundry in lieu of rent, while hotel laundry went to the public washhouse a short distance out of town. They were an amazing family in many ways; foremost for me, was the blend of what seemed to be Xhosa ancestry on the maternal side and San from the father's roots.

Leeu, father of the house, was short and slight. He and his mother, Ouma Siena, seemed as close to pure San as one could still get, with prominent cheekbones, a hooded slant to their eyes and skin the colour of moist river sand. She was shorter and slighter than her son, with a generous behind and her face wrinkled like an old hunting pouch. I never knew his father, who had passed on by the time I became aware of the family.

Leeu's wife, Ma, as everyone knew her, was a large buxom woman who towered darkly over him. She was a real earth mother, but ran the home with a firm, sometimes-heavy hand, and we all had an unhealthy respect for her. Her parents, Ouma Sarah and Oupa Klaas, were tall, lean and leathery and seemed to have the durability and colour of well-seasoned mahogany. The old man was introspective and seldom spoke but I can't remember hearing any of the Black dialects and during that age of classification, separation and humiliation, they were all classified 'Kleurling'—Coloured.

The house had probably been adequate when the family first moved in, but as their children arrived, thirteen, in fairly rapid succession, it was amazing how they all fitted into that small space at night. It reminded me of a snug head of lettuce.

One of the oldest three boys, Martin, had initially been my brother's friend, the next two girls were my sister's playmates, but one died young. I don't know the cause, but it was sudden. She was a sweet girl and I can picture the three of them sitting on the storeroom steps, playing with their rag dolls or cutting out dresses for paper dolls. I remember the plaintive keening of the women and the stunned sobs of the younger girls. Her loss affected us all—the first time death had entered our play circle—though Koerie, Ziems and I were a bit too young to register the full tragedy. After them came five more girls and a laatlam, Mannetjie, rounded off the baker's dozen.

Koerie and Ziems were 'there' as early as my first recognition of life around me. Although Koerie was sturdier than his brother, he had the San characteristics, while Ziems was dark and slight. I cannot recall any rivalry, we were just three good friends. Coal mates. We would sneak in behind Ou Willem, one of our earliest yard-boys I remember, when he unlocked the coal shed. This corrugated iron building was diagonally opposite their house and Willem would collect a wheelbarrow of coal once or twice a day, depending on demand, to feed the boiler furnace or lounge hearths in winter. We would play on the dusty sacks of coal, stacked to the rafters—looking like Welsh miners when we emerged into sunlight again—and as we got older, we ventured higher and higher until at the age of eight or nine we began shinning into the rafters.

Willem would lose his patience and a nervous little giggle, if we disturbed the neat conical piles of coal he used for the hotel, and storm at us, a threatening shovel above his head, cursing in his healthy but unrepeatable vernacular. Everyone was petrified of Ou Willem and we treated him like a semi-tame tiger, never taking our eyes off him as we pushed his endurance to the limits while trying to discover our own.

When I went to school, aged six, I became friendly with kids from the large farming community and one or two who lived closer to us in town, but back home Koerie and Ziems were my friends. We played in our house or theirs, on the hotel premises or in the massive yard that backed their house and sometimes in an even larger garden, which lay between their yard and the edge of the sloot or stream.

This stream usually oozed through town, its pace set by the rhythm of rainfall on the higher southern plateau. Very rarely, it clattered and rumbled after a cloudburst, gnawing at the banks

93

and retaining stone walls of the houses above, and sometimes it chatted and gurgled quite merrily, before slowing to a sluggish trickle again as the rains tauntingly stayed away.

Our territory included the sloot, the veld and low hills and koppies along the northern end of town, where we hunted and collected or played our various games. Although my collection of toys was minimal, it took another good friend to show me that they need not be bought or specially crafted items.

Jasper was a pale skinny lad with tousled blond hair, who lived lower down the road from the Plaatjies. They were a poor family, and his toys were a collection of sash window counterweights, large and small cogs from old machinery, brass doorknobs, mortise locks, discarded perambulator wheels and an assortment of bric-a-brac found on junk heaps. He had a kind of magic, the way he brought those dull, inanimate things to life; making them scrape or compact roads, bore holes, climb hills, carry heavy loads or plough fields, simply by the way he handled them. His sound-effects could indicate engine size, manoeuvrability or power and they made my few shop toys seem dull and uninteresting.

Ann was not impressed when I brought home a rusty cog with wire hook attached, having swapped it for a plastic steamroller for which I had begged for weeks. Somehow, it never played as nicely with me as it did with Jasper. It would also be my father's first dour prophecy as to what direction my future would not follow. 'Oy ah clog! (misfortune), from tsatskehs (odds and ends) he knows; but from business...?' he said holding out a palm negating any financial acumen, 'he knows nutting'.

Antie Bee occasionally prepared dry mealie-meal porridge as a treat for us, but I often ate it with grid-roasted sheep intestines, thoroughly washed and cleaned by one of the grandmothers in the Plaatjies' home. Occasionally Leeu brought a sheep or goat's head from the butchery, wrapped in newspaper, which Ouma Siena would sear with a length of red-hot iron to remove the hair and then roast it over a fire in the back yard. Every morsel, including eyes and brain, were eaten with relish, the bones carefully scraped with pocketknives and the last little flakes and gravy soaked up with crusty home-baked bread. A simple banquet that still has me salivating.

Twice a month the old red and black 'South African Railways' bus delivered hake, which came by train from Port Elizabeth in wooden crates packed with ice. Antie Bee cleaned them in the back yard and gave the heads and fins to Ou Willem, who would grill them over a few coals scraped from the geyser furnace and then tuck into them with such gusto, he got us drooling. He ate every vestige of edible flesh with his pocket-knife and then popped the eyes into his mouth as the *pièce de résistance*. The way he prepared them, brown and crisp and 'smelling just like the sea,' was like any other braai to us and we learned to eat the eyes with equal gusto. He had been in the South African Coloured Corps in North Africa and that could have been the only time he had smelled the ocean.

Ma sometimes made ginger beer during the summer, strong and tangy, and we were each allowed a few sips from a tin mug. The bottles, neatly sewn into sacking by Ouma Siena and periodically doused with water from the tap outside their house, hung in the shade of an ancient fig tree, which stood in Miemie's chicken run at the far end of their yard. Like Jasper's toys, her ginger beer tasted so much better than the lemonade, ginger ale or ginger beer I used to cadge for us from the bar fridge.

Wood smoke and a pot of porridge waiting for tomorrow; paraffin lamps and the smell of new loaves; freshly washed and ironed clothing, reed ceilings, crumbling red brick and the occasional splash of 'white-wash,' sketch the old Plaatjies house as readily as a photograph, which I do not possess. A table and sideboard, under many layers of flaking paint, stood in the voorhuis with a few assorted wooden chairs. There was one bedroom, where a sagging katel (iron bed) and a patched cupboard took up most of the space, while afternoon sun slanted through the tiny kitchen window, highlighting tumbles of

95

smoke exhaled by the little stove.

The bulk of the food was first shared amongst the children, and I often joined the sedate circle of the porridge spoon. From hand to hand it went round the table and no matter the need or hunger, there was never bickering or grabbing, but simply the quiet, dignified process of sharing and eating. Like an old masterpiece, I remember them in the dull lamplight, each mouthful carefully chewed, rolled around the mouth and savoured until the spoon returned.

They also taught me how oranges or any other fruit should be eaten. If a bag or two were purchased for the hotel, Antie Bee occasionally handed us each an orange if we were playing in our yard. Initially, I had watched as Koerie and Ziems lifted the first bit of rind with their teeth and patiently nibbled the pith until only the bitter, translucent skin remained. The same was done with the rest of the rind until finally, the flesh was halved, each segment slowly relished and every drop of juice carefully licked from the fingers. Even at a young age I was awed by the simple economy of simple eating, never wastage. We totally devoured stalk-less apples and pears. Peach and apricot pips were cracked open and the seeds eaten, or we would sit for hours, grinding apricot pips on a whetstone, until a small hole appeared, dig out the seed and the hollow pips made fine whistles.

Our youth was shaped by myths. One, incriminated the pith of orange peel as causing witseerkeel (diphtheria). Could the leathery white membrane that lines the swollen throat have mimicked the pith? Not to worry, the Plaatjies family very quickly put that fable to bed.

When the kids did their homework at the table, the lamp threw whorls of soot up to the reed ceiling and wavering shadows across their faces, as they poured over schoolbooks, whose pages had been stained by many keen or listless fingers before theirs. Elbows on the oilcloth, the younger kids thoughtfully sucked the tips of slate pens while the older ones did so to their precious pencil stubs.

96

'Coloured and Black schools get bogger-all when it comes to books and stationary, but the White schools get everything,' one of the teachers told me, the imperceptible dance of his eyes indicating 'and that's not all!' I was at varsity by then and this well-spoken middle-aged man, who always seemed weary and depressed, would exchange views with me when he came in for his half-jack of brandy or occasional bottle of sherry. Despite my confirmatory nods and agreement, it did not help the situation and at times like that, I hated myself for not being more politically supportive or vocal at least. Like so many others, I would later learn, despair and cirrhosis nabbed him early.

When conditions were favourable, very rarely, Ann read me excerpts from Grimm's Fairy tales for Children. Our main intake of bedtime and other stories was often around a paraffin lamp in the Plaatjies voorhuis or beside the tin brazier glowing in their back yard at night. They invariably involved the shenanigans of 'Wolf en Jakhals'—the scheming old wolf always outsmarted by the wily Jackal in the end—or a healthy combination of ghost, trickery, bloodcurdling and 'tokoloshe' yarns. Between those terrifying Grimm drawings and our stories, full of grim bogeymen and cruel grandmothers, I was 'poep-bang' of the dark as a child. My two mates were not much better, but then they never had to go to bed on their own.

They were a close family, kept on the straight-and-narrow by Leeu—who now and then would have to unbuckle his belt to lay down the law between the boys as they got older and Ma took care of any female fandangle before it got out of hand. The grandparents were respected and revered. Ouma Siena would throw in her quiet, sibilant tuppence-worth when necessary and Ouma Sarah did so in a more strident tone. Oupa Klaas, as far as I can recall, enjoyed the company of his thoughts more than the large family bourgeoning around him.

Recycling—the fancy name for handing down—began many years ago amongst the poor. It could possibly explain why I have never been clothes-conscious, although a good deal of that

97

could have spilled over from Ann's amazing dress-mismanagement. The family inherited our clothing and theirs were patched, darned and handed down until they finally changed shape and lost their original colour or utility. When they were too tattered to mend, salvageable pieces—as well as other small items of society jetsam—went into Ouma Siena's toorsak (magic bag), for patching other garments. Canned food tins were turned into mugs by Leeu; mentholated spirits and paraffin were kept in old wine bottles, whiskey crates served as stools or storage and the metal straps from heavier cartons were riveted together and could batten down loose rafters or zinc roof sheeting.

I was amazed how Ouma Siena could sit for hours, legs crossed at the ankles; feet calloused and cracked, her back stooped as she went about her chores. Summer and winter, I cannot recall ever seeing her in shoes. She would spread her 'kaross' in the shade of the fig tree, the old Jackal-hide blanket as bald and dark as her brother-in-law's pate, where she sewed and darned.

We sometimes watched as she sifted and foraged through her bag for suitable thread or swatches amongst half-empty cotton reels, a treasured thimble, two equally treasured darning needles wrapped in stiff brown paper, odd lengths of wool and an old polish tin, full of mismatched buttons. She scrutinised broken zippers, lengths of riempie, eyelets from old shoes, sections of crumpled ribbon—which she ironed on her lean thighs with the palm of her hand, for one of the younger girls—off-cuts of lace and a collection of smoothly polished 'dolosse'; the knuckle-bones of sheep or goats which often make up the paraphernalia of Sangomas or witchdoctors.

'My ouma kan toor,' Ziems once told me, suggesting Ouma Siena could perform magic and in my younger days, I was always a little wary of this petite, apricot granny. In stories told by the older Plaatjies children or staff members, 'toor' was not necessarily good magic. It mostly implied sorcery, which involved nasty old men and women, who were not adverse to

98

locking children in cupboards or doing them fatal bodily harm, if a farmer or virtuous maiden did not happen to be passing by and save them. It seems the benign brutality of fairytales is universal.

With time, I discovered her mischievous sense of humour and good-natured ragging and my fear turned to fondness. When I brought her a few 'fingers' of chew tobacco pilfered from the shop, she would regale us with weird and wonderful stories in the vapours of the kitchen or under the old fig, where even Miemie's poultry approached the fence to cock their heads attentively. If we badgered her long enough, she would smooth the ground beside her with a claw-like hand and then throw the bones. Sometimes she uttered immediate fruitful or frightful visions, while doing a litany of birdlike clicks and clucks and filling us with the wonders of her past and long-gone ancestors. Other times she would stare towards the hills across the stream and by the forward jut of her head, puckered lips and hooded eyes further narrowed to the setting sun, it seemed like the timeless gaze of an ancient tortoise, wise but indifferent. And we fell for it every time. Mesmerised by her mystical silence, we leaped like springhares when she suddenly turned to us and snapped 'Voertsek nou! (scram!) Can you not see that a person is busy?' An impish smile, showing teeth worn down to the gums, took the sting out of the lash, but by then our hearts would be galloping well ahead of us.

I used to wonder how or where Leeu and Ma found the opportunity to produce so many children in a tiny house, until the three of us were having yet another of our 'birds and bees' conversations. We must have been about seven or eight, and I thought I knew everything there was to know about sex and making babies.

The word 'steek,' in Afrikaans, means stab or a colloquial 'quickie'. I told them their father had steeked their mother thirteen times and my father had only steeked my mother three times. They both giggled and then Koerie shattered that myth. 'Our father does it very, very many more times,' he said and

99

Ziems nodded corroboration. It was quite a long walk to their toilet in the yard, so some nights, when the kids were getting their sleeping places and bedding ready, Leeu would accompany Ma across the darkened yard to perform their ablutions and sneak in a quick service.

Every Sunday the kids scrubbed or were scrubbed by older siblings until their noses shone, dressed in crisply-ironed clothes and shod or barefoot, they set off to church. Occasionally they held evening Bible-classes and through my bedroom window I could hear their voices lifting through the peppertrees. The Plaatjies taught us the real meaning of sharing, caring and appreciating the simple things in life. We have had our disagreements over the years, but there is still a closeness, a bond, that has withstood the corrosion of social and family dynamics. We are forever reminiscing our childhood memories and now and again a name, a dish or some forgotten game will unexpectedly surface—like a Karoo fossil—to be greeted with praise for the 'palaeo-anecdotalist' who unearthed another gem for our collection.

When I went to boarding school in nineteen fifty-one, Koerie, Ziems and I would take up where we left off, on my vacations. It was only after I went to varsity that things began to change. We were no longer children. Koerie left home to seek work in a Northern Free State town; I had to do hotel duties, and Ziems had reached the age of doing his own thing, although he occasionally popped into the off sales to chew the fat.

On our trip to Anysberg, we had returned via Colesberg. It was a Sunday afternoon and the town was still as a cemetery while I showed my wife some of the more accessible spots. We pulled up in front of the park and I remembered the tall maypole. How we could swing in dizzying circles that made the sun spin, and every two or three years one of the council workers would slap on silver paint. Now it stood motionless, and in need of a fresh coat, but I clearly remembered the melancholy clanking of chain handles after the last kids had dashed home to dinner.

100

A familiar middle-aged woman came out of the park and I introduced myself. She told me her name was Rebecca, fondly recalled my family and asked after Boris and Beryl. During our short conversation, she told me one or two of our former staff members left for greener pastures many years ago, while the rest were all deceased. Each name I mentioned she met with a sad shake of the head: 'Weg'—gone.

When I got to the Plaatjies family, I was shocked to learn only Ziems and a younger sister, Meisie, were still alive. He was living in the (moderately) new Coloured settlement called Loeriesville, on an open plateau near the old Parkie outside town, and she was in Kimberley. Rebecca, who worked for the municipality, explained how to get to his house and that she would tell him of our visit.

We purchased staples and a few 'luxuries' at the supermarket and drove out to Loeriesville. A chill breeze tugged at papery thistles between the little houses and we found him, hands deep in the pockets of a shabby overcoat, already pacing in front of his tiny two-room council house. He seemed smaller, as if he had shrunk in the intervening years, but his hug was firm. I introduced him to Ferdi, whom he addressed as 'Nooi' (Miss) and invited us into the voorhuis, which served as lounge, kitchen and storeroom.

He tried to poke some life into the tiny stove and came to join us at the table. He confirmed Meisie was the only other surviving sibling. Koerie could still be alive, but he doubted it, 'I have not heard from him for a very, very long time.' Reading between the lines, it seems alcohol—the scourge of the Platteland—malnutrition and hopelessness had taken their toll with most of the family and others I asked about. HIV and Aids related diseases, especially TB, are also reaping the wild oats sown across the Platteland.

Before we sold the hotel and left Colesberg, he and Koerie had discovered comfort in the bottle and some of his younger siblings followed suit. I remember after Ma died, the steadfast salt-of-the-earth Leeu, would sometimes wind his way

101

unsteadily down the back road to their house and it was sad to see how poverty, loneliness and dejection could steer even the hardiest over the brink.

Ziems told us he had already buried his wife and son. His daughter came in a little later to check on him, an icy breeze and flurry of dried leaves swirling around her legs, and indifferently made us coffee. Here was a further sadness. I was just a strange whitey in her father's house; the chain of events and memories that bound us were of no interest to her. I could not blame her; more important things loomed in her colourless young life.

Now as we sat around the small table, he seemed to recall our past more eagerly, reminding me of Ou Jasper and our childhood games under the pepper trees. Did I remember how the older boys had tricked us once with melkbos, he asked, too discreet to elaborate further. 'Melkbos,' they conspiratorially told us—and it seemed like yesterday—'will let your ball hairs grow wild like willow sprigs.' I remembered the three of us stone-stepping across the sloot and up into the koppies, pleased as punch with this new discovery. In no time we each had a generous handful of the pencil-like euphorbia stems, pulled our shorts down, rubbed on lavish amounts of the thick milky sap— the more we used, it stood to reason, the faster the hairs would grow—and leaned back against the rocks, our little peckers pointing to the sun.

That was the age of wholesale gullibility and we fell for anything that might enhance or advance our manhood. All it did was stir up an angry rash, a burning itch and if anything, possibly delayed the appearance of our pubic hairs by a couple of months. Another gem of adolescent advice that occasionally did the rounds, was, that rubbing chicken shit on your upper lip, preferably the soft green (smellier) component, nurtured an almost instant moustache! One more nostalgic, but foul facet of my past.

'Daai, was lekker dae,' he said, his 'good old days' bringing me back from the hills, our carefree youth and innocence.

Of tops and clay and trapping fish...
Evan & Ziems (1999)

When it was time to leave, he became more emotional, as though he could read the future. 'Moenie my weer vergeet nie, Ou Evvie'—my nickname slipped out as though he had used it only a day ago—and he shook my hand, 'asseblieftog'. Don't forget me again, please. The irony was I had never forgotten any of them. Memories of the whole family, Colesberg and the hotel were constantly with me, but yes, I had forgotten his plight, and in my own 'benign negligence,' had missed another golden opportunity. I left a sum of money, reassuring him I would send more, we hugged again and then he watched us drive away, a forlorn figure with his collar turned to the wind. In my journal of that trip, August 1999, I mentioned 'clubbing (of his fingers) may be chronic lung disease, hope not TB...or other??' (HIV/Aids).

We spent the night with Stephan and Rina de Wit, son and daughter-in-law of one of Miemie's half-brothers, Barrie and Lettie de Wit, in their hospitable home, where they treated us to an 'opregte Karoo braaivleis'—a pukka barbeque. Uncannily, their house was built on the exact site of Jasper's old home.

Next morning, we stopped at the offices where Rebecca worked and I told her about my concerns and that maybe she could look into it and see if there was anything that could be done for Ziems, leaving my telephone number and address with her.

As we were leaving, someone called my name. An elderly Coloured man introduced himself as Adam Thobias, reminding me he had driven my mother to Cape Town when my father took ill. How I had kindly taken him to the station and seen him safely onto the train. 'I would never even have found the train in that busy place.'

I remembered his father, Ou Thobias, the Waggoner, and his two placid mares. They always seemed to be deep in thought, as they plodded along behind well-dubbined blinkers or snuffled their nosebags when he stopped under the trees. He carted equipment, furniture, small livestock or rubble, for a nominal charge, and looked so stately up on his seat, (superfluous) whip and reins in one hand, the other politely doffing his hat to passers-by.

Back in Cape Town, I phoned Rebecca a few times and she thought Ziems was looking better and nothing seemed buitengewoon (out of the ordinary). Not long after that, I received a letter to say he had died, adding no further details but that she paid for the funeral arrangements, which I reimbursed.

It was the severance of a tie that had lasted more than half a century, and took with it many beautiful memories of my childhood. Ferdi took a photo of us in front of his house, arms slung over each other's shoulders, the breeze tugging at our coats, and he stares forlornly at the camera. I was grateful for the providential timing of that trip, to have seen him one last time, but disappointed I had let him down.

Chapter Thirteen
THERE'S A TIME AND SPACE...
And the highway van came riding, into the old inn door...

S omeone passing through, apparently took pub-crawling to the extreme and very nearly popped his van into the pub for a drink. Fortunately, only the frosted door panes were smashed, and it took a good few weeks before similar glass could be found. Before the Municipality laid proper sidewalks, sometime in the 1930s, one could step out of the bar directly onto the road, which would one day become the N1.

Not quite as she looked in her heyday,
The Colesberg Hotel (1999)

I got to know the hotel intimately. Every door and the sound it made; the scuffed or shiny fields of linoleum; bright curtains and dull couches...as if I had worn the old building all my life. Maybe I had, as a tortoise must know its shell.

I could sense its moods. The late-night kitchen's silent anticipation of a new day, the reassuring hum of bar and pantry refrigerators signalling enough ice and cold beers would be at hand and that all would go well with meat, butter, milk and cheese. I felt the satisfied ease of the dining room after the last family had given their dessertspoons a final lick, and the bar's stoic independence, knowing that it needed no shop, bedrooms or kitchen, but was an entity on its own. I knew the lounge's simple pride, the old trading store's earthy presence and most of all; I was comfortable and assured by the camaraderie and loyalty of the folk who made it possible for this halfway house to function. We were all part of it and like a true friend; it became a part of us.

The hotel spread its length beside Kerkstraat, the main street that bisected the town as neatly as Lodewyk's central parting. There were still a good few of those to be seen, but Lodewyk's, somehow made more of a statement. The tall, pedantic, middle-aged bachelor with gold-rim glasses, was one of a handful of telephonists who worked the exchange for many years. On hot days, when the door to their little room, next to the post office, stood open, I was in awe of the way he hitched or unhitched those black spaghetti tangles with such casual ease.

Thinking back now, the way the hotel rested on its solid foundations, it seemed both at ease and instantly ready to entertain at a moment's notice. Its arched colonnades, like bemused brows, reminded me of a Sphinx, stoically proud of its unpretentiousness. Not smug or self-satisfied, but content, knowing that in its day the dining room, bars and lounges had hummed with jovial activity or the serious press of the passing-trade seeking bed and board for the night.

Bedrooms were clean and somewhat Spartan, with porcelain chamber-pots and hand-basins in the absence of en suites. The plain but spacious dining room hosted sumptuous dinner parties and still boasted one of the finest menus between Magaliesberg and Cape Agulhas. Our coarse home-baked Boermeel breads and sour white loaves were delectable and booked months in

107

advance, when reservations were being made.

The writing room—long unused for such noble purposes—served as a venue for poker games, where some innocent silver could cross palms, or for meetings—business or otherwise—away from prying eyes and ears. Small towns are renowned for their friendliness and generous hospitality, but notorious for intrigue and pithy gossip.

There was the 'big' (main) lounge and 'small' (smoking room) lounge on the ground floor and another lounge off the upper landing. Each had a fireplace, nestling under simple mantels, which were a comforting presence once you had experienced your first Karoo winter. A coal bucket and fierce looking tongs, trowels and pokers rounded off the hearths. Art Nouveau prints in dark frames—where skimpily-veiled maidens, pale and Rubenesque, patiently strummed lyres while waiting for curly-haired beaus to leap from the foliage—hung from brass hooks on picture rails circumnavigating every room.

An upright Steinway held its own in a corner of the main lounge. It somehow always gave me the impression of being lonely, in spite of occasions like a birthday or someone spontaneously syncopating the worn ivories. Old favourites, like Daisy, Moonlight Bay, Irish Eyes, Blue Danube, Anniversary Waltz—Natie's favourite—and other ditties would flow and ebb along the passages. 'It's all so merry and gay,' Ann would inform us, casually tapping a foot and everyone suddenly had a rhythm to their stride. Sometimes furniture was moved aside and the room vibrated as couples waltzed, quickstepped, foxtrotted, flapped the Charleston or jitterbugged. Extra rounds would be ordered, as ten p.m. approached. Women dabbed perspiration with little white hankies and the men simply replenished theirs with more brandy 'n coke, beers or Scotch.

The White Bar was our flagship, buoyed by gallons of liquor. There was a fine length of solid mahogany with a curve at the far end where it met the wall. It was worn dark and smooth from years of patient, anxious, or troubled hands, and liberal

108

spilling of spirits. A brass rail clung to its base and a collection of butts smouldered in the spittoon by closing time. Sturdy mahogany barstools had their seats honed to a silken sheen by the bums of bullies, businessmen and occasional upper crusts of the Broederbond, who were invited to winter hunting trips on surrounding farms.

As any publican will tell you, 'tis the bar that generates the income, and shelves were laden with bottles; from the most banal of plonk to imported cognacs, liqueurs and whiskeys. The rich brown of Hennessey, cloudy green Chartreuse, 'poison green' peppermint, the warm red of cherry liqueur and dark ruby of Port, lent a touch of colour to the otherwise uniform rows of 'soldiers,' as some folk referred to a booze bottle. 'There goes another dead soldier,' someone would utter as the barman dropped an empty into the basket under the counter.

I recall a joke once told by a passerby. About the chap who fancies a new receptionist at the office and invites her out to dinner and then to his home. He offers her a Port, which she declines. Why not, he asks? Well, she says, brandy, makes me feel languid and ethereal and I get the urge to compose. A whiskey makes me feel naughty and adventurous and ready for some sinful excitement; gin turns my thoughts inward and I become melancholic and philosophical; but Port?...Port simply makes me fart!

Then there was the alluring violet of Parfait d'Amour; Lover's liqueur, as it was known. A bar-room myth went— (what we kids fantasized about)—that a woman would open her legs after one tot of Parfait d'Amour. 'Daar kom nog 'n pomp'—another poke—one of our barmen used to say, as the steward ferried a round to the lounge. We got to know the bitter orange smell of Cointreau, the honeyed-whiskey background of Drambuie and the burnt almond smell of Amaretto, not long after we began recognising the sauces and jellies that accompanied different cuts of meat! A wide variety of cigarettes cut a New York skyline, indicating their popularity, and glasses for all types of drinks crisply reflected and refracted the overhead globes.

A more austere Coloured Bar, with a separate entrance, was connected to the main bar by a passage running through to the Bottle Store at the far end. There were no fittings or fixtures other than the high counter, with a linoleum top. Morose brown oil paint on the walls for easy cleaning, and raw wooden floorboards that had absorbed almost every fluid one could think of. It was a far cry from its pale White counterpart, yet it turned-over a better trade in the long run. The incongruity of it all.

The Liquor Laws—curse of Natie's life—had to be strictly adhered to. Theoretically, police could demand to see the registers at any time, but in small country towns things like that were not done, unless there was obvious indication of spiritual malpractice. There was a period, when a resident sergeant would make oblique threats that he could come and peruse the books, 'any time it suits me,' but that was for, shall I call it, ulterior motives? Not only was each customer's name, address and type of spirit entered in a Record Book, but the Coloured community were only allowed a certain quota of alcohol per day: two bottles of sherry and a half-jack of spirits. Many complained it was too little…while others argued, too much!

The Black community were banned from the Bottle Store and bars, and had to make do with a beer hall in the location. Here they could drink the sour, fermented brew known as 'Kaffirbier' or 'Umqombothi' in the vernacular. The hall was fenced off and on cold days the men would sometimes drink their beer in the sunshine, thus warming themselves inside and out. They would quaff it with such 'geshmak' (relish), that Ziems, Koerie and I thought we would like to try it. We were in the vicinity one day and cadged a sip through the fence, but it was much too raw and fermented for our sweet palates.

Almost every public amenity had to be segregated, but for reasons I never got to know, we were somehow exempted from having a White and Coloured Bottle Store. The 'Orentlecher weiser'—Natie's reference to the everyday Whites—would

110

enter the Bottle Store trying not to touch or be touched by the clamouring masses and as far as I know, no one contracted TB, Leprosy or Treponema pallidum, the svelte little sexually-transmitted spirochete, willy-nilly sowing syphilis. Some folk did appear a little skittish, like Wildebeest crossing the crocodile infested Mara-Mara River, though guns, knives and violence were very much less of a threat and the system seemed to work reasonably well.

Years later, our Professor of Pathology, a brilliant man from Germany with a desiccated sense of humour, would explain that syphilis could only be acquired through intercourse. Someone in the class told him that he'd heard of someone who got it on a public toilet seat. 'Vehl, awl I ken zay, it must heff bien vary uncalmfortable!' he said, with a rare smile.

The tapkamer, in the bar yard, was wonderfully cool in summer but Arctic in winter, with its thick walls and cement floor. It had a timber ceiling, shelves were stained black from untold years of spillage and carried the heavy tang of sour sherry, in spite of the room being sloshed and scrubbed down with buckets of boiling water after each tap session. Bakkies, leader of the bottling team, sat beside the trough and nimbly juggled bottles filling from the spigots. Stoof, was the corker, Jan did the labelling, Big-Eyes packed them on the shelves and Duimpie made sure enough empties were at hand.

One of the forty-gallon wine barrels was rolled into the room and the gang manoeuvred it up onto a sturdy trestle behind the cast-iron wine trough, which had six adjustable teat-like spigots dangling over the brim. Bakkies would remove the bung and get the sherry flowing by inserting a short length of hosepipe into the barrel, give a healthy suck at the other end—sometimes healthy enough for a few swallows, if he thought we weren't watching—and lay it in the trough to fill.

This was the only time resuscitation required sucking and not blowing. The spigots, designed to fill spontaneously, would occasionally get clogged by sediment and required a little mouth-to-mouth. That was when the overseer would have to be

111

doubly alert, as Bakkies went down on his knees and sucked life back into the system. When his knees became too arthritic, Stoof took over from him. Every cask had a tight deck of labels banded to its lid, though to us, they all tasted sour and rough as a cat's tongue. Names like: Ship Sherry, Rock 'n Roll Sherry, Ryperdjie or Vaalperd adorned those bottles of plonk.

As city kids collected stamps or sport-cards, we collected labels from the wash-room. It was situated next to the tap-room, with a built-in concrete tub where all bottles—except malt, which were returned to the breweries—were washed, rinsed and stacked upside-down in their crates. Ziems, Koerie and I would go through the slush trying to find undamaged labels that we would stick onto the walls to dry. Our sharing was usually amicable, until now and again one of them would come across a real 'newie,' from an imported liqueur bottle, say, and my generosity would dry up faster than a bottle of sherry before closing time. 'They're my father's labels, anyway,' I would announce and then feel trebly terrible after it was handed over. I will say that I was generally a giver, not a taker…only those bloody labels!

In the same premises, one door down from the Bottle Store, was the treasure-trove of treasure-troves. One could fill a ledger on country stores, and our shop had only partially freed itself from the late 1800s. It was the equivalent of ambling around a game park and coming across a dodo or quagga, as we eagerly stalked behind the counters.

Shoppers had very limited income, every piece of material, pair of trousers, a skirt or jacket was meticulously fingered and tested, and if there were three or more colours or patterns, that would further complicate matters. Folk would have to decide whether it would be a shilling, two-and-six or five shillings' worth of 'Boermeel,' called a bucket, depending if a shirt, a pair of shoes—the old pair long past un-roadworthiness—or a few dates and raisins for a Christmas pudding, were to be bought. I was amazed how those women could hoist a 'bucket' of meal onto their heads—25 lbs in a large brown packet—duck under the doorway and then walk up the uneven gravel road and all the way to the Black location, only now and again having to put a steadying hand to one side or the other.

Not many folk carried a purse or wallet in the Black and Coloured community. Coppers, silver and the occasional note were tied into the corner of a hankie—'ah knipple' in Yiddish—which was either stowed between the breasts, in a pocket in an under-underskirt or hidden in the folds of a 'doek'. Men often kept change in their tobacco pouch or a note would be folded into the inner hat brim. For many, with little education, having to put together a sum of two shillings and nine pence three farthings, from an assortment of farthings, 'ha'pennies,' pennies, tickeys and sixpences, took time and unending patience. Sometimes their coins nestled in a bed of pipe tobacco or between tacky segments of chew-tobacco, buttons, loose matches and safety pins. It could have tried the patience of mother Theresa.

'Slegs vir Blankes' or 'Whites Only' signs were everywhere, though shops were granted permission for Black, Brown and White pigments to mingle, but not blend. Friday afternoons and Saturday mornings, bars, Bottle Stores, beer-hall and shops hummed, whether there were a few shillings or only pennies in the pocket. A little well-earned rest or possibly, a bit of fun, lay ahead and folk frenziedly went about their shopping.

Colesberg had its menagerie of naughty children and my brother had once been an active member of that fraternity. Pensie, short and plumpish—well, fat—was at the pinnacle of this illustrious bunch and occasionally came to play with me. We were strolling up town one afternoon when we saw Sakkie, the post boy, park his bike outside Patterson's, one of the two larger and smarter 'departmental' stores. When saddle springs gave in and you stood a chance of being impaled by the post, you did not buy a new one but forced an old tennis ball between the coils, giving a bit of bounce for a few more years.

Pensie's mother was a dressmaker and he just happened to have a darning needle with him that day, which he pushed

113

through one of the saddle vents into the ball and advised me 'Now we must fuck-off, quickly!' He did, not Einstein, who in his naivety saw himself as an innocent bystander and decided to watch the show. Sakkie came striding out, gave me a friendly nod while donning his cap, snapped the bicycle clip around his trouser cuff and swung his leg over the saddle with the satisfied look smart fellows, in smart uniforms, inevitably develop.

For a second or two I thought the needle may have dropped out; but next moment his eyes, which were normally prominent—proptotic, as they say in the trade—almost popped from their sockets. We had cut our milk teeth on every expletive in the book and even unprintable ones, but I was shocked by the guttural 'Ffff-aawk!' that bellowed from somewhere deep inside the man as he levitated and clawed at the seat of his pain. I should have registered the murderous telegraph in the airborne postman's eyes, but I doubled over instead. Next moment I snapped back as he delivered an open-handed slap across my cheek, a galaxy of stars exploding in my head and I must have been temporarily concussed, as it took me a few seconds to orientate myself.

Fridays after work, Sakkie would pop in for a glass of Ship Sherry before going home. With Kierie at my side, just in case he got the urge to deliver another slap or two, I apologised and told him I was not the culprit but happened to see someone fiddle with his saddle. He thoughtfully sipped his drink while assessing my story, nodded acceptance and our good terms were re-established.

(The next time I would be that stunned was when I charged down a kick, playing in one of the cake-divisions, and got the rugby ball between my eyes. I did manage to keep running, but in the wrong direction.)

Ann was in charge of accommodation and bookings. The gilt embossed 'RESERVATION BOOK' —the cover, was the only legible script in that entire tome. Her scrawl crawled across page after page, some deleted with a few ink-strokes, others smudged by tea, some in tentative pencil, and a bizarre

114

display of crosses, arrows, circled dates, question marks and an assortment of biscuit crumbs trapped in the creases.

A study of spiders showed the crazy webs they spun on LSD, and I imagined Ann's writing resembled the tracings of a fly that could have fallen into a 'Quink' Martini. Seven years at boarding school, many more at varsity, and I don't think I deciphered a quarter of her letters.

The Colesberg Hotel had its loyal customers who visited as regularly as the Lesser Kestrels or Greater Striped Swallows. Months and months before the Christmas holidays, letters seeking accommodation would arrive by the bushel and as time grew shorter, telegrams or 'wires' replaced them. Sakkie, in his smart olive-green cap and uniform, would park his bicycle at the kerb outside the Bottle Store, take the telegrams from his leather satchel and hand them to my mother for signing off.

I recall some of the less pleasant scenarios—fortunately not that many—and my stomach would give a nervous twitch when I heard Natie send for Ann, while studying the reservation book in the office. There was a controlled flatness to his voice; the tone a doctor might use when the diagnosis could be bad but he does not want to alarm the family unnecessarily, tinged with a caustic underlay only we could decipher.

How accepting the world seemed. A good example was what we affectionately referred to as 'the office'. Before it was officially baptised 'office,' it started life as a telephone booth. An old, crank-handle phone, 'XO1' spelled our telephone number in red letters, was still set against one wall and a narrow dividing counter, for the Visitors Register, further reduced this tiny space. At best, it was a crush. A friendly sort of country-crush, where a couple or family came to register, happy and contented and looking forward to a great dinner, a hot bath and a sound night's sleep. But if those delights were possibly in jeopardy, due to a mis-booking, even one person could make that little office seem terribly crowded. Things could become a 'biessel heis!' A little heated, indeed. In retrospect, now that those angst-filled moments are memories, I can hear folk

115

reminiscing with their friends, many years later '...and that quaint (rustic?) little reception area, you remember, dear, where was it now...?'

Extremely rarely a 'booked' visitor had to be referred elsewhere or simply stormed out, to seek solace in Hanover or Richmond, Philippolis or Reddersburg, depending if they were heading south or north. We were fortunate enough to have a handful of close neighbours, long before the explosive boom of B&Bs, who were prepared to take our over-flow. When glitches occurred, alternative arrangements could be made, and if we kids were away, our flat was home to many tourists.

By far the most common reason was tourists who did not, or forgot, to book, often with irritable babies or restless young children. Their gratitude, when alternative accommodation was found, compensated for all the other problems and pitfalls of running an inn. It is a small world, and I have met quite a few people who were thankful to have been put up in our flat or a nice country home.

There was not much relief we could offer on summer nights—opening doors usually brought in nothing more than an eager posse of thirsty mosquitoes—all windows had fly screens. But there were plenty of thick woollen blankets, eiderdowns and hot water bottles for the really frozen midyear travellers heading for the Natal coast.

Considering the times, I think the hotel ran reasonably smoothly. Nothing modern or luxurious, the rooms were kept squeaky-clean thanks to the ever-watchful eye of Miemie and her room girls, Miena and Daisy. Miemie later passed the housekeeping-baton to the capable Anna; our big-bosomed, round-shouldered and moustachioed new housekeeper, who reminded me of Droopy, even when she was happy.

One of Ann's less subtle tactics was to facilitate in the dining room on busy nights. Miemie and the waitresses would think of ways to subtly lure her out, but if the ruse failed, visitors were in for some nifty eating. She had no qualms strolling amongst the diners, often removing plates from under their noses before pudding spoons were down and mentioning, in her friendly manner, that a second sitting was in the offing. Miemie finally managed to quell this zeal, reminding her that the waitresses were more than adequate to the task. And that, they were, I marvelled at the way they quick-stepped from table to table, soup, main course and desserts stacked all the way up their arms—like dancing jugglers—remembering each table and order.

As wines have their particular bouquet, I began associating the various rooms and amenities with their breath. They ranged from subtle, to almost tangible, from earthy to unnatural and from delightful to obnoxious. There were certain smells that defied definition, but were blended by weather, mood and mythical associations through the many stories we were told.

Setting off upstairs, the smell of dark red polish that brought a weekly shine to the concrete staircase, and the copper handrail buffed with Brasso, was carried up into the corridor. Bedrooms had their own lingering aroma of miniature Lux soaps, starched bed linen and the transient tourists; those ordinary men, women and children, honeymooners, lonely passers-by and commercial travellers, who left their collective smells—I imagine, universally—that mark hotel bedrooms.

Our regular customers knew they were not coming to a luxury spa, but to clean premises, excellent service—'P.G. everyone will be at work today,' my father would intone—and a table, like most country inns boasted those days, that was discussed far and wide. They would often enquire in their letters or telegrams if such-and-such a dish would be on the menu that night, or whether they could purchase a loaf or two.

Miemie and the girls kept the bedrooms and bathrooms spotless. It was like a kind of low-grade Obsessive-Compulsive Disorder; all that scrubbing and polishing of floors; buffing of taps and basins and dusting walls and picture rails with short or long-stemmed feather dusters.

Kasper, one of our drivers, delivered linen to the washhouse at 'Klipkuil' in the old Ford truck. 'The bleddie tranter (wreck) is more stubborn than a mule,' Natie bemoaned the jalopy, which over years of misuse, had developed an erratic nature as its gears were grated and worn into new shift patterns. It had reached the stage where only Kasper, and occasionally Kierie, knew how to operate it. The washhouse was named after a nearby pool along the stream, where local women came to do their washing on rocks glossed by hands and eons of sporadically flowing waters. It was a low brick building with a wire mesh frontage that not only welcomed a soothing February breeze, but the bitter July air. Washing was hand scrubbed in cement tubs—water boiled in cauldrons over wood or coal fires—then 'Reckitt's Blue' added for extra whiteness and starched for symmetry. Pegged to wires held up by rickety posts, washing hung stiff and motionless in summer or snapped to August breezes like skiff sails before a south-easterly.

The driver would bring back clean washing and offload it in the laundry behind the garages, where three full-time women did the ironing. Here, the smell of irons heated over Primus Stoves and starched linen, mingled with African ditties tranquilly harmonised while they pressed away. Somehow, the smell was never quite the same, when they occasionally worked in silence, a sign of discontent or unhappiness.

The Bottle Store and Coloured Bar carried the tang of bottled sherry and sour glue from the labels. Wood wax and linseed oil, for the thick mahogany counter and shelves in the European Bar, added their touch to the subtle airs of cellophane cigarette jackets; the musty dampness that escaped each time one of the fridge doors opened and the yeasty sweat from empty malt bottles.

From a very young age, I would stand at the street door of the bar and plead for a cool drink. I had developed a fine stutter in those days and was too young to remember this specific incident, but apparently after begging for some time and my father repeatedly telling me to buzz off, I went on tiptoe and bellowed: 'J-jou b-bleddie suinige J-Jood!' 'Did you hear,' the story soon went around town, accompanied by hearty chuckles, 'old Kappie's toddler called him a stingy Jew?'

In the early nineteen-forties my father did major renovations, and although I have no clear picture of the construction work, the acrid smell of flux and molten lead for sealing the elbow and T-joints of cast-iron outflow pipes is my one key. What I do remember is the plumber inserting a bending-spring into pipes, lightly touching the flame of a blowtorch until the copper skin turned dusky and then deftly shaping the angles.

Our kitchen could have done with an upgrade over the years, but there never seemed time for change again. Miemie and Antie Bee ran a tight, if occasionally explosive ship, assisted by a number of able-bodied galley girls, which included the two cabin (room) girls, who also did kitchen duty. Just as well the old ship was not battling at sea, but securely anchored in terra firma, as there were times when mutiny could have marred the usual calm.

Fired by a massive cast-iron coal stove braced in an alcove, the old barque generally sailed on placid waters. Miemie and crew kept it on a tight course, breasting innumerable seasonal holidays, dinner parties and functions, sometimes through stormy waters and high winds, but invariably disembarking satiated passengers. There were far too many aromas to pin-point the kitchen, but from a young age we knew that mint sauce was drizzled over roast leg of lamb, quince jelly meant roast pork, aspic went with fish and apple jelly glistened beside slices of mouth-watering roast beef. These days I find it hard to re-capture the smell of crisp-skinned, succulent-breasted, brown-thighed, pukka home-range-chicken; or Springbok venison jugged with naëltjies (cloves). Those dishes just don't taste the same.

The dining room had a wooden floor with linoleum runners down the two main aisles and the overriding smell was of Cobra Wax and Floor polish. During summer months, the after-breath of Flit or Doom added their sharp contribution, possibly saturated in the floral curtains. A large sideboard gave off a pleasant mustiness that brought to mind years of condiments,

119

fresh or drying Coleman's Mustard, seasons of marmalade and forgotten Christmas bunting.

Seventeen shillings and sixpence bought you dinner, bed and breakfast. Menus allowed one to savour the entire fare, or as much as one could handle. There were a handful of locals, who would come for Sunday Lunches and pass effortlessly through that lengthy list. Miemie or Ann typed the menus. Breakfast included the usual fare, but was in fact a 'mixed-grill,' with bacon, grilled chops, sausage and minute-steaks. A typical dinner menu got the taste buds going with a wholesome soup: bean, pea, barley, vegetable, macaroni or chicken. Grilled fish, was followed by savoury mince or marrowbones on toast; two or three meat dishes such as roast leg of lamb, roast pork or beef. Springbok venison in season and roast duck or turkey. Those days roast chicken was a delicacy, saved for Sunday lunches—which was the highlight of our week. Other popular standbys included: tomato-, green bean-or cabbage 'breedie'; steak and kidney- or cottage pie, 'ou vrou onder die komberse' (mincemeat wrapped in cabbage leaves, with lemon and nutmeg) and one of Miemie's all time winners, a minced chicken-loaf shaped like an aerodynamic rugby ball, the crust glazed crisp and brown with egg-white.

Lamb chops were already seasoned by the scrub they grazed on. Those drab but nourishing little Karoo bushes with wonderful names like: skerpioenbos, doringvygie, 'skaapertjie,' kwaggavy and katdoring… to name a few. Boerewors was so meaty and deliciously spiced that we ate it raw. There was silverside, salted beef, tripe and onions, and another all time favourite, locally and with regular tourists, sheep's head, stomach and trotters. That is probably why very many years later, while working in Scotland, I took to Haggis with the ease of a Highlander.

Every few months a large wheel of strong cheddar, ensconced in its waxed-gauze shell, arrived by train from Cape Town; so heavy, someone had to help Antie Bee lug it into the pantry. Although it was kept refrigerated and under damp cloth,

by the end of its run it would have crumbled like an old ruin—
too hard and dry for biscuits, but it made outstanding macaroni
cheese.

Our Christmas luncheons would be booked at the previous
year's banquet and on occasions, two sittings were required.
The menu would have all the above, plus Miemie's free-range
turkeys, served with cranberry sauce. Dessert would include
her homemade vanilla ice cream, which was the one time we
kids prayed that the PowerStation would not let us down. The
Christmas pudding was studded with tickeys. They were first
scrubbed with Vim and then boiled in bicarbonate-of-soda,
before being mixed into the raw pudding. Miemie or Antie Bee
always made sure we kids got one in our helping.

The lounges and writing room had indefinable smells; an
amalgam of old hearths and cigars, gallantly proffered cigarettes
and summer frocks. They told the story of long-forgotten
perfumes, which sad or happy, jealous or contented women
touched to their throats. The pomades used by men who loved
their wives, smug abusers of wives or those indifferent to them,
but longing for another's. This is where young couples met for
the first time or older ones plotted intrigues, where so many had
come to celebrate and as many to drown their sorrows. Those
subtle breaths eddied amongst the old furniture.

The bars being off-limits to minors, the kitchen and dining
room too frenetic for them and the lounges not interesting
enough at that age, the old shop was the first smell or medley of
smells we got to know.

N. KAPLAN. GENERAL DEALER / ALGEMENE
HANDELAAR, declared maroon letters painted above the shop
doors. For us kids it was like stepping into another world; one
from which we were often shooed as nagging youngsters or
invited to give a hand as we got older and more reliable. This is
where the heady mix of smells all came together; the Karoo's
very own 'Spittlesfield' market or a Turkish 'souk'.

The floorboards, scrubbed pale over the years, were dusty by
late afternoon as bare and barely-shod feet shuffled in and out.

Before sweeping each morning, the shop boy liberally baptised the floor with a bottle of water, releasing vapours not unlike those after the first summer rains, which mingled with the rest of the collection.

Paraffin was one of the main contributors, where the ten-gallon drum stood on a wooden trestle between the two doors. It cost a tickey (three pennies or thruppence) a bottle, which the customer had to provide, and we would tap the pungent liquid from a brass spigot at the base of the tank. Enamel posters advertised 'Reckitt's Blue'—showing a shiny Black woman in snow-white apron and headscarf, hanging up snow-white sheets billowing in a breeze. Long bars of cheap yellow and blue-lye soap, raw and caustic, came in wooden crates and released their acrid flavour mingling with the starchy smell of calico, flannel, silk and rolls of dark blue African-prints. Colourful 'Basuto blankets' stacked on the uppermost shelves and army greatcoats hanging from wires strung between the tall concrete pillars, lowered their woollen offerings.

Bins of loose tobacco, small cloth pouches of Springbok and Horseshoe or packets of Boxer-Piet Retief pipe tobacco, threw in their lot with cigarettes like: Cavalla, C to C (Cape-to-Cairo), Du Mauriers, Flag, Commando (For real men), and Max (Men of the world smoke Max!). Later, there would be the gutsier toasted breaths of Peter Stuyvesant—one of the first to introduce those wide-screen adverts of beautiful people, in beautiful places, doing exotic things—Rothmans (Of Pall Mall), Lexington, Lucky Strike (Give a man a Lucky) and Gunston (with its unshaven hero fighting his sweaty way through steaming jungles.)

Rolls of dark chew-tobacco—fresh and damp or old and dry—skewered with bamboo pins and sold by 'penny' lengths, lent their tangy bite. As novices, we were taught to carefully measure off the lengths on the brass yard-ruler nailed to the countertop. As we became more adept we could do it faster with our 'fingers-lengths' and slice off segments with the pocket-knife, dangling on a piece of string. There was no time

122

or need to wrap it, the avid purchaser would immediately bite off a wad, tuck it between teeth and lower lip and stash the rest. Some of these characters, due to poor dental hygiene or good spacing, could spit a brown stream between their upper teeth with deadly accuracy; unfortunately, all too often while still in the shop.

The relish with which they tucked in made it look so delectable that one day I began nagging my mother to let me have some. I must have been about six, and she repeatedly told me it was not for children. I finally pushed her too far and she lost her cool. By the brisk way she hacked off a piece, an alarm bell did ring and I should have made a dash for it, but I was too busy savouring my victory. Quick as a mantis she snatched my jaw with one hand and jabbed it into my mouth. A nauseating bitterness—that seemed to stitch my tongue to my palate and my cheeks to my teeth—welled in my throat. She had timed it beautifully. As I was about to spit, she held my jaws together and commanded: 'Now go on; chew the dammed stuff!' I wailed, wept and squirmed until Miemie came to the rescue and broke up this macabre fandangle. 'Next time you'll listen when I tell you something for your own blessed good,' she tossed after me as I ran out to rinse my mouth, but the taste lingered much longer than I cared for.

There was also, what I thought of as mechanical smells. The darkly-greased wax-paper protecting bicycle chains, cotter pins, ball bearings and Yale locks; the rubber of new bicycle tyres and inner tubes and the brass parts of Primus Stoves. Long rows of deep drawers belched the metallic tang of hardware, every time they were opened; pliers, fretsaws, shifting spanners and chisels, as well as packets of nails, screws, bolts and nuts.

The aroma of Koffiehuis, FG and raw coffee beans, tempered some of those other smells. These luxuries were weighed using mainly the petite, brass ounce or one-pound-weights. The dark cast-iron weights—with non-slip grip-bars—were used for weighting heavier commodities, the everyday staples such as mealie-meal—fuel that fed the masses and (barely) kept starvation from the door—Boermeel, samp, dried beans, white or yellow mealies (large as filly's teeth) and tacky brown 'Goewermentsuiker'. There was a scarcity of white sugar, rice and cake flour during and after the Second World War. A sweet, dusty smell rose from the white sugar bin, when the shop boy emptied a 100 lb bag, while unrefined, 'the poor man's sugar,' carried the whiff of molasses and reminded me of smoky little houses. We weighed off brown paper packets of dried goods during lulls, and for smaller quantities, we could twist sheets of newspaper into neat cones with the flick of a wrist.

Miemie's heavy accountancy tomes, their page corners yellowed and curled from finger-licked-turning, were kept under the counter next to large tin canisters filled with Pyott's, Baker's or Baumann's Cream Crackers, Salticrax and Lemon Creams. Penny-line sweets were my undoing and I must have nicked a great deal of the profits before, during and long after my milk teeth came, and ditched me. We would put our tooth in a slipper, where a 'mouse' exchanged them for a penny and I remained gullible long past the age of innocence.

I drooled over the small neat boxes filled with 3-X Extra Strong peppermints, Mint Humbugs, Barley Sugar Sticks, Wilson's Toffees and Motto sweets in different colours, shapes and messages. Rock-hard 'Blackballs,' what the Yanks refer to as Jawbreakers or Gobstoppers—and in the style of those insensitive times, 'nigger-balls'—could be sucked for hours and changed through pastel shades as they ever so slowly diminished in size.

Jasper's older brother Kobus, had a pet Vervet Monkey that quizzically raised its brows at passers-by while nonchalantly fiddling with an erection. 'You must get him a wyfie (female), that hard-on is wasted!' Ziems used to rag Kobus. He would spit on a Blackball to facilitate the monkey popping it into its mouth, but due to the direction of their teeth and small aperture, it would be a battle trying to get the sweet out again. That would be Kobus' highlight of the week and we all unfortunately derived great entertainment watching its efforts.

Occasionally a crate of dates, raisins or sultanas would arrive, usually before the festive season, fresh and spongy and exuding the scent of their distant origins.

The sun relentlessly bored through the two large display windows, where posters for Boswell's or Pagel's Circus were pasted for a handful of free tickets. It sizzled flies and moths and baked a different aroma. Each time the small wooden doors to these windows were opened, the metallic tang of hot tin mugs, zinc buckets, enamel food pails and three-legged cast-iron cooking pots oozed into the shop, as well as the smell of 'pre-heated' cheap crockery, school slates and an assortment of knitting and crochet needles.

Even the old shop ladder, which looked like something from a Heath Robinson exhibition; strapped, patched, splinted and reinforced with wire, imparted a smell of stoic antiquity. How no one came a cropper and broke any bones is another measure of good fortune. 'Neitin, I am still going to break my neck on this (verdomde) ladder!' Miemie would tell him on his periodic visits to the shop, usually when one of the waitresses had brought morning or afternoon tea and biscuits. That the Rubenesque Anna did not was even more amazing. Watching her, as each rung sagged and squealed under her weight, the supports bowing and quivering as she nonchalantly leaned towards distant shelves, gave me the same goose bumps as the trapeze artists looping amongst the spotlights above the circus floor. Later, it would be up to one of us, or the shop boy, to do the acrobatics, handing items down or re-stocking shelves under the high concrete ceiling, where cobwebs rounded off corners that were beyond the reach of even the longest feather duster.

Then there were smells generated by the human body. Degrees of body odour, brought to its pinnacle at the height of summer, could be asphyxiating. At times it overrode the combined output of all the above commodities and, adhering to the laws of pheromones, had the ability to linger well after closing time.

125

Another of my favourite places was the corrugated iron sheds, of which the largest stood back-to-back with the Railway Depot beyond our stables. Here were stacks of sheep, goat or cattle hides, a leftover trait from my father's old 'smousing' or speculating days. Crystals of rock salt clung to the stiff skins, waiting until enough had been collected for railing to Port Elizabeth. Antique furniture stitched with spider webs, as well as forgotten treasures like wooden wash-stands with tiled tops and backboards, porcelain basins with matching pitchers and soap dishes, which were put out to rest when they renovated the hotel.

Exploring the dark, cavernous interior with my sister many years later, we came across brand new women's shoes of the early nineteen-twenties—silk and satin, colourful bows and flowers, cross over buckles and stubby heels—still in their original boxes. She took one or two pairs back to Paris, where she was living at the time, and they caused quite a stir. How mindlessly Koerie, Ziems and I hunted through those outbuildings, where snakes, scorpions and spiders made their home. We found grease-encrusted engine parts from another era and discarded snooker table paraphernalia. Ornate lamps under a pale coating of dust—the icing sugar of time, as someone once said—bronze mouldings and glass shades, with a collection of flies and moths interred in their fluted sumps. Obsolete scales weighed the heaviness of time in rusty pans and there were old crank-telephones that once sent or received messages from far-off places, on lines scratchy with static. Who knows what other lost treasures might have been buried deep under Hessian bags, tarpaulins and years of clutter.

For me, part of the magic of those old sheds, was the gloom, which seemed to be suspended on fine cables of sunlit motes, focused through boltholes in the high-pitched roof.

Chapter Fourteen
IN SEASON, OUT OF SEASON...
Some commercial travellers, the butterflies, who regularly pollinated our town

Like insects and flowers, country hotels shared a warm relationship, a symbiosis, as the naturalists would say, with Commercial Travellers. They were the Reps of today and the smouses of yesterday. No matter how long their absence, they were familiar and welcome as old friends, or the seasons.

Many had emerged from the old-school; Jewish 'smouse' (speculators or itinerant traders) that survived into the suit-and-tie, driver-and-automobile age, each with their own charm, humour or idiosyncrasies. Sharing a similar trade, their texture of temperaments and personalities was shaped by distinctive backgrounds, which had finally brought them to Colesberg and other small towns dotting the Platteland. In time, they became part of our family and we part of theirs. Most of them I remember as a child, through my boarding school years and finally home on varsity vacations as a young (irresponsible) man.

There was the diminutive Mr. Jackson with pink cheeks and elfin ears. Like a pair of parentheses, his eyebrows arched steeply above sad hooded eyes, apologetic as those of a jester who had seen the best and worst of life. Small hands with delicate fingers, rusted by cigarettes, animatedly shaped his sparse conversations or periodically touched his hair, as if confirming he had not suddenly gone bald. In his dark three-piece suit, white shirt and starched collar that bit into cleanly-shaven jowls, he cut a sombre little figure in winter; while his summer tan- or cream linen suits gave him the crumpled air of a Peter Lorre, in one of his private-eye roles. Unlike many of his counterparts, Mr Jackson was not outgoing, 'not much of a mixer,' as my father sometimes classified clientele.

'Vot voz...?...voz!,' he would say, when anyone asked him

how things were going, pulling down the corners of his mouth with a discarding shrug. He always travelled with 'Rex,' a small dog, who shared the apologetic manner of his master. Mr Jackson's speciality was men's and women's overalls and uniforms. When he used to hold up a crisp pair of blue overalls, for Miemie's perusal, the pants would lie crumpled on the floor, while he was hidden from view by the upper half. He would sit at the bar enjoying a few whiskeys and soda after work, or occasionally one or two with my father, and as the evening wore on, a further blush rose to his ears, his eyes became even sadder and then he would carefully make his way to the dining room to eat a lonely dinner.

His driver George, on the other hand, was a dapper, snappily dressed middle-aged gent with a neat moustache, a gold incisor and a glint in his eye for the girls. Early evenings he would take Rex for a walk, before going to have his own dinner. 'Non-White' drivers or nannies took their meals at the large kitchen table, when the worst of the dining pandemonium was over. Lenie, one of our feistier waitresses, told me George and Sanna, an equally feisty kitchen girl, 'played lekker cowboys and crooks'—her codename for sex—and she didn't seem surprised when I told her we knew.

Old Mr. Baumgarten was also short, but jocular and rotund. Metal frames, with bottle-end lenses, pressed neat grooves across his temples and a rim of wiry grey hair seemed to further prevent his shiny pate from sliding off his head. A large mole perched on his cheek reminded me of Khrushchev, especially with his heavy Eastern European accent. In spite of his eyes being small and rheumy, they flashed a genuine twinkle when he removed his spectacles to buff them with his tie.

Miss Lourens used to visit him in the evenings. She was a fine teacher who had a short temper and a long reputation for instilling fear into all her past, present and future pupils. I was greatly relieved to learn I was not going to have her in senior school, though it was difficult at times to weigh the pros-and-cons between her and boarding school. I knew nothing of their early or younger days but by the time I came-of-age—'Toe jy mens geword het,' Miemie would say—they were old friends.

He let her know when he would be in town and towards sunset, she took a slow walk to the hotel, where they would have a few pre-dinner drinks and then a couple more with their meal. They would then adjourn to the stoep, during the hot months, where if they were lucky, a breeze groped its way between the cane chairs to cool their legs. In winter, they sat side-by-side on the couch in the 'little' lounge, chatting over coffee and a last schnapps or two. Gradually the conversation waned and they fell silent, possibly rummaging over well-spent years or unfulfilled aspirations, or memories reawakened by drinks and embers settling in the grate. Sometimes they would nod off, one or the other would suddenly wake and so the evening ended. Occasionally he accompanied her, but mostly she saw herself to her spinster's home while he unsteadily climbed the stairs to his room.

One evening, possibly after one or two too many, Mr Baumgarten had gone to bed early, while Miss Lourens decided to sit on the stoep and freshen up before trudging home. She nodded off, firmly wrapped against the icy night in her thick herringbone coat, as a trickle pooled under her wicker chair and meandered towards the next. I was confused and a little devastated to see someone, whom my brother and sister had always described with such awe and fear, looking so vulnerable and oblivious. Someone must have told my mother I was gawping, because she came to fetch me and asked the incumbent barman to drive Miss Lourens home.

Max Schneider peered challengingly at the world from beneath a thick, heavily pomaded blond thatch. With impressive horn-rimmed spectacles and a large agate ring, black and shiny as a panther's eye, he had the look of an ex-vaudevillian or a movie impresario. In keeping with his persona, his range was men's suits and (slightly smarter) ladies' dresses. An old bentwood chair was passed over the counter for Max to sit on, puffing his cigar and holding the hand with the

129

big agate, like an auctioneer, while his driver unpacked and held up the various items to be perused.

Max loved a game of poker with the boys and not only did he bring an air of excitement to town, but we could always tell he had arrived by the aromatic waft of a large cigar clamped in the corner of his mouth. He was popular with the locals, and their poker games in the writing room sounded like a bachelor party in full swing, the stewards constantly on the run. Booming laughter, shouts of success or disappointment and the genial chatter of friends. He also brought with him a colourful collection of jokes, rough and raunchy, as I later learned, remembering the sudden lowering of his bass voice on my sorties past the lounges, followed by loud guffaws.

I remember my father and Max, coaxed by the crowd in the pub one evening, doing a resounding duet of the 'Anniversary Waltz'. It must have been good—or maybe the good spirits lifted them all—because they received an equally resounding ovation. He enjoyed ragging Miemie, the ever correct and serious Miss de Wit, in a friendly, older-brotherly kind of way, and she would humour him with a thin-lipped smile and unwavering stare. 'Uh,' or 'Ja-nee'—the ubiquitous Afrikaans stopgap to start, continue or end a conversation—was all she said when he was done, and then continue examining his wares.

'I'm in ladieth underwear!' Mr Rozovsky used to joke in his soft catchy lisp, which I forcibly had to stop myself from imitating. With cropped jet-black hair and a neat parting, a prominent nose, dark amused eyes, a liking for bright ties and chewing gum, he reminded me of a Jerry Lewis recently gone to seed, as rosettes of pleats tugged at his shirt buttons.

He appeared to be unflappable with his warm, quiet sense of humour and addiction to Wrigley's gum, which he chewed with small, mincing movements. There was not much of that going around during the post-war years and the odd stick or packet he gave me—unopened, with tear-tag intact!—was divided and sub-divided and if need be, re-sub-divided and usually shared with Koerie and Ziems. Each piece was chewed all day, if we could help it, and then left in a cup of water overnight, to be chewed next day. When it became too hard and tasteless, it was tossed out or traded. Trading chewed chewing gum was nothing new. A marble or a 'go' on someone's bicycle, the chance to play with a friend's newly made 'draadkar,' a toffee?—whatever was barter-able for a piece of chewing gum could do the trick.

What I remember most about Mr Rozovsky, were his eyes. Whether he was speaking to Miemie, my parents, someone in the bar or to me, they never left your face. It was the look of someone who genuinely listened and whenever he questioned me about school or in general, I had the feeling he was interested, nodding or shaking his head, and his jaws would stop working the Wrigley's for a second, as he took in a new fact.

Mr. Walters was one of the few non-Jewish Commercial Travellers. The kind of man who, other than a highly polished bald head, would have gone unnoticed in a crowd, blending well with his grey slacks, pale understated sports coats, sombre ties and brown rubber-soled shoes.

Tricks were his forte and he had a new one each time he came around. He would try to demonstrate them, between the sample cases lugged in by his driver and heaved onto the countertop for Miemie to inspect. If she happened to be on her own, she would have to juggle his sleight of hand, his wares and her customers. The most impressive one, was how to slice your finger with a pocket-knife. It necessitated a touch of self-mutilation and self-discipline. We watched spellbound—and with a little queasiness—as a fine line of blood erupted along the 'cut' around his finger. I was astounded by his bravery. He was a good fellow and always imparted, 'The secret, my friend, is…' with the same panache as he demonstrated them.

The trick, he told us, dabbing blood on a piece of toilet paper, was to administer a surreptitious pinprick beforehand; he kept one in the fold of his lapel for easy access. A hankie was then slightly tightened around the base of the finger, increasing the pressure, which facilitated a drop of blood that a blunt

131

pocket-knife dragged from the puncture site and around the digit. My attempt that evening was painful and unsuccessful and that was when I decided to scratch magician off my 'one-day' possibility list. After seeing Max Collie on one of his country tours, I was mesmerised into becoming a hypnotist, until the glib moves of a travelling magician—and one of our customers, Mr Rhodes, who could make a penny disappear and then 'pull' it from my ear—got me interested in magic.

I fell in love with Miss Berman the first time I saw her. As a young boy, I realised most of the men who frequented the hotel shared that emotion and there would always be a press of younger men in the bar when they knew she was in town. Not that I understood what it meant, but she had the most sensual mouth this country bumpkin had ever seen. Dark crimson lipstick defined full, expressive lips and in the age before lip-gloss, hers glistened tantalisingly when she spoke; drawing the listener closer and closer until one could sniff its intimate warm tang. She had a smoke-husky voice and I remember how she threw her head back when she laughed. It was a deep throaty purl and a well-manicured hand, with crimson nails and an assortment of rings with large semi-precious stones, lightly touched her voluptuous bosom.

My mother described her as 'vivacious'. With her thick black tresses bobbing and swinging as if they had a life of their own, the striking Miss Berman, probably entering middle age, could have stepped out of a Peter Cheney novel. My brother was (still is) a besotted Ava Gardner fan, with a huge poster in his bedroom, and Miss Berman reminded me of a more buxom version, especially when those locks fell across her face. I used to think her dark eyes were devouring everything in sight, and she epitomised a wantonly elegant, smart but sassy, big-city lady. That she behaved more sultrily when she spoke to me, was all prepubescent daydreaming, but watching their change of behaviour whenever she was in town, some of the local men seemed to suffer the same delusions.

Chippy Morkel was the exception. Young and brash, he had

a mop of ginger hair and two obstinate cowlicks that gave him the careless dash of a stuntman. He was born with a lekker-bek (gift of the gab), as the locals would say, and a disarming smile that must often have sold more units than customers needed.

He travelled for engineering equipment and lubricants, servicing garages, the farming community and council workshop. Brimful of endless jokes, old school stories and self-confidence, he entertained his clients on their premises by day and in the pub at night. He must have had a royal entertainment allowance, because when Chippy was in town, he was the heart and soul of those get-togethers and usually buying the rounds. When I was old enough to work the bar, watching him, and the local lad's body language, it was not difficult to realise his one major drawback was that he was as subtle as a starling and his jokes were often at someone else's expense.

*

Miemie faced this troupe with the same firm but polite reserve. The awe, crushes and eagerness for rewards of a young boy were nowhere near this professional and unbiased woman, who knew exactly what and how much was needed for shop or hotel and no matter how they played the game, no ball ever passed her. As suggestively as Miss Berman tried her 'sell-the-sizzle-not-the-steak' technique, Miemie treated her as a kindly teacher would an incorrigible child. I never came across a Commercial Traveller, no matter how slick or experienced, who could change Miemie's mind. Those who knew her never tried. In their day, new boys would have to run the gauntlet of being assessed for integrity, their knowledge and dependability and their wares painstakingly scrutinised and tested—repeatedly fingered for stretch, possible shrinkage, 'hoe was hulle' (colour fastness?)—and the all-important considerations: cost and saleability.

She treated them all the same, as though she could accurately weigh-off exact portions of her time and patience to spread

133

amongst these good men and occasional women. Although she favoured no one, I think she may have had a kind of maternal soft spot for Mr. Rozovsky. It reminded me of Pope, when he said something like: 'Bright as the sun, her eyes the gazers strike; and like the sun, they shine on all alike.' Well, similar in a manner of speaking.

The larger wholesalers would now and again hire the Methodist Church hall for a day or two, and for us kids (and many adults), it would be the equivalent of a trip to Disneyland. Star-struck, we wandered between trestle tables decorated with crinkle paper—which for me usually spelt Christmas—where better-class (shiny) or cheap (dull) cutlery; plain or coloured glass dishes and porcelain dinner services were on display.

Other tables had African bangles, brooches and necklaces; acoustic guitars, concertinas and mouth organs. Tight rolls of African Print and other imported materials, the latest clothing and underwear. Fancy suits with wide lapels, mantillas and black African 'tshalies' with friendly tassels, hung from shiny chrome frames on magical wheels. 'I will still rap your backside for you today,' Miemie would warn when I tried to give them an accidental nudge.

Beneath the arched 'holy windows' stood shiny bicycles, display stands with aerodynamic cycle lamps and dynamos—so one could ride up and down Church Street on hot evenings, a cone of yellow stabbing the darkness between streetlights. Board games like Snakes and Ladders, Ludo and Tiddlywinks; tubular metal containers with Pick-up Sticks; Dinky toys with rubber wheels, balsawood aeroplane and boat kits, marbles, Plasticine and spinning tops in all shapes and colours.

Miemie came out of these extravaganzas as unimpressed as she had entered, never blasé. She would put in an order for essentials—at the right price—and may have fancied a 36-long, in black gabardine—not the right price. As I said, she was simple and unpretentious as a landscape, and like a landscape, only God and time held sway over her.

Then there were their drivers, who played a big role in our practical sex tutorials. None of us learned about sex from our parents or nature-study classes; we picked up tips from our Coloured and Black friends, staff members and sometimes an older sibling. On one occasion, my brother cagily broached The Birds and the Bees. 'Oh no, not that again,' I moaned, 'I've just had it from Beryl!' That would have been the closest scientific validation we got.

For practical classes we relied on these drivers. There were a couple of rooms in the back yard, next to the garages, that accommodated these hapless chaps and they inadvertently tutored us in vivid, varied and vigorous ways of 'pinching the cat in the dark,' or light. They were the proverbial sailors of the lost seas of the Karoo and just as every Jack Tar had a gal in every port, so many of these chaps must have had a poppie in every dorp. When the travellers clocked in for a few days, the scene was set for a bit of real-time instruction. 'Castle' and 'Lion' beer came in sturdy, lidded crates that we used for building ramps below their bedroom windows and in a matter of minutes, we had instant ringside stands.

I only have a clear image of George, Mr Jackson's driver; the others somehow remain faceless tutors. Some got down to business with the lights on, others preferred the dark, which was the opposite of silent movies; plenty of sound but no picture. The chaps who did not mind the light afforded us good viewing. We noted every stage of those conquests. How they handled themselves and their women, whether it was smooth patter or stern coercion, silent trysts or vocal couplings, remembering exactly what or how things were said and most important of all, 'Die eksin' (action), as one of our bar boys referred to sex.

Bo told me that in his youth, an Amazonian young woman was boarding in one of the rooms on the first floor. They discovered that a local mechanic, Spier (muscle), was servicing the lass. Boris and a mate would time his visits, then scale one

135

of the drainage pipes festooning the back walls and cautiously peer through the window.

When they reached it on one occasion, the couple were not in bed, but going about it upright and starkers in the middle of the room. While they were torn between the choice of excellent viewing, but bad timing, the two-backed monster pivoted and next moment Spier was staring them in the eye. 'In that split second,' as he likes to say, he decided falling to his death would be the nobler, if messier, option and was about to let go and plummet to the concrete screed, when Spier gave a wink and a frisky thumbs-up behind the maiden's expansive back, turned up the revs and gave them a show to remember.

Chapter Fifteen
WE CHANGE, AND TIMES WITH US...
Rights of passage, vinegar dressings and a dollop of benign neglect

How I never turned out to be a kleptomaniac or other felon remains a mystery. No matter how busy the shop was, the moment I walked in, two or three pairs of eyes would follow this raider of the archaic till; a simple drawer that could be silently opened and closed. If the cash drawer appeared to be monitored, I turned my talents to the sweet counter that was not always manned. Later there came a time when I nabbed the odd packet of Cavalla Tens, which Koerie, Ziems I would take to the koppies, for a bit of adult sublimation.

Occasionally, in my naivety, I ransacked my father's trouser pockets, where they hung over a high-backed chair in their bedroom. No matter where I tried to spend the change, storeowners informed my parents and, when these antics outgrew the cute phase, it earned me a spanking. I heard Natie tell an early customer one morning, he was just going to the shop to get 'kleingeld' (change), and I told him not to bother, I had some. He took my change, helped the man, then took my hand, led me to the flat, took my head between his knees and gave me a good 'patzen toches' (smack on the bum).

One did not have to be a genius to swear, that was our lingua franca, especially in or around the shop, Bottle Store and bars. I believe my vocabulary was impressive, not only for its fruity content, but the very young age I began expressing myself. 'Whole strings of them, with very little repetition...' one of the townsfolk reminded me many years later. For a three or four-year-old to be earning cash-for-cussing, I must have had quite a repertoire. In addition to cash, it also earned me mouthfuls of mustard—strong powdered Colman's—or Miemie's other favourite, a slice of caustic blue soap.

I have another early memory. It would have been a Sunday

morning—both parents lying-in—Ann reading a book and Natie swathed in newspapers he may have cadged from a tourist the previous evening. Einstein is busy studying the dynamics of light at close quarters, despite dour warnings of doom from the elders. Finally, through trial and (a massive) error, I manage to unscrew one of the oval switches dangling from the headboard and in a flash of singed flesh and frightening static, 220 DC volts hurl me across my father and onto the floor. Too stunned to cry, but realising my folly, he pushes aside the fingers I hold up as a burnt offering, clamps my head between his knees and gives me a walloping with his slipper. Coming in that order, those shocks put an end to my scientific spirit of discovery, but not for the fauna and flora that was all around us.

My siblings (jokingly) remind me of having killed untold chicks and ducklings. In a court of law I would have to admit, Your Honour, I did do-in a few, but the foul acts need clarification, there were mitigating circumstances. I cannot remember a time when at least one of the chicken, duck or turkey hens in Miemie's menagerie were not drawing a clutch of fluff-balls in their possessive wakes. (Ask me; I've been attacked by brooding hens—don't laugh—more times than I had poached eggs.)

Children seem to bath in an armada of toys these days, but never having had bath toys, I used to play with the real McCoys. Watching how their adult counterparts would tail-up as they searched for subterranean morsels down at the sloot, in the freedom of our 'benign neglect' I did drown a couple of ducklings in the process. And, like 'Lenny' and his mouse in Steinbeck's masterpiece, I did squeeze—cuddle, sounds better—the occasional baby chick to death: out of sheer love! I rest my case.

On holiday in Colesberg, the young son of one of our city friends came into the shop one day with a sturdy turkey quill stuck into an old jam tin filled with soil.

'I have just given it water,' he informed my mother and in reply to a silly question: 'Because I am growing turkeys,' he

138

told her with the direct naivety of youth.

I remember another February. My mother on vacation in Cape Town, the hotel busy, kitchen frantic and I was getting in everyone's way. Miemie had repeatedly warned me to stay out of the pantry 'en onder ons voete uit!' I finally snuck back in, clambered onto the table so that I could reach the cookie tins on one of the high, 'childproof' shelves. Clutching a biscuit in each hand I decided to jump, but as luck would have it, my toe snagged and next moment, the floor came up and smashed my right forearm.

'FOOSH,' as the E.R. boys and girls refer to it in this age of acronyms; 'Fell on out-stretched hand'. Even in retrospect, my 'dinner fork' greenstick fracture was one of the worst angulations I have seen. It was so grotesque, it made me howl more than the pain and as I ran into the kitchen holding up this malformed 'thing' in front of me, the women shrieked and scattered in all directions. Not the morose Lena, who foamy arms and all snatched me up and told Miemie to sit and hold me tightly to her chest. One good yank and my arm straightened like magic, as, untrained and instinctively, she executed a perfect reduction on a severe 'Colley's' fracture. An old flannel rag was wrapped around my arm, liberally doused with vinegar—the age-old antidote to everything and anything that befalls man or beast in the country—and Miemie's lazy right eye gave an involuntary twitch of relieved anger, as she rather harshly sat me on the chair. 'You are very lucky I did not warm up your backside with a good hiding,' she scolded, 'just you dare creep into the pantry again, do you hear me?' Her threat was unnecessary. I would not have lifted my backside off the chair for all the cookies in Colesberg.

When the last sitting finally ended, she led me to the office and sent for my father. He and the barmen were too busy to get away right then, so the two of us walked up to Doc Cooper's surgery, where a young locum he had managed to get, gingerly removed the cloth. (Our doctors almost never went on vacation and both my visits were simply bad timing.) He looked at my

139

arm, said it did not look like a fracture, got Miemie to re-wrap it and sent us off. I remember odd stabs of pain for a week or two, when the blankets or someone accidentally touched my arm, but it healed in no time. An X-ray, for something unrelated many years later, showed the bones looking as good as new. Thanks to a quick-thinking scullery maid and another use for a tangy vinegar dressing, doctors were rendered superfluous.

In time, we began working in the shop, then lending a hand in the kitchen and later graduated to the bars and hotel reception. It all seemed so easy when one grew up in such a milieu that by the time we were in our early teens, we felt quite comfortable managing the hotel on an out-of-season Sunday. We also had to supervise off-loading the railway trucks bringing shop or bar supplies; wine bottling and when we got our driver's licence, fetching or taking laundry to the washhouse and delivering large shop or bar orders. Everyone tried to avoid taking charge of Ann's Reservations Book in her absence, but we simply had to take the good with the bad.

A cemetery, a blue gum and Kiep-Kiep... our earliest impressions

'Do you know you're at the dead centre of Colesberg?' someone once joked and he was dead right. The cemetery across the road from the hotel dated back to the early 1800s. Some epitaphs were in Latin, while truncated columns indicated a premature departure. The story on one grave, in embossed Latin, indicated the man had been hanged for murder. I have no recollection of any classical scholars in the vicinity, but have a sneaky suspicion the word 'hunc' may have given rise to some fanciful adlibbing, most likely by Balbinus Boris Caesar.

The sun skidded off smooth black granite slabs and brought a glow to long-toed Carrara marble angels with folded wings, who seemed to be gazing on the grave at their feet or longingly beyond the tall spiked palings. We would wonder if it was towards some distant Eden, only they could see, or just to get out of the dreary old cemetery. It was also another test in the rights-of-passage and how we slotted into the pecking order. Let me admit upfront—I failed this exam without sitting, or walking, for it. I baulked as the bolt was withdrawn, the gate swung open, and I would gladly have traded in my bicycle, if that had been the choice. I was in good company; there were plenty of tough kids, who had a healthy respect for the departed.

One of the older boys would put an article on a grave in the furthest corner and then, well after dark, the 'initiate' was accompanied to the graveyard gate and told to fetch it. It was a good hundred and fifty metres, winding between dilapidated graves, stunted pine trees that soughed forlornly and in which owls hooted at night. 'That means the death of a loved one,' the older kids would say, fuelling more phantoms to haunt our bedtime stories. That the love-call of Ollie the Owl could be so ominous. Myths, I ask you?

The tall gates swung open or closed on hinges that squealed eerily enough by day and when they shot the bolt with a clang of finality, quite a few initiates ventured no further than the main path, a few feet from the gate. To demonstrate his fearlessness, my brother would enter, slide the bolt behind him and vanish into the dark. Then we would see the flare of a

141

match as he lay down on one of the slabs to enjoy a contraband Cavalla filter. No wonder they used to call him 'Boris Karloff,' of Frankenstein movie fame. When we climbed these pine trees in search of birds' nests, brave as we thought we were, Ziems and I were always casting backward glances and I could feel my ears twitch and tighten as those primordial muscles went into danger mode...fight?...or flee? Koerie was the bravest, by day, but also failed the night passage. We only relaxed once we were safely out of the cemetery and on the street again.

Aged six or seven, we were already toeing across horizontal drainpipes between the hotel and a large expanse of flat corrugated roofing over our adjoining flat and storerooms. Due to the way the land sloped towards the stream and the lofty ceilings of the time, the hotel roof was higher than a modern 3-storey building. We would dash up the outside concrete fire escape to an upstairs courtyard, shinny up some pipes, ease our way across a narrow archway bridging the back rooms with the main building and then a short clamber onto the shallow-pitched roof. The entire world seemed to stretch in all directions. On our stomachs, we wormed our way to the edge, groping for eggs or chicks in pigeon nests under the eaves, with nothing but the stupidity of youth between us and the ground below.

Sometimes we climbed the partially rotting supports of a tall, corrugated fence separating the garden from the back road and worked our way across to the steeply-pitched roofs over the sheds adjoining the depot. Barefoot, we silently eased our way down the far side, to peer through a gulley at folk sitting in the shade or enjoying a bit of winter sunshine. Going up was usually straightforward; coming down was a bugger, often snagging our clothing on metal scars in our frenzy to reach terra firma. But for us, the sheer fun of having been invisible to the world far below, made the trips worthwhile.

Chapter Sixteen
TIME, AND 'THE RIGHT STAFF,' WORK WONDERS...
Some good (sometimes erratic) men and women to count on

A few staff members arrived and left too rapidly to leave a recordable footprint. Some blended into the background, while others left an indelible impression.

Generally speaking, Black and Coloured folk had very little to smile or enthuse about, but Lena and Jane, mother and daughter, could have been twins. Short, tubby and completely humourless, they made Yuri Andropov—who took over the shackles from Brezhnev—seem jovial. Lena—healer of my broken arm—would scrape the fatty deposits off the first wash-up sink, which she kept in a tin. That was the 'Lanolin' or moisturiser that the kitchen girls applied to face, arms and legs and their skin seemed to glow with health. Some wizard should go into this readily available commodity and could tout it as 'One Baked Bean can suits all skins.'

Jane was the only true narcoleptic I came across in my medical career. (A small percentage of people who nod-off for a couple of seconds or minutes at the drop of a hat...or even, when putting one on!) She also took care of our flat and one could find her fast asleep, hands still tucked under the mattress or leaning on a broom, on her knees (polishing the floor) or sometimes in the kitchen, clutching a handful of cutlery, mouth wide open...mind temporarily shut.

The sisters Miena and Daisy were the exact opposite. Tall, elegant and beautiful, like polished teak, they were always smiling and friendly, yet discreet and decorous. Men of all colours had the hots for them, including Ou Luiperd le Roux.

'Umtshato,' marriage in Xhosa, is also the custom whereby parents give a daughter in marriage to an approved suitor or one who they thought would be a suitable provider. As in most arranged marriages across the world, bride (or groom) might not always have been in favour of their intended partner, but in keeping with those times, they simply accepted 'the good with the bed,' as Natie would have said, and got on with their lives.

'Ukuthwala (kwentombi),' on the other hand, meant the abduction (of a young girl), a custom that was practised in certain circumstances—when the suitor or his representatives arranged 'lobola' (bridal price) and other conditions with the intended bride's family—so as to 'abduct' her for marriage. Infrequently, the suitor would forcibly 'take' a young girl or woman against her or her parents' will and abduct her to his home, where one can only imagine the kind of life she would have led. Daisy's mother and another young girl, whose mother once worked for us, got wind of such intentions. I have vague memories of whispered arrangements with Miemie and my mother, and Beryl, on one occasion. The fearful secrecy and stealth with which these young girls were smuggled into a room on our premises, after dark, and kept there until the problem had been resolved; usually by the father and uncles or older brothers of the intended bartered brides. The ploys worked for these two maidens, but others were not always as fortunate.

Anna came to work for us when it became too difficult for Miemie to run the entire show. She was a dour Afrikaner spinster, pale and thickset with large pendant breasts and her hair cut like a newly hacked clearing. She was not morose, but a permanent hangdog look clutched her face. Stoical as they made them, she came to work for two days complaining of severe stomach pain and cramps. Miemie told her to go and see the doctor, but she shrugged it off and pressed on. She collapsed at home on the third morning and was taken to hospital, where she had emergency surgery for what turned out to be a ruptured gall bladder. In a bad way, she was rushed to Bloemfontein, for further surgical treatment and follow-up.

Returning three weeks later, she had lost a bit of weight and her usual ponderous step seemed chipper. My mother asked her how she felt. 'Thank the Lord, I just feel so much better now, you people won't believe it!' she said with the enthusiasm of a young girl and her glummest expression yet.

There was a chorus of frilly-capped, starched-aproned waitresses, who pranced or danced through the dining room over the years. Those that did not make the grade, might have had the skills but not the temperament and those who had plenty of temperament, did not have the skills. There was a solid core of five, who, depending on pregnancies, domestic upheavals, work-related tiffs, illness or personality clashes; came and went over the last twenty years of my parents' run. They worked in pairs; three were often needed at the height of season, while one, could manage during exceptionally quiet spells.

They were all excellent, but the lean and fearless Livonia was by far the best. Ecological sentiments lay in the future, snakes, having enticed Adam to eat from the forbidden tree, were killed on sight, and she did away with three unwelcome visitors. Admittedly, one was on our front stoep, another in the dining room and one comfortably coiled on a pantry shelf. She had the skills of a Secretary bird, dancing around the reptile on thin pale legs and waiting for the right moment to stomp her heel on its head. A female leguan, laden with a clutch of eggs, had thought of turning the rock wall separating our back yard from the sloot, into a nursery; but unfortunately, Livonia did away with her as well.

Her husband, socially pleasant but domestically abusive— 'smooth on the street, rough under the sheet,' as they used to say—was a heavy drinker. After a particularly violent assault, when she couldn't come to work for a fortnight, he took it upon himself to go dry and, literally overnight, became a changed man. It was only in retrospect, that I could look back and recognise the magnificence of such commitment.

Those women memorised lengthy orders and like a juggler, Livonia stacked plates along both ropey arms, remembering each table and diner, and after a busy night, she could recall the dishes her guests had ordered. Under different circumstances, in another era, a mind like that could have been so much better

145

utilised. Her one drawback was a fiery temper that erupted when provoked. 'I am born and bred a thorough Griqua,' she snarled at a woman who had called her a 'fokkin' Boesman,' before grabbing her by the front of her dress and delivering a faultless kopstamp (head butt or Glasgow kiss, as it is known along the Clyde Valley soccer clubs), that instantly settled the squabble.

The Rubenesque and feisty Lenie came a close second in the service section, but I voted her tops in the saucy raconteurs department. Mild and even-tempered and a bit of a flirt, she would signal me to the serving hatch during quiet spells—or with Ziems and Koerie, on the kitchen steps, in the evenings—and regale me with some explicit anecdotes. 'Kaabies (cowboys) en crooks' was her metaphor for sex, should anyone overhear us. She gave me firsthand tutorials on her deflowering, forced sex and occasionally consensual sex. She must have sensed this pipsqueak had a crush on her, because what she lacked in scientific acumen, she more than made up for with erotically vivid description. Who knows, in more modern times, she could have been the Jackie Collins of Colesberg.

(Another) Meisie had a fine sense of humour and an impressive set of dentures, which clacked when she spoke, ate or laughed and she would periodically assist them into place with a quick brush of the fingers. Either her jaws had shrunk (atrophied), the dental mechanic made them too large or she received the wrong pair from De Aar? The upper set popped out once, fortunately onto an empty plate 'and I juss quickly put my hand over it, like so' she demonstrated, 'before the people could faint from the shock,' she ended with a run of castanet-like clacks.

Sanna was sultry and sexy and hence did not zip about but sashayed between the tables with a smouldering look, possibly thinking about her next cigarette. She was a heavy smoker and would puff away, seated on the kitchen steps before and after mealtimes. Koerie told us the way she let smoke trickle from

146

her lips made him horny and Ziems would laugh. 'Don't even imagine yourself, you're much too light (in the pants) for such a woman.'

'Tinkie'—short, for tinktinkie, one of the tiny wren family—was a petite late teenager who could barely see over the serving hatch. She made up for lack of size by doubling her speed and darting between the tables like a sunbird. She could do two serving sorties in the time it took the others to do one. With her winning smile, she was a favourite with the guests. We thought we were so clued up. She told us that she was feeling nauseous in the mornings and vomiting, and that her breasts were painful. Ziems thought she probably had a cold, Koerie told her if her breasts were sore, that meant she 'needed it' and Einstein thought she'd eaten something that wasn't good. Whatever she had, produced a healthy chubby boy.

More than the summer heat, a different heat was generated by so many women working in a close, frenzied atmosphere. It was further warmed by the stove, which gave off heat long after the fire had gone out. One could tell the atmosphere in the kitchen at a distance. Usually it was the familiar, 'heimische' (homely) rattle of utensils—our kitchen-lullaby we fell asleep to in the flat next door—but every now and again the noise took on a more provocative note, allegro or grandioso, as musicians would say.

The slightest misunderstanding—a waitress accidentally (intentionally?) taking another's order, a mishandled plate, an unreasonable customer (not all that common), a sarcastic remark or that unseen vagabond, PMT, which had no name then—'Sy's al weer vol stront vanaand!'—would trigger a Rimsky Korsakov Concierto. Like one of the modern compositions, acrimonious flutes and oboes exchanged accusations amidst the clash of cymbals. In the kitchen there was agitation in the handling of crockery, frustration rattled cutlery and in the dining room chairs seemed to scrape more annoyingly as fresh settings were arranged and heels stomped a little more peevishly across the floor. We could hear it, but

147

diners barely took their minds and mouths off the tasty dishes, generally oblivious to the change in orchestration.

Miemie could usually bring instant order when her right eye narrowed in anger and she began rolling her wet cloth into an unassuming but devilish baton. The girls had all witnessed her in action, when driven beyond reason, but at times like those, it took longer to settle. On rare occasions, the simmering in the dining room called for higher authority, and a message was sent to my father in the bar. When angry or dissatisfied, Natie's expression took on a hard, chilling set and when he opened the bar hatch with an annoyed rattle, adjusted his heavy 'Clark Kent' glasses and glowered at the waitresses, there was no need to dash into the office and don his Superman suit. It was enough to restore decorum, if not peace, and usually by the next day, things would be back to normal and the previous evening's altercation had settled in the sediment of hotel ups-and-downs.

Antie Bee was second in command and as I said, she performed daily miracles with cinnamon, nutmeg, cloves and coriander. A sprinkle here, a dash there, net 'n 'katspoegie'(cat spit = small amount), half-a-handful or only a finger-length, made it impossible to get a recipe out of her. There seems to be an infinite number of health and whole-wheat breads; 'oysgeshtupt' (crammed) with every kind of seed, pulse, rind, fibre, dried-fruit, trace-elements, nuts and vitamins one can think of, but I have yet to taste one that even comes close to her simple crusty breads.

When kitchen knives lost their keenness—'this knife is again so blunt you can ride on it to Bloemfontein,' Miemie would complain while trying to slice a leg of mutton—Antie Bee honed them with a few brisk strokes across the kitchen steps. For a born-and-bred Plattelander, she was a wizard with fish. They were cleaned on the kitchen steps with deft scrapes that sent scales into the sun and clinging to her arms and bonnet like glitter. She gave heads and fins to Ou Willem and tossed smaller off-cuts to a motley collection of cats waiting around her long skirts.

148

With a mixture of awe and excitement, we watched one of the yard boys bring a chicken, a duck or the occasional turkey to be slaughtered. She decapitated them on a block that stood below the kitchen stairs and tossed the headless birds behind her, to do their last drunken tango in Colesberg. Hither and thither they tottered, blood dulling once proud ruffs, until they seemed to tire and finally came to rest. They were then dunked in a basin of scalding water, plucked, trimmed, eviscerated and ready for the roasting pans. One would think, having watched those macabre dances, we would never eat chicken or meat again, but those out-of-the-ordinary things became part of our lives.

A few wispy grey hairs peeking from her cap, arms flour-dusted to the elbows, I can see her kneading dough in a large zinc tub smelling of sour potato yeast. It was then put to bed overnight under a blanket or two, where it swelled like a portly paunch by morning. I rarely watch TV cooking extravaganzas. It seems mandatory to swill litres of wine, dispense as many F-words as there are grains of rice in a measuring cup, break into tears or berate assistants when some exotic dish implodes in one of their four, high-tech eye-level ovens.

I have no truck with any of those histrionics; they are extremely well paid to entertain. It merely highlights the difference, when time was running out and two sittings were chomping at the bit; the only way we knew Antie Bee was feeling the pressure was the speed with which she whisked egg whites for her Blancmange pudding. There were no 'lectric blenders and she took the constant pressures, plus having to stoke the fire, in her stride, with nary a fuss, cuss or fuck-word.

I remember Wally from my early youth. Natie was caught in a love-hate or to be more exact, a nurture-murder relationship with him. When he was sober, Wally was the equivalent of two good, or three average stewards, but drunk, he was an absolute menace who refused to acknowledge the fact that he was out of control. With suave, dashing eyes—that became lifeless when drunk—heavily Brylcreemed wavy black hair and a festive

Omar Sharif moustache, he bedazzled all women, from stoical verkrampte tannies to hoity-toity English ladies. Black, White or Brown, Wally was a lady's man. He was a lusty fellow and between spirits and sex, many man-hours were lost—(well...depending from whose point of view)—and those were the times Natie could gladly have strangled this talented steward.

He built amazing kites with supplies he sometimes got from an uncle in Durban; tough silk threads, lengths of split bamboo and tissue paper in a range of brilliant colours. He made glue with cake flour, a teaspoon of brown sugar, a touch of vinegar and water. If bamboo was not available, he carefully split and trimmed local reeds and shaped frames into birds, bats, frogs, faces and boxes, as well as regular diamond and bow-shaped kites with exotic tails.

There were the (exceptionally) rare non-fornicating, sober, off-duty Sundays—with a good breeze passing through town—that he took us to the large common down the road. There he would show us how to make them dive, climb, swoop, quiver or loop, but none of us got anywhere near Wally's expertise. He knew where to trap 'blackcats' (Black Heads) and Cape canaries with birdlime, a messy business at best, but he made it seem simple. Quick as a flash, he had each wing splinted between the fingers of one hand, while the other gently released the fragile claws. A piece of cloth touched to a small bottle of paraffin cleaned their feathers of excess lime. He taught us how to make cages from Whiskey crates, a piece of chicken mesh and 'taaibos' twigs for perches. He also cooked up great beef or lamb curries. I was too young for such exotic tastes, but Bo and Bee would commission him when they were home and he used his 'speshul spices and condimuhnts from Duh'bin'.

Wally could hoist a large, fully laden 'Lion Beer' tray above his head and weave between rowdy revellers with nary a spill. No matter how crowded the lounges, with folk milling from table to table, he memorised each drink and mixer, with or without lime, two cubes or plenty of ice, fresh lemon or bitters

150

and delivered them on time. 'Yeesus Wally, but you're a real thorn!' revellers would praise him. Doring (thorn) was an accolade, indicating ace!

It was 'from a different kettle of fish,' as my father said, when Wally was 'shickered' (drunk). 'Oy gevalt, de bugger is ongeshnoskit (drunk!) again!' as though anyone could be oblivious to Wally's drunken state. To compound the problem, he thought he was doing a splendid job and doggedly refused to abandon his post. Natie would finally storm out of the pub, grab him by the back of his collar and frogmarch him out. Usually he returned, adamant he was 'Aw-keh,' bloodshot eyes riveted on a spot in the far distance as he swayed and teetered. He was never challenging or belligerent, but somehow unchallengeable, and that was one of the few times the Old Man became physical and would 'donner' Wally out into the yard.

During one of their many truces, and in a bid to retain him, my father allowed Wally to move into a spare 'boy's' room on the premises. It was close to the Plaatjies house, which gave Ziems and Koerie an early warning system should 'Cowboys and Crooks' be heading that way. One particular Sunday morning Koerie came to knock at my bedroom window and told me to hurry. Within minutes we were on the beer-crate-bleachers, silently cheering our hero. He was no dummy and after some weeks had strung a makeshift net curtain across the window, but, being short of material, a make-do gap remained. Taller, I had a good view, Koerie's was not bad, but poor Ziems was losing out. In his excitement not to miss the finale, which he could clearly hear but barely see—Wally was a vociferous lover—he accidentally bumped Koerie, who tried to regain his balance on one of the loose-fitting lids, and our precarious stairway to the stars began to topple. With Koerie's curses and my banging an elbow against the window as we fell, Wally was at the door in a flash. We weren't waiting for him, but had he not been clutching his little white steward's jacket to his otherwise naked loins, he would have chased and probably strangled us. Along with his other talents, he was also a jolly good sport. Two days later he had forgiven us our tryst-passes and we were good mates, wanting to know when we could go trapping 'Capies' again.

After the final sacking of Wally, sometime in the early '50s, we only had three wine stewards until the hotel was sold in 1964. That bit of information might not mean much, but it was miraculous considering the trade, and I lost count of the number of barmen that passed through our portals in the same period. The three replacements all came from the Black section of the township and not having had much schooling and new to stewardship, Fred, Geelbooi and George coped remarkably well. Maybe not Geelbooi, but I think he may have had a dyslexic problem. Fred was the philosopher and thinker, with a great sense of humour, Geelbooi the cheerful, helpful smiler and George, the unhurried and inflexible introvert. I mention the following bit of scatology both from a physiological point of view—call it a scientific slant—and as another fine postprandial Sunday anecdote.

I was home on vacation, the parents and Miemie had been invited to a farm and Fred and I were keeping inn. The main street was desolate, nothing stirred but the papery Eucalyptus leaves across the road, as the two of us chatted on the veranda. Suddenly there was the hum of a fast approaching car, which squealed to a halt, the driver's door flew open and a young man dashed out. He had the frantic look of someone with a suppressed but now imminent bowel movement, waiting in the wings. Wide-eyed, clenched-jaw and a kind of paleness around the mouth caused by vicious cramps. 'Toilet!' he bleated and Fred jumped up to lead the way.

He returned with a wicked smile, to tell me that as the door banged shut, the silence was broken by strange grunts and intermittent groans, which seemed to be filled with unbearable pain. Across the road, the wife and kids patiently sat in the car, oblivious to this aural drama.

Fred invited me to 'Come listen'. Met by silence and just when I thought the fellow might have passed out, there was something between a distressed whimper and a prolonged sob. It was followed by a splash, which reminded me of an old fashioned bomb-drop into a placid swimming pool and this was followed by a shuddering sigh of relief. Then in quick succession there followed the brisk sound of paper running off the reel, the rustle of trousers coming up and the throaty gurgle as he pulled the chain. Without a hand-wash or thank you—and apparently unfazed by our proximity to the door—the relieved traveller was out, into his car and heading south. A good few pounds lighter, we would discover.

Fred returned to the stoep a moment later, his face lit with wonder. 'Kom kyk die deng,' he said and led the way. There stood, in the same trajectory it had been delivered, a magnificent 'Richard the third,' as Spike Milligan referred to them. Had we not more or less witnessed its birth or had it been lying anywhere else, there is little chance one would have recognised it. Even the tell-tale pinch-off points were absent. We were mesmerised. Fred finally lifted his hand, felt for the chain—and still staring into the bowl with a bemused look—gave it a business-like yank. 'How did that thing come out of the man?' he mused.

In retrospect, 'that thing,' standing perfectly (proudly?) motionless as the third flush swirled ineffectively around its base, must surely have been a cast of his entire descending colon. There could not have been much clearance twixt apex and anus. He gave that slow suck of air from the cheeks—when impressed or annoyed—and told me he was going to look for something in the yard 'To kill that thing'. It would have made a fine entry in a picture quiz; more like a Chocolate Log in a teacup than the real McCoy.

There were quiet a few yard-boys over the years, but Ou Willem had the longest innings and was the only yardman who left an impression on me. Short and squat as a brick, with massive shoulders and the strength of a Clydesdale, he could carry a full sack of coal in each paw. We watched him, barehanded; open a jammed zinc door that two town

153

'specialists' couldn't budge. He may have suffered 'shell-shock' in North Africa, as the old timers used to tell us, and was quiet and retiring with an apologetic little giggle, when sober. He became something else after a few drinks, which happened fairly often.

A collection of empty wine casks accumulated in the bar-yard, standing like tubby monks in hooped cassocks, waiting to be railed back to 'Stellenbosch Farmers Winery.' When enough had gathered, he went on a real binge. He would pour a measure of boiling water into each cask, effortlessly lift and slosh them around like you or I would shake a Martini and allow them to marinate for an hour or more, depending on his thirst, before effortlessly draining them into a bucket. He became belligerent and morose, held long conversations with someone only he could see; gesticulating and shaking his head while ambling around the yard, and, his giggle disappeared. Everyone had learnt to keep out of his way. He reminded me of the Boswell tigers, the way he would threateningly turn and snarl at someone who coaxed or goaded him into getting on with his work.

Those wine-brewing stunts, on the other hand, sometimes left him comatose for an entire day or longer and this started a dreadful chain reaction. One of his jobs was to feed the old boiler, which heated the geyser that supplied the hotel and our flat with hot water. Between winter and summer, its appetite may have varied, but the rhythm of the feeds did not change. Ou Willem also had to fetch and weigh coal for the shop, as well as tend the three lounge hearths during cold weather. Cold-water chaos was bad enough in summer, but a nightmare in winter and was one of the other major calamities that drove Natie to the brink of fury. Fortunately, the bad binges were not that often. In the same way nature adapts to variations that come its way—as Darwin cleverly noted—so do hotels. Everyone had learned that the moment Ou Willem stopped giggling or made his first gesticulation, the other men knew that feeding the boiler was also their job for the next twelve, twenty-

154

four or thirty-six hours.

I got on, well-ish, with the old chap and if I was around, he invited me to join him with the fish heads and fins. He would scrape a few coals from the boiler and grill them on the cement plinth until nice and crisp and I would salivate, watching him tuck-in. The Plaatjies family taught me to eat sheep heads and he taught me to suck fish eyes. In his spare time, he made neat mugs from empty canned food or golden syrup tins and seamlessly riveted on handles, with copper tacks. Some were for the kitchen, while others, we later learned, were used by him and his cronies when serious social-quaffing was called for.

'Ou Kat' was a yardman before Willem, but I only have a vague image of him. My brother has a small black-and-white photograph of Kat, where he looks like one of those Khoi-Khoi leaders seen in old etchings. Tall, thin as a bulrush, with a salt-and-pepper beard, he is the exact opposite of Ou Willem, as he stares past the sun, in a shapeless felt hat and tattered khaki pants barely reaching his lean calves. He apparently had the stamina of a springbok and the rare ability to down a full bottle of sherry by opening his gullet and draining it without the need to swallow.

At one stage, we had Jeremiah, a dignified young man from the far north of 'Northern Rhodesia'. His main job was bellhop—a long hop from Manhattan—and then to lead guests to their lock-up garage. He would trot ahead of the car, waving his torch into the impenetrable darkness, and then light their way back, in case of snakes or scorpions.

This was the only man I knew who kept his two blue overalls in impeccable condition, and his business to himself. When it was his Sunday off, he was one smart dude in pressed slacks, crisp shirt, a natty sports coat and freshly dubbined tan-and-white shoes. His hair brushed into a neat 'Afro,' and a pair of sunglasses allowed him to peruse the women on his strolls about town. After some months, he did not so much fall among thieves, as that they stole his innocence and introduced him to the bottle. As one of the 'upfront' staff members, it brought

155

him on a collision course with my father and this began to happen more frequently. I am not sure if this Jeremiah could foretell disaster. The last time would be, while waiting for the visitor to garage his car one evening, Jeremiah passed out—out of sight—and the poor man was in quite a state when he finally wound his way back to the hotel.

Paulus and Albert, the bar-boys of my youth, taught me how to wash and dry glasses. On hectic evenings, Natie or one of the barmen would send me to hurry them for fresh glasses, or carry them out to the washroom when I was old enough. Part of their duty was to ferry trays of glasses from the bar to the washroom in the yard, where they sat on empty beer crates around buckets of scalding water, washing, rinsing and drying before returning them to the bar. Deep in conversation, their hands flew in and out of the suds, into the clean bucket, and then in a swirl of cloth, brought a shine to the goblets. Only if things became too chaotic and even those two experts could not keep up, one of us would go to the storeroom to fetch an extra box of new glasses.

During the cold months they stoked a brazier or 'drompie'— a four-gallon paraffin tin with a few breathing holes punched through the sides—filled with embers from the boiler, which diffused a constant blanket of warmth that blocked some of the icy air shouldering its way through the open door. On quieter evenings I sometimes joined them, sitting on my crate, as they taught me the trade. How to wash, dry and shine the humblest of tumblers to the most delicate champagne flutes and wine glasses. Cloths had to be bone dry—not always possible in winter—never insert too much cloth, the bare hand never touches the glass and the shine would come naturally; not by force, but the speed with which the glass spun between the fingers.

'Touch, is a move, move, is a bullet!' That was (another) George's terse assessment of foreplay and sex. If a woman allows you to 'touch' her, he explained, holding a glass up to check the shine, that means you can 'move' with her and that will lead to the 'bullet!' He had been one of the bar boys after the first two, and Ziems, Koerie and I would sit and chew the fat with him if it was not too busy. Most Blacks spoke Afrikaans in small country towns and his English was remarkably good. He flashed a white, boyish grin—a friendly gap between his front teeth—and loved ragging the girls, who stoically put up with his jokes. He must have been in his late thirties but could never resist demonstrating his prowess when a serious game of marbles was warming up in the back yard.

Sias, one of the older school boys, was the marble champion, but when George fitted the 'goen' in the fingers of his left hand and his right middle finger took aim, he made him look like an amateur. Sias disliked George, not only for his skill, but because he was Black. There were a few others who shared the same sentiments. George bubbled with a child-like freshness; he was no newcomer to Sias's attitude and his mock subservience pissed Sias off even more.

Old Kasper, the driver, was also an ex-South African Coloured-Corpsman, who looked fragile, but was exceptionally hardy. In spite of extensive burn scars on his face, he had cultivated a robust moustache, whose ends he twirled into fierce-looking spikes, rather like caricatures of elderly Colonels, especially when the old boy was ticking. After my brother's attempt, Kasper gave me driving lessons in the old truck, but its devilish whims and irrational gear system flummoxed me, and Kierie completed my lessons in the Mercury.

Kasper was intelligent and practical and helpful, but impossible after he had had a few 'doppies'. The old army days or ways would come flooding back and he marched (lurched) around the place, arms stiffly swinging back and forth as if he were on the parade ground, presenting arms or standing at ease. When my father tried to caution or reprimand Kasper, he would march up and slam his feet down as he came to a smart halt, inches from Natie, execute a fairly crisp salute (for such a wilted figure) and bark 'Yesh Shir!' We thought it hilarious, but it obviously triggered other visions for my father.

Night porters were another unavoidable cause for Natie's prematurely grey hair. The incumbent porter would report for duty at eight pm, lend a hand where he could and when my father closed the bar at 10 pm, he would be given a list of room numbers, what time the occupants wanted to be woken, tea or coffee and so on. He also had to polish shoes, neatly parked outside bedroom doors, and feed the furnace. Fortunately, most tourists clocked in late afternoon or early evening, as I think quite a few late-comers possibly had to carry on to the next town, while the porter dozed in a comfy spot.

After they had cleaned the shoes and given the boiler a head of coal, boredom and the heat took over, while on cold winter nights, a fire in one of the lounges could put the best of men to sleep. There was a particular felon, who put the premises to good use for his nocturnal carnal pleasures during his short tenure in orifice. Clues were discovered by the room girls and he was fired. It would only be Lenie, to come up with a pithy quip: 'Never mind night porter, hy's 'n bleddie naaiporter!' ('Naai,' in Afrikaans, means 'sew' or 'darn,' but is slang for sexual intercourse).

Going by facial features, the short, muscular Kierie must have had San blood coursing through his veins. He too was unbelievably powerful and I often saw him vault the high bar counter, agile as a cat, and physically throw troublemakers out the door. He had patience in abundance—I could imagine him tracking or crouching near a waterhole—but anyone who pushed him too far would unleash a silent burst of energy, like lightning, that was both frightening and awesome.

Before my age of duties set in, Ziems, Koerie and I would sometimes go on a Saturday afternoon to watch him play rugby on the stony field with rickety posts, amongst the koppies. He played for the Coloured first fifteen, at almost any position, but preferred inside centre, due to his slick footwork. He never ever sold a dummy...he gave them away, left right and centre. When Kierie got the ball on the wing, his speed, strength and nimbleness invariably took him over the try line. Had

158

integration been around, he would have been a provincial player and who knows, he might even have worn the Green and Gold.

Over the years some of my father's racehorses periodically came home to recuperate or retire in our stables, before returning to duty or being farmed out. The gloomy stalls, exuding the pleasant smell of manure, baled Lucerne and their powdery warmth, were cool in summer. If new arrivals weren't too skittish, the groom would sometimes let me brush them, their hooves anxiously clattering on the ancient cobblestones. A few were cordial and relaxed and enjoyed the odd titbit of fresh lucerne or mealies I fed them, but on the whole they were mostly uppish and aloof and one had to be watchful for flashing teeth or hooves.

Hendrik, a later groom-cum-yard boy, was a strange fellow—'a little loose in the head,' as his colleagues described him—but one who got on with his job and never needed reminding. It was only when he took over after Ou Willem died, that there was a regular flow of hot water. Sometimes too hot, and the overflow pipe on the roof would rattle and sway as it ejected spouts of scalding water. He could have been O.C.D., a bit obsessive compulsive.

It was therefore strange when he did not appear for yard duty one day and someone was sent to look for him. They found him in the stalls, dazed and even less coherent than he normally was; bare from the waist down, his troozers neatly folded on an empty crib and boots side-by-side on the floor. I leave the rest to the imagination.

The mare was fine. Possibly a bit long in the tooth: Who the hell did he think he was, anyway? But she had made quite an impression on Hendrik. Fortunately, it was only a tangential quarter-moon abrasion to his forehead, but it would be a permanent reminder that taking a 'flutter' on a filly did not always pay dividends.

Chapter Seventeen
SANDS OF TIME, AND FEET OF CLAY...
A flagon of barmen

'I can't live...with or without you...' goes the U2 song, and it could have been Natie's refrain. 'You don't get managers, you only get damagers!' Whenever we asked him to hire one—'It will give us a chance to all go on holiday' (Ann); 'Less of a strain on the three of you' (Beryl)—we invariably got that answer. It was one of his favourite dictums. From what I gleaned over the years, I think our old man may have had a point. We never got a manager, but plenty of barmen.

If there was a flagon of barmen in my time, I can imagine the numbers who flowed through in earlier years. He viewed every barman with the same caution and suspicion one would a snake in the garden, and, like motorcars and refrigerators, thought of them as a necessary devil. He trusted none further than he could throw them, as he sometimes lamented, and that ranged from a seven-foot-something giant to a young fellow who had a congenital deformity of the spine; the only barman I knew who had to stand on tiptoe to serve a tot at head level.

Clocks were tuned more closely with the seasons out there and the hotel was no exception. In similar vein to Commercial Travellers, barmen came and left, sometimes faster, sometimes slower than the solstices, though never as seamlessly and often rather explosively. CVs were scarce and those who had good (genuine) ones stuck to their jobs, while the average 'floaters' seemed to concoct their own as they saw fit. A reference letter was usually hand-written, probably by the aspirant himself; creased and stained by many expectant presentations, and as Natie added, 'not worth the paper it's written on!' Old, young, pedantically neat or shabby, fat, thin, tall, short, massive or puny—and that was only the visual impression—one never knew what was coming until the day they arrived and presented themselves at the bar.

'Nu?' my father would later counter with that age-old expression, if Ann or Miemie had given the new man a dubious look, 'What did you expect? A Lamed-Vov?' ('Nu,' can mean many things, including so? why? when? what? don't tell me! enough already! get lost!)

When Beryl first read André Schwarz-Bart's 'The Last of the Just,' she told us the sad history of this Jewish family, including the 'Lamed-waf,' (also known as the 'Lamed-Vov'), the 36 'just men'. The latter is a bit of a 'drossche' (long story), but numerically, those two Hebrew capitals add up to 36 and legend has it that at any time, in our history, there are always 36 just men in the world, the 'Tzadikim Nistarim'. They are usually good, pious, poor and obscure men, who bear all the worldly sorrows and for their sake, God does not destroy the world. We had been deeply impressed by the story and apparently, so was Natie.

Unfortunately, when my father was in a pickle—the last one had either gone AWOL overnight, or been dramatically fired—a bad barman was often better than no barman. If one of us happened to be home, he had a little leeway, but usually it was a case of beggars not having the luxury of being choosy for boozy barmen. There was half a tumbler-full of good ones. Before we got Kierie as full time Coloured Barman, we had a giant called Petrus, tall and solid as a silo, and Louwtjie, a short chap with a bad limp, who could barely see over the counter. Quite a pair they made and were often good-naturedly ribbed by the locals.

A story no one believes happened when Louwtjie and I were on duty one Saturday afternoon. It was during that lull, the drinker's doldrums; late lunchtime customers had gone home for a second-breath and early-evening revellers had not yet sauntered in, when a stranger did. There was nothing extraordinary in his appearance, other than a long overcoat protecting him from the autumn chill, and Louwtjie poured his drink. He had another and then asked if we would like to see something interesting?

I was not keen on getting too friendly with this character, but

161

my co-host was a gregarious little fellow and eager to befriend anyone who came through those doors. 'Ja!' he invited the man, who then asked for a hammer and nail. Louwtjie took one from the tool drawer, removed a nail from a crate under the counter and handed them over. With that, the stranger stepped onto the rail at the curve of the bar, opened his coat, then his fly, and laid a well-hooded penis on the counter. He set the nail on his foreskin and with two or three nifty taps, sunk it. 'Ag nee!' Louwtjie said, as the fellow now gripped the edge of the counter with both hands and leaned back, like someone on a Hobycat, increasing tension to prove he had done a proper job.

Louwtjie was stunned. 'Yee-sus!' he murmured and by this time, I had risen from my chair at Natie's post and stood closer to verify that this had not been a trick. With an aloof grin, the fellow wiggled the nail free, flipped his pricked-dick back into his trousers, buttoned up, finished his drink and left. We were dumbstruck. Neither of us even thought of going out to see what kind of car he had or where he was from. There was no blood or mess and it all seemed a little surreal. Could it have been mass hypnosis? I remember many years later watching the 'Khalifas'; where men pushed skewers through their tongues, cheeks and earlobes, while in deep trancelike states; but knocking a nail through your penis! A tiny hole in the mahogany, that darkened and blended with other scars over the years, was the only visible proof of his visit.

I was reminded of this strange incident many years later, by the joke about a soldier who sustained multiple shrapnel punctures during the war. He went to see an urologist, who told him there was nothing he could do surgically, but taking piccolo lessons might be an option.

In those days, if you were 'European'—the generic name given to Whites, irrespective of their origin—you could buy a firearm as readily as a shifting spanner or a steel cutter, and Louwtjie got himself a handgun. ''n Opregte cowboy rollie,' he said and invited me that first Sunday to do a little practice shooting. We drove to a suitable area on the desolate

162

Petrusville road and climbed through the fence to get to a natural depression between the hills. He had brought along a couple of empty veggie cans, which he went to set on some rocks about twenty yards away.

He was almost drooling as he threaded his belt through a beautifully tooled and tasselled leather holster, hung it at his hip, and with an attached thong, secured the tip around his thigh. Then the *pièce de résistance*. From an old satchel, he took a long-barrelled six-shooter, all in silver, that flung sparks of sun in our eyes as he gamely tried spinning it on his finger, before clumsily sliding it into the holster. I noted the point of the barrel seemed pretty close to his ankle, as he crooked his legs, cowboy-style, while relishing that blissful moment. Comfortable with the feel, he took it out and began loading with the dedicated expression a mother bestows on her first-born. He turned to the cans, legs apart, both arms crooked at the elbow— John Wayne or Gary Cooper, no doubt—took aim and slowly emptied the gun in their direction. There were the deafening reports, the whine of bullets and the hills were alive with the sound of echoes; but the cans remained spitefully dead. He quickly reloaded and did a second round, with the same results.

To add some measure of credibility to this poor show, he went into a stealthy Yul Brynner crouch—á la Magnificent Seven—and with his finger still in the trigger guard, made flicking motions with the gun, as we used to do with toy pistols. 'Pow! Pow! Pow!' he mimicked, 'firing' at imaginary Crooks or Red Indians in all directions. It included mine, and as I saw him pivoting on his heels, I had hit the dirt, almost winding myself landing on my stomach.

I lifted my head and yelled: 'Are you bloody mad, Louwtjie? You never point a gun at a person!' 'No need to worry, it's empty,' he reassured me. His little pirouettes had taken him closer to the cans, and to prove he had emptied it, took aim and squeezed the trigger. A tin looped into the air before the boom ricocheted between the hills, and that was the only time I saw the cocky fellow shocked. I could have sworn he paled, and

163

immediately packed up without giving me a chance to do my Roy Rogers impersonation. Back at varsity, a barely legible P.S. in one of my mother's letters informed me that he had to sell or have his gun confiscated for reckless handling. Pity, he could have turned out to be Colesberg's very own Hopalong Cassidy.

Rosy cheeks and a boyish smile could not dispel Petrus' formidable presence. My brother, who by then had become quite a gymnast and rugger-bugger—and was only a third of the giant's size—would lie on his back behind the bar, get Petrus to step onto his tummy with his size sixteen barges and then jiggle him up and down much to the delight of the regular patrons. In his hands, a quart bottle of beer looked like a pint, and a goblet, like a thimble.

We had a Hitler look-alike who could have been the right age. I am not sure whether the Führer had grubby fingernails and picked yellowed teeth with a pocket-knife, but his hair, moustache and fierce faded-blue eyes were uncannily similar. This clone was so lethargic that he appeared to be dozing while pouring a tot and his wife probably never ironed, because he looked as if he had rolled out of a tumble dryer.

They had a pretty, coquettish young daughter; twelve or thirteen she could have been, who periodically came to ask him for money and would sometimes have to wait outside the bar.

'That girl is a fine one, I must tell you...' my father occasionally mumbled.

My mother was much more generous and insisted 'she's simply wanting to be noticed.'

Later, we would learn he was right, but by then the trio were probably ensconced in another small hotel, in another country town, plus a babe in arms. No matter how much my father tactfully asked him to tidy up, to look a little more presentable, he became progressively shabbier and that brought to an end his tenure at das bunker.

In spite of a stoop, Oom Boet was a tall, gaunt old geezer, placid and unhurried as a heron, but with a large hatchet shaped nose and prominent Adam's apple, reminding me of a Pelican that had swallowed a fish. During quiet spells, he told stories about 'Die Laeveld'—the bushveld—where he had dispensed spirits in the surrounding towns, before moving to the Karoo and finally, Colesberg. People he had known who had had close encounters with some of the big five, and his timing and descriptions had me dangling on every word. He seemed a very genuine old chap and the fact that none of the incidents involved Oom Boet, somehow made them more genuine. If nothing else, I thought he was a spellbinding raconteur. A bad chest, probably emphysema—and definitely not assisted by the troops of 'Commandos' he still puffed—had him incapacitated some months after he started working for us and we genuinely missed the old chap.

Then there was a dapper smoothie with two gold teeth and the gift of the gab who did a very short stint with us. He rather fancied himself a ladies' man and was constantly smoothing back pomaded hair in the large bar mirror, which also reflected those glittering dental inlays as he smiled.

'A bit of a nancy boy, if you ask me,' was Natie's candid opinion. He brought a new meaning to pathological liar, when it came to discussing his amazing job résumés, worldly travels and sexual prowess with the ladies.

His downfall, like some of the others, was greed and sticky-fingers. Rather than subtle pilferage, he went for the big ones and he was not prescient enough to realise that my father was. Natie might have looked like a soft touch, but years in the trade had sharpened his eye and intuitions.

It later transpired, through someone who knew Don Juan's parents—'Opregte (good, genuine) and really loveable old people,' as someone described them—that he always was 'a bit of a skelm' and had never been out of the Platteland.

I remember a crotchety retired farmer from up country, Ou 'Ram' Cronje, who told us from the start, 'My one problem is that I take no shit from no one,' and we soon learned why he had inherited that nickname. In spite of Natie's other dictum:

'The customer is always right,' he either gave them hell or stony silence when they became boisterous or over-demanding. From him I heard stories about crippling droughts, the helplessness of watching animals die and your fields wither, or the blessing of soaking rains and a good harvest. He was honest and reliable but his initial popularity with the crowd soon waned and unfortunately, votes count when it comes to cash flow and my father's dictum unfortunately held sway.

There were other faceless transients, who sometimes moved in and out before they had put their Brylcreem on the bathroom shelf. Some listed steeply towards the till; some, it seemed, had never been weaned from the bottle, while others were blessed with a fondness for both. There were those who never stopped babbling—'Can drive a person med'—my father would moan, and a few who were ominously silent. In-between, as I said, there were a handful of honest, decent men, who could tell a good story and left something of themselves with us, before sooner or later, gravitating to pastures new or more rewarding.

Chapter Eighteen
IN THE RIGHT PLACE, AT THE RIGHT TIME...
A Town Like Colesberg...with apologies to Neville Shute

I don't know many people who re-live the past like my siblings and I. Memories lie in wait and like a red-lipped smile or a long-forgotten wink, Colesberg has the knack of discreetly inviting itself or brazenly gate-crashing our conversations. Images are instantly brought to mind by a passer-by, a tree or a peculiar taste. Others might be subtle but familiar, teasing the memory until they finally click into the right frame. 'Out of the blue,' as Ann referred to serendipity, we remember long-forgotten characters, a childhood myth springs to mind and something will remind us of our old medicine chest, or the sound of a fly worrying the windowpane.

We were raised on a blend of Black, Coloured and White myths, bedtime stories and home remedies. Saline gargles for sore throats, or if that did not work, an aspirin crushed between two teaspoons and dissolved in half a cup of warm water. Headaches could be eased by a cloth soaked in cold water and placed on the forehead (Ann); sprigs from the peppercorn trees under a hat or 'doek' (Ouma Siena); or a string tightly knotted around the head (Lena and Alfred). Bad abrasions or sprains could receive the vinegar-cloth treatment, 'twakblaar' (Nicotiana glauca, the Wild Tobacco weed) or if severe enough, 'Iodex' ointment from our medicine chest.

A clove, steeped in 'medicinal' brandy, (thus making it kosher to keep a bottle or two in the kitchen cupboard), or 'Grandpa Powder,' usually did the trick for toothache. Warm olive oil on a tuft of cotton wool occasionally relieved earache, although I remember the odd times when Doc Cooper had to administer something more potent. Tummy ache, constipation, listlessness, not eating well or not wanting to go to school, got a good dollop of castor oil or Milk of Magnesia. A half teaspoon of 'koeksoda' (bicarbonate of soda) instantly relieved heartburn, while 'tea' brewed from a few cloves and dried ginger eased abdominal cramps.

There was also a clutch of Dutch remedies with wonderful names like Rooilaventel, Witdulsies, Dassiepis, Lewensessens and Bokvet. They reminded me of horoscopes; just as any prediction could fit any birth date, so many of these remedies were quoted to relieve liver problems, kidney ailments, cystitis, constipation, diarrhoea, cramps, loss of appetite, obesity, ingrown toenails or alopecia! It reminds me of the story a colleague once told. A hypochondriac was running off a list of ailments to a weary GP late one afternoon, when the distraught doctor reputedly slapped his desk and shouted, 'Listen, my good man, the fee is seven-and-six, now choose any one symptom and get done with it!'

There were the usual myths that kept us on the straight and narrow. The fear of sprouting goat horns if you eat while lying down probably prevented choking to death, and fear of the church bell curbed many of us from pulling faces. Not wanting their finger taking root in a nostril or 'looking like a gorilla one day,' put a slight brake on our bogey-hunting expeditions. Being terrified of mealies—or other veggies—sprouting in dirty ears, we diligently scrubbed them inside and out. I can hear Miemie's: 'Liewe Heiland, lop was jou ore, mens kan koring saai in hulle!' (Dear Saviour, go wash your ears, one can sow corn in them!).

A clove of garlic sewn into a flannel sachet and worn around the neck prevented the visit of illness or evil spirits, while a healthy fear of the 'tokoloshe' stopped children and 'pretty young maidens' from straying too far from home after dark, lest they be abducted. My mother's closest call to voodoo, was having us bite the tip of our shirt collar, if a button had to be sewn on, in situ, lest some tragic event befall us or our souls accidentally get sewn into the fabric. Rather than loose the button, it had to be replaced immediately, probably on the same principle as 'a stitch in time saves nine'. Then there was the ever-lurking presence of the evil eye, 'kayn aynhoreh,' whose ability to spoil the party at the drop of a hat could be prevented by three generous spits. Fortunately they were modified over the years to a more socially acceptable 'Ptoei! Ptoei! Ptoei!'

Childhood can be a beautiful or dreary, a happy or frightening, memorable or best-forgotten mosaic of tastes, smells, sounds and visual or tactile memories. There is a fourth repartee, when someone discovers where we came from: 'Colesberg! That's a one-horse-town and the old nag is long dead!'

Not at all. A large district sported racehorse and Merino stud farms, as well as a flourishing wool centre and occasional stud cattle. Many famous racehorses were bred in those stables and thanks to Gary Player's input, many more will hopefully canter forth in years to come. The dorp lies on the N1 in the heart of the Great Karoo. Northwards, it snakes about 30 kilometres to the Orange River, also known as 'Die Grootrivier,' where it crosses the bridge and heads for Bloemfontein, Johannesburg and as far north as one would care to venture into Africa and beyond. At the other end of town, it branches southeast as the N9 and later the N10 to Port Elizabeth; or continues south-westerly to Cape Town. In the early days, before they cut a by-pass between the koppies, the National Road passed through town. On chilly Sunday afternoons, folk parked at this three-way junction to bask in the warmth while doing a little car spotting. The number of registration plates I recognise on the road still surprises me.

It was a thriving centre. Originally, there were two hotels: the 'Colesberg' and 'Central,' but later a motel was built at either end of the village. It boasted three banks, four garages, two cafes, two large—call them pre-departmental—stores, four small General Dealers, two butcheries, two doctors, a large suite of lawyers, two hairdressers, a barbershop, hospital, dairy and a bakery.

Along the dusty town square, the solid Town Hall and library, sandwiching an open market between them, squatted on

169

the high bank overlooking the sloot. On the opposite side, on another dusty square, the post office, magistrate's offices, police station, Methodist Church and a small play-park faced the Town Hall across this stream.

The imposing Dutch Reformed Church, 'Die Nederduitse Gereformeerde Kerk,' stood sentinel at the top of 'Kerkstraat,' while its breakaway half-brother 'Die Gereformeerde Kerk,' took refuge across another bridge, at the base of more koppies. The acrimonious breakaway occurred circa 1859 and because the splinter group thought the town sinful—after all, the 'Nederduitsers sang 'man-made' songs, rather than only God-given psalms—they built their church with stone hauled in from an outlying farm. There were ructions at the time, but nowadays they are all friends and the Nederduitsers jokingly refer to the others as 'Doppers,' while the latter call them, 'Gaaitjieponders'.

'Kerkstraat' was the only surfaced road, topped with a thick layer of concrete. Strips of tar set in the expansion joints would turn rock-hard in winter and almost run in summer. We gouged out pieces to model or sometimes chew on, following another myth that tar was similar to liquorice. 'Hondebloed' was the vernacular for real liquorice.

Initially nestled in the centre of a group of hills, the town grew by insinuating itself between them, as molten metal finds its way into a mould. The Coloured and Black locations would be relegated to an area behind 'Kiep-Kiep,' the large koppie that loomed behind the much smaller one in front of the hotel, with a chain of smaller hills separating them from town. The Coloured School and homes belonging to fractionally better-off Coloured families: teachers, nurses, builders, carpenters and the Waggoner, were at the lower end of Campbell Street, the road in front of these hills. The Gentle family lived there and never has a name been more fitting. The elderly couple were quietly spoken, courteous and the gentlest souls I can remember, always smiling and willing to be of assistance. Mrs Gentle had been a teacher, and I think her daughter may have been a nurse, while father and son were in the building trade. It was people like them who made the ironies of apartheid—other than the schism itself—so blatantly nasty.

White homes began further up. The blacksmith, whose sprawling work yards, forges and sheds took up half a block, was one of the latter. He was not a friendly old chap, but we sometimes played amongst a collection of carts and wagons in various stages of repair, as well as old engines, discarded ploughs and car chassis.

Those were the days before Hennie Sieberhagen and his beautiful wife Louisa came to settle in Colesberg. 'No, not Uitenhage,' he said, accentuating the rough Afrikaans 'g' of the town they hailed from, 'rather say, U-tannagee, sounds more posh.' He was a swarthy young man with bushy eyebrows, a barely-contained moustache, high tanned forehead and jovial hooded eyes. He bought the garage diagonally across the street from us and built a house in the open space at the base of the koppie, which put our old playground out of bounds forever. But by then we had moved on to wider and browner pastures.

Pepper trees, Acacia, Eucalyptus and Casuarina lined most streets; Italian Cypress, tall and funereal, speared the cloudless sky, while Willow and Poplar grew along the stream flowing through town. With a touch of spit, we decorated our faces with the conical Eucalyptus seed casings to look like spiky zits or weird shamans, until the saliva dried and they dropped off one by one. Summer winds rattled their papery leaves and swirled up dust that tap-danced across windowpanes or soughed forlornly through the metal frames. Dusky-pink flowers brightened the otherwise drab casuarinas and we made endless chains from their multi-jointed needles. A few blocks up the road from us, possibly planted by one of those first English missionaries, a massive oak tree spread its arms across the entire house and garden, casting a wide circle of shade. Every spring we watched, awestruck, as the miracle of new leaves pushed through those gnarled, seemingly dead branches.

Tucked between the hills, summers were hellish hot and

171

mostly dry. Attracted by the massive mounds of volcanic rock, sporadic storms released deafening peals of thunder and lightning. May to August sparkled with hoar-frost, crusts formed on ponds, taps dripped frozen stalactites and pipes burst. If a proper plumber was not in town, the same angst and infectious dread percolated through the hotel as when there was a power failure or one of the main refrigerators packed up and help had to come from further afield.

Hardy or foolish, we broke off shards of ice and sucked them on the way to school, in spite of my chilblains. Woollen balaclava caps Ann knitted for me seemed to make very little difference. 'Dos vet helfen vi ah tayt'n bankess,' Natie would say when something turned out to be useless: (it helps like a dead leech (or a heated cup), one of the old shtetl remedies for drawing out illness and fever. Chilblains sprouted painful scabs on my ears and split the skin over swollen knuckles. Some winters my heels were so bad that I found it difficult to walk. At wits end, Ann berated me, 'But ice you can suck, you blessed idiot!'

Then a passer-through dropped in for a warm up schnapps one day and noticed my hands as I tried pouring his drink. 'Chilblains,' he stated rather than asked, and I nodded, spilling a few drops in the process. 'You probably won't do it, but piss will clear that up. Every morning and evening for a few days.' He buttoned his coat. 'Try it,' he threw over his shoulder when he left. I was so desperate I would have stuck them in pig shit, so I did just as he told me and voila! Hands and feet and ears improved and the blains were banished forever.

I related this incident to a medical colleague years later and he told me it was probably getting better, anyway, the urine played no role, but as far as I was concerned, it cured my malady. At the risk of bringing the medical fraternity down on my head, should anyone be interested, it also 'cured' my athlete's foot problem—(Taenia pedis)—that I picked up at varsity. That bit of naturopathic advice also came via a passer-by popping in for a drink.

172

The sudden halt of the power station's low throb was the only time silence was not golden. While candles and lanterns are associated with romantic evenings, hotels do not run well without electricity. There would be no ice, plenty of lukewarm drinks and the dread of all those perishables going off in the pantry fridges. Hot water fortunately came from the boiler—unless it coincided with one of Willem's binges—and the coal stove could still deliver good food. But it was a perfect setting for chaos by candlelight.

Like a modest woman, the Karoo wears only a few simple dresses. She has been honed through untold millennia to toughen bark, reduce leaf size, produce toxic or bitter saps that make them unsavoury and one of the few times when a thorny aspect and a thick skin are admirable and life-saving qualities. Some learned to mimic stones (Lithops), while others found it safer getting a good root-hold on steep cliffs (Gasteria rawlinsonii). Resilience, that's the name of the game. Came the first rains and there was a hint of pale green, which changed to lush green and by late summer, yellow swathes of wild grass covered shallow depressions or swayed along the dongas. During periods of drought, the scrub turned from drab green, to drab brown and finally a sickly grey, as if a veld fire had recently licked the earth.

Most birds regulate body temperature by opening their beaks, gular fluttering, to lower body heat. Discussing the drought in the post office or at the barber, folk would remind each other, 'It's so hot, the crows are yawning'. Farmers watched their crops and stock wilt as weeks and months went by without a cloud on the horizon. Windmills stood motionless, birds fell silent, and the only sign of life was the screech of cicadas by day and crickets at night, part of the Karoo silence. In the absence of shade, sheep had learned to stand head-to-head, while cattle turned their rumps to the sun and lowered their horns.

Winter sun felt weightless and nourishing. Those were the days when children needed plenty of sunshine for healthy skin

173

and bones, before ozone punctured the stratosphere and malignant melanomas and skin cancer changed our way of thinking. Summer sun had weight. It flattened mirages; tested joists and caused hardy acacia to droop. I remember Miss Graham, the librarian, as she was crossing the square one day; the sun had squeezed a shade of blue onto her pale skin through the umbrella. Cypress laid crisp shadows; cats found shelter in shady nooks and gardens were reduced to wilted cannas and marigolds. Only in the dry heat of the Karoo, could curtains and shutters be closed against the sun, as brommers buzzed in the gloom and pendulum clocks seemed to tick more loudly.

My mother's toughest set-tos with us were about hats and siestas in summer, shoes and jerseys in winter. Our spats became more vocal with each change of season, and she would insist we have a rest when we came back from school. As we grew older—still healthy in spite of those pitfalls—she finally threw in the towel. What a thrill it was, to splash barefoot in irrigation furrows along the streets, when sluices opened on watering days, revelling in the coolness and summer delights to come.

I have wonderful memories of Doringvlei, the farm belonging to Oom Petrus and Tant Marie, where we often went on Sunday afternoons. There would be melktert or lemon meringue pie and chunky Boerebeskuit under crocheted doilies; adults had tea or coffee, and there was home-made ginger beer or Exa cordials for the kids.

Occasionally I took Ziems or Koerie along; the rule was I could not take both. After greeting the family, we immediately set off to the river—where we swam in deeper pools, wary of crabs that burrowed into the mud banks with their fearsome claws. We learned how to pick them up, the hard way; if a finger got caught in their pincers, we would 'speel kitaar'(play guitar), as the Coloured kids used to say, trying to shake them off.

It was along this river that I witnessed the arrival of my first flash flood. Fortunately, it was only a mini, and announced itself like the rustle of field mice cavorting through dry lucerne. When we looked around in surprise, a low ripple of muddy froth had already crept up behind us, but scarcely reached our calves, at its peak. Many years later, I was flagged down by a policeman and some farmers at the Leeurivier on the N1. How apt, the name Lion River. Not long after I got out of my car, a low growl turned to a roar, as a tumbling wall of chocolate water came surging around a bend. It was packed with debris and the bobbing carcasses of sheep and goats, the bloated body of a cow came rushing by and water began lick-licking the bridge. A larger branch must have tangled under it and the level began to rise. 'Dié brug gaan nog wegspoel,' someone announced. Then something small probably worked loose, the level dropped and the flow continued, sucking and slapping at the crumbling banks. It was scary.

We explored the low surrounding hills and occasionally played in the sheds and paddocks, until one of the maids came to call us. Refreshments were served on the shaded stoep or in the voorhuis, depending on the season, and if one of the brothers was with me, we received our share at the base of the steps or in a small courtyard next to the kitchen. It would not have been proper to serve one of them with the rest of the people in the parlour. The old couple seemed kind and considerate to their housemaids and labourers, but a definitive line separated that from fraternising. 'Every person in his place,' was as common as 'good morning.'

I liked the smells of the old house and the cool-room. The barns had packed earthen floors and in the toilet (long-drop) some distance into the garden, pages from 'Outspan' or 'Huisgenoot' had been cut to size in lieu of toilet paper. I recall someone once commenting that he'd wiped his arse on the Queen's face that very morning.

During school holidays, I sometimes spent a couple of days on the farm and I must have been there once, towards the end of a drought. Some weeks before, clouds had appeared each morning, their bellies slowly turning a promising grey, but they

175

would take fire in the late afternoon, turn charcoal after sunset and spitefully burn themselves out. In town, the mood had changed; clouds meant hope and hope meant renewed faith.

I would accompany Oom Petrus on horseback to check for ailing or dead livestock, by truck to drop off dry fodder or simply do chores about the farmyard. I remember us walking up the low rise to the sheep pens one morning, the air filled with the earthy smell of dry dung. He put a veldskoen on one of the rails, lifted his hat to the glare and narrowed his eyes to where a dark smudge lay on the horizon, fuzzy as a charcoal sketch. 'That could mean something…' he said, in deference to failure. Groups of sheep stood motionless and the sun glinted along phone wires undulating into the distance. 'Party lines' connected farms, and each household was so attuned to their particular ring, that they were deaf to other calls. After lunch, we again trudged to the pens. A light south-easterly herded a scud of cloud, like beaten egg white, and sent dust-devils swirling across the veld. The windmill had been the first to sense a breeze, wrapping its vanes around this flimsy draft. The old man studied the pump, possibly nervous it might lose its purchase. 'The wind looks good,' Oom Petrus said and his step seemed lighter on the way down. The drought broke a few days later and the land healed with amazing speed.

On trips through the Namib Desert to the Kunene River many years later, the locals showed us the miraculous 'eight-day-grass': Enneaeeogon brachystachyus. They told us it takes eight days from germination to producing viable seeds, but like all good myths, it was from the time those dormant seeds first taste the rain, that it took eight days to reach maturity. That in itself is a miraculous adaptation.

As kids, we were aware of an approaching storm by the bruised colour of the sky and we detected those faint distant rumbles, softer than a marble rolling across a table, long before guests could hear them. 'Listen, auntie…' or 'Can you hear, uncle?' we asked in our bumpkin naivety. They would be sitting on the stoep after dinner, hoping to get a little relief, oblivious to the approaching storm as the air took on a violet tinge. Cumulus clouds were even more striking in that arid climate, their moist interiors crisp as children's cut-outs against the dry air. Ann always reminded us that 'Every cloud has a silver lining,' if things hadn't gone our way and the Karoo gave us some stunning examples. As the day progressed, thunder slowly rolled closer, more insistent, until deafening peals and ragged bolts of lightning shook the town.

Large raindrops released the smell of damp earth and wet vegetation. They reminded me of tiny figures dancing in celebration, where they struck the main street, lifting vapour off the hot cement. Adults took shelter in doorways or in shops, while children cavorted, bare feet revelling in muddy water, arms outstretched, faces to the sky and mouths wide open to catch every precious drop. Those were the days before Acid Rain, when womenfolk collected rain water to wash their hair and most homes had a rainwater tank.

Frogs appeared, seemingly out of nowhere, and their croaks joined the chorus of nocturnal crickets. 'They actually fall out of the sky,' oldsters used to rib us, or they possibly believed. 'Bufo gariepensis,' the Karoo toad, can hibernate or aestivate underground in their keratin-like shrouds for an entire season or more, and surface after the first drenching rains. They tucked into their special delicacy, juicy termites, which the coming rains seemed to have prepared for flight. Fascinated by their rustling swarms, we watched them jettison wings, specially grown for their house-hunting trip, so they could start digging. They were also a delicacy with some of the Black and Coloured community, who taught us how to eat them. Lightly fried in a pan, with a sprinkle of salt, they had a crisp, nutty flavour.

Occasionally, if the timing was right, these rains were a two-edged sword that released swarms of hoppers or voetgangers and the Brown Karoo locust 'Locustana pardalina' that darkened the sky and cleaned out everything edible in sight. It has been discovered that in (bad) swarming seasons, it is the rubbing of young hoppers against each other, which releases a

177

compound, serotonin, which stimulates wing and muscle growth to almost double their normal size. No wonder they are the major crop busters in Southern Africa. We witnessed those living carpets or passing clouds on two different occasions. A dense, undulating clatter of millions—prolonged swarming can apparently go into the billions—of wings, legs and mandibles in motion, sounding like a strong wind rattling eucalyptus leaves. Armed with planks, sticks or damp Hessian bags, we joined adults in the veld. It did as much good as trying to stop kestrels from visiting each year, or holding back the sloot, after a cloudburst up country. Once they were on the march, only spraying could stop them in their tracks and that had worse repercussions, taking out birds, rodents and reptiles that took care of these blighters under normal conditions. Listening to townsfolk, I was impressed from an early age by the resilience of farmers, struck by one uncontrollable blow after another.

In a manner of speaking, small town siestas lasted from two pm on Saturday, until eight am on Monday morning. Barring a bit of Saturday-night-fever enjoyed by a small crowd of regulars, they literally became ghost towns, with only a few dogs and a couple of mad Englishmen out in that doomsday sun. On Sunday mornings, the Church bell, with its distinctive timbre, would call the congregants to service and later in the afternoon for evensong. During the day, radio broadcasts sent hymns or sermons spilling across gardens smelling of sweet pea and simple or sumptuous lunches.

Banks, and an occasional private deal, necessitated a signed contract, but many deals, whether a private loan, purchasing livestock or selling a car, were sealed with a handshake. Everything worked on trust and honesty. (Gambling debts, unfortunately, fell into a different category.) Only once was there a tragic sequel that draped sadness on the town for many years. Although the 'deals' were signed, stamped and sealed, it seems a case of paranoia might have triggered the gruesome outcome. Not only were the victims popular and dynamic young men, but that something so foreign and violent could

178

have touched that community, was undreamt of. 'Such things only happen in America,' someone commiserated in the bar.

Spirited farm parties arrived with Christmas and New Year. Meat sizzled over glowing embers; tables were laden and enough alcohol was in stock to last through the night and into the next day, if necessary. They could also be the setting for a little benign flirting, ongoing intrigues or some serious hanky-panky. I heard a game old gal, her whiskey clasped in one hand, telling a friend that 'Colesberg could've been another Peyton Place!' I suppose that could be said of many country towns, where trysts and cross-bed-couplings were not easy to disguise, and especially in the mini-microcosm of small town hotels.

My father and Miemie never took part in gossip and Ann might have enjoyed a juicy titbit, but never had a bad word to say. We (kids) got the gist of 'who and what' via the bar, lounges or shop. When these characters came into the hotel, we would be amazed to find them looking so normal, just like everyone else. Wife abusers, philanderers, flighty housewives, double-crossers, alcoholics; they all blended like squares on a patchwork quilt.

Those were the years of white nationalism and apartheid; that nine-letter thimbleful of vowels and consonants that caused such havoc and heartache. It was also the time of wilful or genuine innocence. There were plenty of people who meant well. But, added to what every man expected from his car or tractor—efficient and economical service on demand—two extras were expected from their staff: subservience and gratitude. While an occasional backfire or erratic starting was part of a vehicle's nature, backchat or self-expression were unacceptable in the workplace. Any type of fraternising across the colour bar was not only frowned upon, but came with a label: 'Kaffirboetie'. It was probably levelled at the Kaplan kids on numerous occasions.

On vacation from varsity, an old school pal and I attended one of the yuletide parties. A large throng was already on the veranda when we mounted the steps and a young maid, on her way to the barbecue with a tray of potatoes, was accidentally jostled. I instinctively crouched beside her to help, when I felt his hand tighten on my shoulder. 'Let the maid pick them up, what the hell are you crawling amongst the people for,' he growled in my ear. I recall a weekend on their farm. His younger brother was playing on the stoep one morning while a maid scrubbed the stone tiles. She sat back on her haunches; patiently waiting for him to retrieve his ball, then reminded him that she had other work to do. He stared down at her and in a friendly tone, from which the line of authority could not be mistaken, told her never to rush him again.

There were those who politely referred to brown-skinned or Coloured folk as 'Kleurlinge' and Blacks as 'Bantu,' while others used the general category of 'Nie-blankes' for anyone who was not White. Others used the derogatory 'Hotnot' or 'Kaffir' either as direct communication or in everyday conversation. There were cases of physical abuse, but at a time when it was considered an employer's right to hand out any punishment he or she saw fit, those incidents did not always register on the Righteous Scale. The Immorality Act was another political ace that came back to trump the very hands that dealt it. I cannot recall anyone ever being brought-to-book in our village, but we kids had first-hand knowledge of some of those supposedly 'immoral' shenanigans around our premises.

'I am a Smuts man,' Miemie used to say and after '48, when most Afrikaners saw him as a traitor, she and a handful of diehards remained firm Sappe. She was never outspoken but made no bones about which team she supported.

In the late '50s and early '60s, an entourage of parliamentarians would be invited by their country colleagues on springbok or kudu hunts and sometimes they came to the hotel for drinks or jolly old dinner parties. I remember the bear-like B.J. Vorster, with his brooding-brows, who would become Prime Minister after Verwoerd got the knife. There was Jimmy Kruger, who later carved a name for himself in the Steve Biko

180

saga and a much younger P.W. Botha, who would take his index finger to 'Tuinhuis' after Vorster, but refused to cross the Rubicon while the tide was right. Or, was it left? No matter. Miemie spoke of others who graced our tables and would in time grace parliamentary benches.

Towards the end of a meal, our local parliamentarian would send for Miemie, who had orchestrated those sumptuous banquets. She was not one for the limelight, but Ann would finally persuade her and she would take off her apron, touch a hand to her bolla and enter the dining room to receive praise she never asked for, nor enjoyed when it came. The family would also be invited to the table, though Natie's rare appearances were short and reserved. Now, as I look back, it would be interesting to know what he and Miemie thought about those Broederbond banquets. Being a publican, Natie felt he had to be friendly and neutral to all, but Miemie—in whom he probably confided much more than to the gregarious Ann—reassured us, 'Your father talks Nat, but votes Sap'.

Chapter Nineteen
PROCRASTINATION, IS A THIEF...
The last years of a once thriving 'shtetl' in the Karoo

Once upon a time... a doctor named Braham Kisch came to South Africa during the early eighteen thirties. He was a medic from London and in 1837 he had added 'Licensed Chemist' to his credentials and opened an apothecary shop in Colesberg, making him the first Jew in town. In keeping with the epochs of the Karoo, his appointment as 'temporary' District Surgeon in 1846 lasted a mere 20 years.

A son, with the imperial name Tiberius Benjamin Kisch, who was born in the village, went to study in Scotland and returned to Colesberg in 1862, where he opened a General Dealer store and auction rooms. Being a keen photographer, he set up a studio in 1863, supposedly becoming the first professional Jewish photographer in the Cape.

Then he delved into diamond prospecting, became a member of the Colesberg Party, who were some of the first to peg their claims at 'Colesberg Koppie Alluvial Diggings,' when diamonds were discovered in 1871. Of interest, is that not only would an entire hill, the so called 'Colesberg Koppie,' be erased by the frantic efforts of 30-to 50,000 diggers; but between 1871 and 1914, 25 million tons of earth would be removed to carve The Big Hole, 'Umngxuma Omkhulu,' in its place. The town of 'New Rush' would bloom around this manmade crater...and later become Kimberley.

Since those early days, more than 92 family names have been recorded for the town and Colesberg had one of the largest Jewish communities. A Jewish (Hebrew) Congregation was established in 1901, with a Reverend Matz being the first Rabbi, Julius Gordon becoming the first president and Morris Stern, first secretary. Services were initially held in the town hall and later at Morris's home, the stately old 'Mimosa House,' which became the hub of Jewish and other cultural activities.

Tirelessly motivated by Morris Stern, the foundation stone for a synagogue was finally laid in October 1919 by Julius Gordon and the 'shul' was consecrated the following year. It was modelled on the old 'Vilkomir Shul' near Kovno in Lithuania, where Morris's father had once been a Rabbi. Regular afternoon 'cheder' (teaching classes) were held for youngsters and many Jewish families came from smaller neighbouring towns for the major festivals or 'chagim'.

A Jewish cemetery had been set out in 1908 and when Zvi Zalman Kaplan—not one of us—died in 1909, he became the first member in perpetuity. By 1930, a flourishing community of 35 families spread themselves across a wide spectrum of trades and professions. There were general dealers, farmers, stock speculators, produce and ostrich feather buyers, businessmen, an attorney, a doctor, several hoteliers, a district surgeon and a fashion salon.

In the time of my brother and sister, there were still twelve or thirteen families comprising about fifty people, and when folk came from nearby towns for the High Holy Days, numbers could swell to almost eighty. That was quite a robust figure for such a small town and our simple Synagogue.

The music associated with 'Rosh Hashana' and 'Yom Kippur,' (New Year and Day of Atonement)—the High Holy Days, known as 'Yamim Noraim'—are the most heartfelt of all the festivals and commemoration services and contain some of the oldest (liturgical) phrases of music. There was a Rabbi Yaakov Halevi Möllin (1356-1427), Chief Rabbi of the Rhineland, who apparently went from one Jewish community to another, crisscrossing Central and Eastern Europe while gathering traditional prayer melodies, and laid the foundations for the uniformity of future services.

Thus, on High Holy Days in Synagogues across the world, the 'Chazzan' (Cantor) will sing melodies that are unchanged since the fourteenth century, and a few even dating back to the eighth. The atmosphere created by these familiar themes, especially 'Kol Nidre,' the poignant opening supplication on the first night of Yom Kippur, is what binds, humbles and yet lifts the congregants from their everyday lives.

I am not religious and not fully observant, but more of a traditionalist. My crash-course to study for my Bar mitzvah lasted only two years. Children normally go to 'cheder' (Hebrew / Bible studies), from a very much younger age, and although I read Hebrew, (not very well), I cannot understand nor speak it. Yet, wherever I have been, the haunting melodies of those prayers, beseeches and blessings always take me back to the old 'Shul' in Colesberg and the warm huddle of congregants. Now, all these years later, I can only imagine what their anxieties must have been through those early years of nineteen-forty, changing to fear, then horror and their ultimate loss and anguish.

The synagogue was shaded by Acacias, where kids could play when services were too long or the nature of the prayers precluded the very young. Rough timber floors, pale wooden pews and simple steel pillars, painted a dark brown gloss, supported the women's gallery. A small anteroom on either side of the entrance served as 'cheder' rooms, in the days when Colesberg still had its own Rabbi, or where men and women could separately retire for a breather. What the 'shul' lacked in class and old world trimmings, it made up for with soul and 'heimischeid'.

The last of the local Rabbis left in 1942, six months before my brother's Bar mitzvah—(could that have been the reason?)—and our maternal grandfather, Oupa Traub, who was staying with us at the time, taught him his portion from the Torah, as well as the umpteen blessings or 'brocheh'. After the 'Reb' departed, the congregation would arrange for a Rabbi to come from Johannesburg or Port Elizabeth, for the major religious festivals such as Pesach, Rosh Hashanah and Yom Kippur.

In the old days, the lesser festivals: 'Purim' (commemorating the deliverance of the Jews from the slaughter planned by the wily Haman), 'Simchatorah' (when the last book of the

Pentateuch has been read and blessed in the Torah, to be started anew), 'Chanukah'(festival of lights commemorating the rededication of the Temple by Judas Maccabaeus, 165 BC) and 'Sukkoth' (Feast of Tabernacles or harvest festival, when the Israelites lived in the wilderness) would also be celebrated. In my time, family numbers had dropped quite radically, most having left for larger centres, while others had gone to rest with Zvi Zalman Kaplan.

*

Right next door to us lived the Kawalskis, who also owned a shop attached to their home. Their son and three daughters had already moved to the cities when I was a lad. After his wife died, the old chap spent many evenings sipping a cold lemonade on our veranda, or wrapped in his overcoat, scarf and fedora, he sat in the 'little lounge' staring forlornly into the embers until it was time to go home.

Dora and Mitchell Lichtman lived with their children, Mark and Faye, further up the road, behind a screen of tall pepper trees. She was a kindly woman who seemed to have unending reserves of patience and made 'imberlach' (grated carrot and ginger), 'pomerantzin' (baked orange segments in sugar) and 'pletzlach' (minced apricot squares), which were delicacies usually enjoyed on festivities. Mitchell was a tailor and wore three-piece suits to work. He cut a portly figure in his waistcoat, sleeves caught up with silver armbands and a tape measure permanently dangled around his neck. He lightly sketched patterns on lengths of smooth worsted gabardines, heavy winter tweed or flannels, with a flat disc of marking chalk, before bringing out the heavy scissors that croaked its way across the table. A bronze hound stood by their fireplace, its serrated lower jaw acting like a tong when the tail was lifted or lowered. When it was not cracking nuts for guests, I would gingerly insert my finger between the jaws to test my pain-threshold, in case the Gestapo ever captured and questioned me.

(Just as well they didn't.)

On the next corner lived the elderly Sterns, a couple whose children and grandchildren had long flown the coop. Morris and his wife Helena were tall, courteous and refined. He had one of those classical patriarchal faces one sees in Michelangelo sketches, tinted with a mood of long-suffering and understanding. His spectacles usually perched on a high forehead, glowing with a healthy year-round tan, or low on a fleshy nose, and kind brown eyes looked at the world from beneath tangled brows.

His garden was a tranquil paradise, where fig, pomegranate and grape, peach, apricot, loquat, almond and aromatic Satsumo plums flourished, like his luxuriant snuff-yellowed moustache, which lent him the appearance of an old prophet. He dug, pruned or irrigated, dressed in linen shirts, large black boots and suit trousers held up by braces. A massive old Mimosa with wide-spreading branches cast dappled shade over the house and garden in summer, while its pompoms added their perfume to rose, honeysuckle, sweet pea, jasmine and my all time favourite, purple Iris.

Ann was particularly fond of Mr Stern and when he brought her baskets of fruit or bunches of flowers, it would have the same effect on her as when she took her first deep breath of holiday 'yam luft' (sea air). We had to accompany her when visiting the ill, elderly or lonely, which she insisted was the correct thing to do, and most of our Cape Town holidays were often a dreary mix of uncles, aunts and friends, but I enjoyed visiting Mr Stern whenever I came home from boarding school or varsity.

If he was not in the garden, I would find him in the sunroom, perusing religious journals, gardening magazines or the papers. He immediately offered something hot or cold to drink, fresh fruit, nuts or biscuits, and then enquired about boarding school and my aspirations. Sooner or later he would lead the way to his perfumed garden—the Mimosa almost eclipsing the sun and scarabs droning between the flowers—pointing out new shrubs,

186

a young tree he had set to root or a bed of flowers about to bloom.

Their home, 'Mimosa House'—as stately as the old couple—was cool and dark inside. Spacious rooms with high ceilings complemented antique furniture, antimacassars draped couches and easy chairs, while small marble statuary and old prints added culture, not clutter. The wooden floors were immaculate and tall sash windows met their images on the grey and black marble tiles in the large entrance hall. Had it not been for the dry summer heat beating to the shrill of cicadas and the thorny Mimosa with Oryx-like thorns, I imagined the interior could have been Dresden or Warsaw.

I only have vague memories of his wife, an elegant woman with neatly set, blonde hair, a string of pearls glowing on her neck, and she wore fashionable, pale-framed glasses with thick lenses that magnified her blue eyes. I have flashes of Doctor Cooper and 'nurse' (Sister) Maine, fussing in her bedroom, where she sat bolt upright in their large four-poster, possibly in terminal heart failure. I had gone with my mother to visit her and she passed away that day.

On one of my later visits, the maid let me in. I found Mr Stern sitting in the sunroom, his large gardener's fingers resting beside a delicate China cup of lemon tea on the table beside his literature. He seemed to have been staring out of the window and turned to welcome me. The powdered track of a tear disappeared into his moustache and I thought it might have been an age related thing. He indicated a chair next to his and it was only then that I noticed a photo of his wife on the picture rail between the windows, a string of pearls at her neck and a wistful smile on her lips. He was the last man standing for the once thriving Jewish community and passed away on June 18th 1965, aged 94.

Beyond the Sterns lived David and Bella Gordon and their three young sons. He was a speculator, short and slight with permanently clenched jaws as if he had toothache or just received bad news. Bella gave piano lessons. With curly hair,

187

pink cheeks and doleful eyes, she watched her pupils and it sometimes seemed to me that her smiles were not an inner reflection.

Mister Cohen ran a small dairy in the road behind the Gordons. I cannot recall if he was a bachelor or widower, but I remember his shabby clothes and shapeless cap, and the ramshackle cart, with a dented can or two, from which he ladled milk into proffered pails or bottles along the way. Years later, when I saw Fiddler on the Roof, 'Tevyah,' the main character, would be a replica of Mr Cohen.

Doc 'Bill' Cooper and his wife Haidee lived further up the main street. His 'White' surgery was attached to the house and the 'Non-White' set of rooms was in the yard, overlooking the stream. Soft-spoken, empathetic and gentle, he was a man who had dedicated his life to the people and treated everyone equally. I heard my mother once mention that 'Bill was not happy having two surgeries'. In my innocence, I always thought the Black and Coloured patients were luckier, as the greenery and rock-pools were at their best below their home.

One of the highlights for my siblings and me, was an invitation to Sunday luncheons at the Coopers. It was somehow different, more exciting than 'onse kos' at the hotel and it was a treat to watch 'Doc' carve the chicken, his thoughts possibly elsewhere, while Haidee nonchalantly dished the veggies. The impression I gathered over the years was that she did not 'appreciate' her husband nearly as much as the townsfolk did and I was aware of strange eddies—raised brows and unspoken words—whenever her name was mentioned.

'Doc,' or Bill to his friends, had a true gift and was one of those rare combinations of bedside manner and brains, a splendid diagnostician and practitioner. By simply sitting on the bed, quietly taking the patient's hand, and with his soothing voice, like the slow pouring of a potion, he immediately eased both the family and patient's fears. Very often, patients only needed a sympathetic ear, a warm touch or kind word and Doc Cooper could sense that long before he examined or took a detailed history. He steered my course to medicine. He suffered Rheumatic Heart disease as a child, which became progressively more debilitating until he finally realised his time as a general practitioner was limited. He interviewed a long list of aspiring applicants and finally handpicked 'Dok Dupie'. Although his retirement was sad and painful to a town he had long loved and cared for—very often pro-deo (plus umpteen un-cashed cheques which were found amongst his papers)—the transition was seamless.

Unless he was out on call, a couple of evenings a week his grey Packard, under a layer of dust, would pull up outside the pub and he came in for one, maximum two Scotch and sodas with Natie. They would sit side by side on easy chairs, and knowing my father was not into gossip and a taciturn man at best, Bill took him into his confidence on certain matters that he probably could not share with anyone else. I have a feeling that when they were too painful, my father may have let drop an abridged version to my mother, who adored Bill, but other than that, Natie treated his friend's confidence with reciprocal Hippocratic allegiance. Their friendship, an elementary closeness of trust and respect, endured many years. When Bill became too ill, he returned to Johannesburg, whence he originally came, and where he discreetly arranged his departure.

In keeping with the times, pomade had left two darkish halos on the wall where the two old friends had sat so many evenings, through a rapidly changing world. In summertime, when crickets and Christmas beetles added their input, and on winter nights, when the old paraffin heater lent its quiet hiss, they must have discussed their fears and concerns about an imminent war; then the reality and inhuman ravages, so much worse than anyone would have imagined. Finally, after all that carnage, there was something to celebrate, the establishment of a postage-stamp, a piece of land for the wandering Jew.

They also would have speculated on everyday matters such as the collapse of the feather market, the ascent of wool, dour changes on our political front and their personal business or

189

socio-domestic foibles. My father was not what one would readily call a sentimental man, but for many years, he would not allow that section of wall to receive a fresh coat of paint, in memory of Bill Cooper.

The old Central Hotel lay at the angle of Church and Murray Streets. Before it was sold sometime in the mid-forties and turned into one of the up-market hotels on the N1, it was still owned by the Levine family. They had three sons, who could at least boast a town hall and library across the road, and not a cemetery! One of the boys used to rag and pester Bee. She somehow coaxed him into a cupboard in one of the 'cheder' rooms, one day and locked the door. Neither he nor the Rabbi were impressed when they let him out a couple of hours later...but he never teased her again.

My Uncle Max Daniller, his wife Zelda and their three children, Hillel, Shaynah and Avron lived next to the Central Hotel. It was a large double-storey house that had a high cement stoep, shaded by Casuarinas. Max still had interests in Ladismith and was often away, but Zelda opened a dress salon on the ground floor, where the ladies of Colesberg could browse and buy more classy creations.

Zelda was short and feisty with cropped grey hair; a *pince-nez* hugged the bridge of her nose and a black cigarette holder protruded from her lips. She was always peering through a haze of smoke as she measured or professionally perused the clients. Her husky voice had a strong eastern European flavour, reminiscent of snow, samovars and hot 'borscht'—beetroot soup with a baked potato and a dollop of sour cream. They later moved to Cape Town, where my mother would take us to visit them in their home, high up amongst the pines of Oranjezicht, where turtledoves and resin tinted the air. Zelda opened a dress shop somewhere on Adderley Street, where she soon gathered a much wider and more elite clientele.

After the Danillers left, Isaac Gordon and wife Bessie became the new owners of the house, along with their children Alec, Joe and Natalie. Isaac or 'Ikey' was a farmer-speculator,

190

in that he hired a huge tract of veld around Coleskop, where he kept the sheep and cattle he had bought at stock fairs.

Bessie took over the dress shop. I occasionally accompanied my mother, as there was usually a tempting supply of tasty nibbles on the counter or upstairs. I watched her and Aletta, the red-haired assistant, deftly running their hands through rack after rack of dresses, skirts and blouses, selecting fresh choices for the women as they came out of the changing-rooms and posed before the mirrors. Here, too—as in other public places—the smell of paraffin heaters filled the cosy space on days when the air cut my ears and fingers like a razor. Each time the door to the staircase opened and closed, the delectable aromas of lunch or dinner would waft in and mingle with eau de colognes and the smell of new dresses. Those narrow stairs rose so steeply in the gloomy well, how no one broke a bone was a miracle.

Two fans managed to stir the hems of light summer dresses, but they sure as hell couldn't camouflage the foul airs escaping from the rear end of 'Rosebud,' Bessie's English Bulldog and loyal companion. She was a demure, friendly old gal and a prize specimen, but what a price to pay; her face was so fallen-in through centuries of (good) breeding that her rheumy eyes were almost level with her nose.

On the eve of High Holy Days, Jewish families from nearby towns would arrive, some staying with family or friends while the rest clocked into the hotel. From Norval's Pont came the old Barishman couple with their daughter and son-in-law, the Millers and two young daughters. Mr and Mrs Seligman and his elderly father were hotel owners from Middleburg, and the large Jacobson clan had farms and shops in Philippolis. There were the elderly Plottels (brother and sister) from Petrusville and the Levitans, who owned the Hanover Hotel, and their two children. Mr Levine, the shy, lisping old bachelor from Naauwpoort, was a shopkeeper, who rather late in life found himself a feisty wife, Bella, from Johannesburg. His suits always seemed rumpled, as though they were too large, while

191

she was smartly dressed and never a hair out of place.

The atmosphere was 'liebedisch' and exciting. Depending on the occasion, there would be pots of chicken soup and 'kneidelach' (matzo balls), 'floymen tzimmis' (braised beef with prunes), 'lockshen,' 'perogen,' 'gehakte' (chopped) herring and chopped liver, potent homemade 'chrein' (horseradish, that exploded into our nostrils and brought tears to our eyes), plenty of pickled gherkins and tasty chicken 'schmaltz'. Certain families made their own 'kosher' wine, purple nectar which we kids would try and get stuck into at every opportunity. There were the usual after dinner treats like those Dora Lichtman made, as well as dark brown tacky 'taiglach,' (crisp pastries made of matzo meal, stuffed with raisins and coated with sugary syrup.)

Best of all would be the camaraderie. We kids would be ecstatic with the 'balagan' or 'gezundte toemmel'—words that just sound like healthy-hubbub or sociable-pandemonium—as some of the old timers referred to controlled chaos. Pesach was the more stringent time for us, as everyday goodies such as cool drinks, cakes, biscuits, sweets and bread, as well as certain other foodstuffs, were off-limits for eight days! The old Jewish sentiment somehow filtered through, for even though they were not our longstanding childhood friends, we somehow gathered from adult talk that they—the parents—were 'landsman,' someone from the same town or country of origin or 'aygene menschen' (our own people), hence we automatically had an affinity with them.

The rafters in the old synagogue rattled to the booming voices of Messrs Jacobson, Gordon and Levitan—our very own 'Three Tenors'—as year after year they vied with one another to see who was the most melodious, whose voice took the high or low notes without a tremor and who could hold a note the longest. Mister Jacobson would hook his left thumb in the sleeve of his waistcoat, wrap the folds of his 'tallith' (prayer shawl) around his elbows and hold the prayer book up at arm's length. This was not done to read the Hebraic prayers—they

192

knew most of them off by heart—but it allowed him to eye the ladies up in the gallery.

On Yom Kippur, during the silent prayers of atonement and for the dead, their thoughts must have strayed to towns and shtetls they had fled or sadly departed. There were so very many Jews, who had had the means of leaving Germany and Europe, but kept putting it off, unable or refusing to see or believe the danger signals, as time and Hitler marched on. We are Germans, foremost, then Jews, many of them reasoned, why should Hitler do us any harm? But these middle-aged men and women had left their childhood, their family and homes, and still dreamed about it. Now, when they saw their children seated in the pews or playing outside under the trees, happy and carefree as pups, how much more they must have cherished them, the horror of the recent war still fresh in their memories.

On Yom Kippur, the men were not supposed to shave, but on all the other 'chagim' (festivals), the smell of Ingram shaving cream was fresh and sharp down-stairs, while up in the women's gallery, talcum and an array of perfumes struggled to get the upper hand from fur coats recently dusted with naphthalene for summer storage. The women would be in their best or latest outfits, smart hats and beady-eyed fox stoles, biting their own tails.

Depending on how fast we grew, kids sometimes also got a new outfit. I remember my first suit, a grey one, which I was going to wear to synagogue. First, I had to show it to Koerie and Ziems—proud of this 'set of clothing'—so I decided to ride my bike down the back road. Ann told me not to, it was getting late, but I said I would be quick. It was an old cycle; back brakes no longer functioned, and the front ones had to be carefully manipulated with the toes, so they could take evenly. I got up speed, felt the wind whipping past my ears and at the last moment tried to jiggle the brakes. I sailed over the handlebars so gently—my toecap jammed between the spokes—that the painful scuffs, bruises and a battered suit came as a double shock. A treble shock: a couple of smacks from

Ann, despite the solemnity of the occasion, which taught me that even benign boasting, was not profitable.

I was in Standard Three, the year before I went to boarding school, when one of the chaps called me a 'Bleddie Jood' during break time and we got into a scrap. He was a bit of a 'windgat,' the succinct label for show-off or big deal and I had a silent crush on his older sister. I remember us punching and wrestling in the dusty corner of the boy's playground, where the high wall separated us from the girl's side. We were finally pulled apart and I felt a stab of pride when I noticed tiny red blooms on his shirtfront. 'You're just lucky my nose bleeds easily,' he said, nipping my bloom, in the bud. I was never vindictive or aggressive and could not understand why I was involved in so many scraps, especially at boarding school. It could have been due to my brother telling me I should never let others take advantage of me and if a fight was inevitable, I was to strike first. I don't think so, but, so be it.

When I was fresh at boarding school, our maths class was about to begin one morning when a lad in the next desk, who had been needling me from the start, levelled a similar jibe. His, however, was accompanied by an upper-crusty sneer and a bit of nose rubbing with index finger, a little pantomime I have always detested. It was not like the down-to-earth statement of my former provocateur and we went down between the desks. Unlike other fights, where I could remember our blows and onlookers crowding round and egging us on, I had no recall on this occasion, only the teacher lifting me off him and giving me a good telling-off!

Other than my Standard Three experience, I cannot recall other anti-Semitic jibes or remarks worth any mention in Colesberg. Amongst the Afrikaners we were almost endearingly referred to as 'Boere-Joodtjies' and what with being 'God se verkose nasie,' we seemed to be reasonably well accepted in the community. Whoever invented the maxim of us being 'God's chosen race,' must have had a fine sense of humour, because, by gumption! as my mum used to say, our long history of being abused is not exactly flattering to the Big Man. On the other hand, I suppose what we were chosen for was never specified! It's rather like saying Idi Amin had a fondness for Asians or that Verwoerd (Hendrik Frensch, our Prime Minister from 1958-1966) had the Black man's honour at heart. Only the other day, while phoning an association in Pretoria, I switched to Afrikaans when I heard the woman's heavy accent. There was a sudden pause: 'But isn't Kaplan supposed to be a Yewies surname?' I told her it was, but that I came from the Karoo. 'Ooo,' she crooned, 'dan is jy mos 'n Boere-Jood!'

There were one or two in the English enclave, of whom I got the impression that they beheld us with a slightly raised upper lip...but overall, I think most of us grew up feeling part of the picture and fitting in with the rest. For our parents, many having hailed from Eastern Europe, things were probably different. They were more attuned to the subtleties or boldness of body language, the unspoken word or how the word may have been camouflaged. Anti-Semitism need not be overt; if it isn't, then it lies in the eye of the beholder, and it is amazing how quickly and with what uncanny acumen, the eye can behold.

By the mid nineteen-thirties, Jewish folk began leaving the small towns and the exodus became more noticeable after the Second World War. In 1955, the Colesberg Hebrew Congregation officially ended and they sold the synagogue to Volkskas Bank for £4,250. As a synagogue may never be destroyed /desecrated, a large portion of the proceeds went towards the building of a new 'shul' and hospital at Ashkelon, in Israel, and the balance was donated to the Colesberg Hospital and municipality, towards upkeep of the old cemetery. The Torahs, which had stood dozing in their velvet and satin covers from one festival to the next, were donated to other synagogues, and never again would the plaintive strains of 'Kol Nidre,' drift out into the quiet Karoo evenings.

195

Chapter Twenty
A STICK IN TIME...
A Town's a Town, for a' that and a' that

From the tall sash windows of our English-Medium classroom, we could see the homes of 'Vaalbank' and out across the veld to Coleskop, which even at that distance, was a towering block of sandstone and dolerite. No wonder the old ones referred to it as 'Towerkop'. Although Mrs Van was our teacher, I associated her with her garden. Whenever we arrived for extra lessons, she would be busy staking and tying dahlias, a wide straw hat protecting her shoulders from the sun and bunches of honeysuckle wrapped around the garden fence, filling the air with its perfume.

Labor omnia vincet
Colesberg High School

We were a class of twenty-odd English-speaking boys and girls, from Sub A to Standard Three. Single-handed, she taught, supervised, scolded, comforted, restrained or cajoled, punished or praised this motley bunch of kids; all in one classroom. 'Too many cooks, spoil the broth,' 'A stitch in time, saves nine,' were some of her favourites that she drummed into us. In spite of her wooden hairbrush, bald as a tonsure, with which she paddled our behinds when necessary, we all adored her.

As we progressed through the Standards, we in turn supervised or helped the younger ones when she was too busy clearing the undergrowth into uncharted territory with an older group. She was like a Mother Hubbard, who, thanks to the generous government subsidies of the time, kept a supply of nuts and raisins or dried fruits in her cupboard. White schools were heavily subsidised, Coloured schools received much less and Black pupils received a pittance. She seldom had time to join other teachers in the tearoom, and she would bring a thermos of tea or coffee and a packet of sandwiches to school.

I remember when the oilcloth World Map, with a patina of fine cracks like a Dutch masterpiece was unrolled for geography lessons, she nibbled and sipped in Colesberg, while outlining the borders of Belgian Congo...Persia...or Siam. Arithmetic was taught with cardboard pennies, tickeys, shillings and florins that looked like the real thing, as well as an abacus with bright shiny beads. Had those coins clinked, I might have nabbed some. We learned our multiplication tables by sing-along sessions each morning and should we forget one or two, we always remembered the tune.

Once a week we joined an Afrikaans class across the corridor for Nature Study. I sat next to a girl with a large chin, whose skin was ablaze with acne, and who in retrospect must have had a learning problem, as she was a good deal older than the rest of us. On one occasion, the teacher put cut-outs of a housefly and a honeybee on the blackboard and asked which one we would rather be? The girl nudged me and whispered: 'Say the housefly,' so I put up my hand, proudly announced my choice

197

and received loud booing from a usually disciplined class, and a puzzled look from the teacher.

Town kids were besotted with the bioscope. The possibility of missing a 'serial' or 'Gene Autry' if we didn't complete our homework, kept our noses in our exercise books and out of trouble for a while. The old 'bioscope' was reached via a long, echoing passage, impersonal as a stadium corridor. It led to a small, equally impersonal foyer, with a hatch-in-the-wall that served as ticket-office, and one then entered the cinema through a pair of simple swing doors. It was a cavernous hall under a corrugated zinc roof, ideal conditions for a sauna in summer and a freezer in winter. Besides being togged out for Antarctica, Ann and some of her cronies took hot water bottles, mohair rugs and occasionally a flask of hot tea or coffee to see them through the epics.

Thunder or hailstorms totally obliterated an already muffled sound system and only the deaf, unperturbed, could follow the plots. Seats were on the hard side and some of the older folk took pillows along. 'Good God, for one (shilling) and four pence a ticket (adults) did we expect the London Palladium?' Doc Cooper once remarked. Stalls were 'Whites only,' while 'Non-Whites' entered the small gallery via an outside staircase. We awaited forthcoming attractions, especially Tarzan, Westerns and horror films with unbearable impatience. Not to mention the weekly 'serial,' cartoon and, best of all, The Three Stooges, Bud Abbot and Lou Costello or Laurel and Hardy.

Kids naturally gravitated to the front rows, older children held the middle ground and adults brought up the rear. My earliest memory of the bioscope was probably during a matinee screening of Pathe News, when my mother sent Boris to keep my head down. I have vague images of grainy black and white flickering, as rows of trucks with people crowded on the back drove by and there must have been other disturbing scenes, which, circa 1943-1944, may have been Jews on their way to or from camps.

A few years later, I was using the bookcase in my parent's

bedroom as a shortcut through the window, when I spotted a bizarre book cover. It turned out to be 'The Scourge of the Swastika,' and I was devastated and a little frightened by the haphazard piles of skeletal naked bodies and vacant stares of barely living survivors. I asked my mother about it and she was terribly upset by her negligence. In her defence, it was on the top shelf, almost level with the abnormally high windowsill, and the possibility of someone clambering up there was the last thing on her mind.

For years, I couldn't fathom how those actors got onto the large screen and I remember asking Boris and Beryl how they got people 'up there'. They tried to explain that they were not the real people, only pictures on a flat sheet. But how can pictures move, I wanted to know? I wasn't convinced. There were large openings on either side of the screen that led to storage space at the back and I would sometimes dash to the side, to check they were 'flat'.

The projector was antiquated, each reel ended with strobe-like flashing of black on white numbers and changeovers could be a lengthy process due to faulty sprockets. Ou Naatan, owner of the cinema and a friendly, convivial chap, was an experienced projectionist; but these films did the country rounds, and must have taken quite a beating in less competent hands. Reels were often poorly labelled, or put back into the wrong canisters, and the word anticlimax reached a new high when the final reel of a long awaited James Mason thriller or Boris Karloff horror was slipped in second and the second reel then still had to follow. This caused a barrage of boos, whistles and angry foot-stomping on the wooden floor and separated the purists—those who left immediately—from us louts, who found it better to sit through the middle sequence than go home early.

Frequent projector breakdowns added to the fun. If, after a few stop-starts it appeared to be a lengthy business, a hastily scribbled apology appeared on the slide projector. It gave us time for a quick dash to the Palace Café, across the road, to stock up on refreshments. Up in the gallery, late-comers or early leavers passing the projector hatch momentarily eclipsed the screen, to more angry boos and shouts of 'sit bliksems!' The dimming lights seemed to suck the excited prattle from the hall. Loud shushing warned persistent chatterboxes that the picture had begun, although it was only a series of adverts on the slide projector, faded and colourless as if bleached by the sun. They started the evening's entertainment, and a brassiere, or model with short bobbed hair in a one-piece bathing suit, would get piercing wolf-whistles and catcalls.

That would be followed by Pathe News for some overseas headlines and then South African Mirror brought weeks-old news clips of quick-stepping, dark-suited parliamentarians, mounted police, jerky cricket or rugby matches, spring floats and political rallies. Its catchy introductory tune always got us stamping our feet. One of the comedies brought light relief for the adults and raucous laughter and more animated stomping from the kids, until it was time for our weekly highlight, the 'serial'. Cowboys and crooks, 'Skop skiet en donner,' as Westerns were referred to, and now and again a 'Tarzan' series, to the accompaniment of much louder and prolonged shouts and whistles.

We teetered on the edge of our seats as stagecoaches teetered along cliffs; sugar sticks or toffees forgotten. We craned towards the screen when baddies ambushed unsuspecting goodies or the jungle man swung into the highest tree and called his menagerie to the rescue with chesty yodels. When the tension became unbearable, our feet thundered like a herd of Afrikaner cattle passing through, accompanied by loud 'yays!' when the baddy finally got his comeuppance. Each episode ended as the hero or heroine was irretrievably done for, yet the following Saturday they would make it in the nick of time, hale and hearty, to fight another battle.

The bioscope, like her books, brought some relief and entertainment for my mother. Ann was a charitable soul and her generosity unconditional and spontaneous. She donated or gave to many of the local communities and institutions, including the Coloured and Black schools. Each year the principal of the Coloured school gave her complimentary tickets for the concert and she purchased extra seats for family and friends. We all had our turns accompanying her, and the excitement in the hall was palpable, everyone waiting for the moth-eaten old curtains, sagging on wires strung across the stage, to be drawn aside. Meagre subsidies barely took care of tuition and luxuries such as curtains and props never entered their budget.

The cast waved unperturbed at parents and friends, faces shining like the newly polished shoes of those who could afford a pair or the scrubbed and Vaselined feet of those who could not. The rest made do with freshly whitened takkies. They entered into the spirit of the evening with gusto, singing, reciting or animatedly acting out their roles and Ann watched with a beatific grin, her foot tap-tapping with their songs.

My favourite venue was the Palace Café and passing through its ornate portals was a treat in itself. I had a silent crush on Electra, the Greek owner's daughter. We were in the same class—eight or nine years old—and she often invited me for a cool drink or milkshake on the way back from school. The fragrance of strawberry, lime, banana or cream soda milkshakes—that lingered around the high stools at the 'soda bar' or eddied between the booths that looped the central tables in a friendly laager—remind me of the last drops spluttering up my straw, while staring at her long-lashed eyes. Kids drooled over display cabinets filled with toys and comics, or the sweet counter. Shelves stacked with Chocolate Logs, Beehives, Creamy Toffee, slabs of Cadbury and Nestle chocolates or glass jars beckoning with multicoloured 'boilings' and mint humbugs.

Gymkhanas were another popular event. We thought it a 'pukka' English word, unaware of its Hindi origin, meaning 'gend-khănă,' ball-house, or could it be the house of balls? Early morning, crowds started arriving at the showground, a mile or two out of town and parked under the eucalyptus trees

201

surrounding the rugby field. Some remained in their cars and trucks if the weather was too bad, while others found seats on the stands or headed for the stalls and paddocks. Lean, wind-dried lamb ribs, loin and leg chops, 'sosaties,' with a light dusting of curry and curls of spicy 'Boerewors' hissed and spat over deceptively dormant-looking acacia embers. Salads were simple: potato, grated carrot with orange juice, boiled baby onions in homemade mayonnaise or grated cucumber with vinegar. Those aromas soon had the crowds heading for the refreshment shed.

Show-jumping and dressage always drew the biggest crowds. Some riders had the gift, an affinity with their steeds of conveying every change of body movement into a well-rehearsed pattern of manoeuvres. Locally bred racehorses and thoroughbreds observed the world down their haughty muzzles; smug merino rams waited for their rosettes of distinction, while ewes and an assortment of disinterested cattle paraded for inspection. Long-horned 'Afrikaners,' humped and dewlapped in their sleek red coats, were another attraction; as were, woolly Merinos and silky Angoras. Judges in dustcoats assessed build, stance, forequarters and hindquarters, size of head, length of neck, pelt, wool texture and curl of horn; while breeders stood around the paddocks, proud as the peacocks that clamoured and paraded in Mrs Brink's garden up on Vaalbank.

Here too, there was audience participation when watching friendly but competitive horsemanship, 'jukskei'—Karoo 'boules'—and a chance for the town hefties to prove their mettle in a bout of 'toutrek'. There was plenty of good-natured ribbing: 'Remember it's rope pulling, Koos, not wire-pulling!' or 'Hey! Jan! You don't have enough beer in your belly yet, man!'

The 'plonks' and 'plunks' that drifted across the sloot, encapsulated lazy Saturday afternoons for me. When the rest of the town had gone into siesta mode, a small but devoted whitewashed group of tennis players went about their friendly or competitive matches on the clay courts. Caps or visors were mandatory. From a distance, on a quiet day, one could hear the scamper of takkies during a hectic rally, the measured exchange of singles or the erratic interaction of mixed doubles. The worst of disappointments would be a shrill 'Damn!' from a damsel or 'Ag noo man!' from one of the men; though I'm sure more devastating expletives may not have carried on the high dry air. 'Shot!' 'Mooi skoot!' or 'Good one!' often rang out as they acknowledged fine strokes, and between matches, players sat under the old peppers shading the clubhouse, enjoying a cup of tea or a glass of 'Oros' and iced water. That is how I remember the tennis club, perched on the opposite bank of the stream. In the late afternoon the decorous bunch would get together in our 'big lounge' for drinks and a bit of light merriment and if they had played clubs from neighbouring towns, someone occasionally tickled the ivories to entice them to a spot of dancing.

It was the opposite in winter. Banging car doors announced the arrival of the rugby crowds, as they stomped through the hotel, some players still in rugby boots, to change and freshen up in the downstairs bathroom. Wives and girlfriends settled in the lounges, while players and supporters made a booze-line for the bar. They only joined the women after escalating threats of dire repercussions, which were ferried by the wine stewards and discreetly announced to the culprits. 'What the hell are you telling me, hey?' they growled, mock angry with the waiters, who deferentially explained: 'No, boss, it's not me but the young missus who says so.'

The town hall was the hub of social and cultural activities. It served as a synagogue during those formative years, and hosted weddings, bazaars, meetings, plays, visiting magicians, hypnotists and dances. The Agricultural Ball was probably the most popular, but there were also rugby dances and the occasional New Year's Eve do. When it was time to air suits and evening dresses, a three or four-piece band came from one of the larger towns and the musicians—fellow country boys trying to be city boys—with Brylcreemed 'kuifies,' shiny suits and smart shoes, eyed the local girls as they glided around the floor.

There were no Arthur Murray studios, but most couples seemed fairly comfortable with the foxtrot or waltz or quickstepping across the boards. The Charleston was still very much in vogue and the 'langarm-lunge' held back for no one. If Rock and Roll supposedly took up the space of three couples, 'long-arm' could take up the entire hall. There was revelling and some social cross-pollination and it was a time of subtle and sometimes not-so-subtle eye contact and body language, in a bid to renew old school day infatuations or wicks lit at a prior Spring Ball. I can't say what other wicks were lit or dipped on those occasions, but they were exciting times for participants…and onlookers.

Max Collie impressed us with his mass-hypnosis, and the audience took great delight in seeing impeccable tannies and staid oomies going through those crazy capers. Occasionally magicians came to town and wowed us with their sleight of hand, the audience oohing and aahing as they linked and unlinked supposedly solid steel hoops, drew yards and yards of knotted hankies from a small pouch or the slightly stunned-looking white dove from a top hat.

The popular NTO, 'Nasionale Toneel Organisasie,' was in its heyday and the town would be abuzz when posters announced an imminent visit. Weeks in advance the town hall was booked out for the likes of Wena Naude, Andre Huguenot and their troop of thespians. Young actors were aged with powdered or floured wigs, thick greasepaint and crow-toes. I found some of them a little scary, especially the gaping green mouth of a 'poisoned' character once—who must have used a full bottle of food colourant—as he took a dying gasp on the edge of the stage. It simply added another bogeyman to my over-subscribed collection.

Small towns and 'bazaars' went hand-in-hand. They were every child's delight and almost akin to Christmas. Friday night we hardly slept and would be 'stomping at the bit'—as one of our boarders used to say—early Saturday morning. (He also used 'preposition,' when he meant to say 'proposition'). In freshly starched aprons, women manned the stalls and tables, which were laden with bottled jams and preserves, tarts, cakes and biscuits, veggies, fruit and jars of honey; knitted baby clothes, crocheted bibs and beaded doilies. They fussed about their stalls before the official opening by Mayor or Minister, seemingly comfortable and contented with their roles as wives and mothers and daughters.

A handful of men, patiently self-conscious, were courageous enough to help their wives, while others took their tea or coffee outside the hall, chatting about the latest trends in harvesting, feeds, fertilizers and the price of wool, or governmental proclamations. Folk could enjoy a 'lekker bord kos' at tables arranged under the balcony, while folding chairs along the walls allowed the elderly to catch their breath or a bit of 'skinder'(gossip). The hall droned with excitement and expectation. Town and farm children were respectfully noisy and impatiently polite, as they dashed around, gawking at all the goodies.

The staid old building once hosted a fashion show organised by women of the ACVV, 'Afrikaanse Christenlike Vroue Vereniging'. They were a large group of 'models' from all walks of life, age and sizes. Ann was one, which made us proud, but nervous and much to our relief—(apart from a friendly wave or two)—my mother behaved exceptionally well, in spite of her ovation. One of the cat-walkers, bedazzled by her 'fifteen seconds of fame,' threw convention out the window and simply kept going. The more the crowd cheered, the more purposeful her stride. Someone tried to signal her at every corner in the wings, but she doggedly ignored them and zigzagged across the stage, always just out of arm's reach. Gerrie Swanepoel, the estate agent and the evening's flustered compere, managed to grab her and with a disarming smile showing large horsy teeth, dragged her off, rather forcefully, for the hale and friendly fellow he was.

Every few months there would be a 'vendusie' or stock fair, allowing farmers to bring excess livestock for auction or to purchase new blood. It was another highlight for us youngsters, and a ten-minute walk out of town. We sauntered down early for good vantage points on the stockades to view the excitement at close range. Sheep, cattle, mules, pigs and Boer or Angora goats were already milling about. Forlorn bleats and lows, the raspy bellows of ring-nosed bulls and the high whinny of mares, mingled with the glib staccato of 'Bek Botha,' the amiable auctioneer. By late afternoon, the slanting sun carved a canvas of light and shade through a convivial pall of dust and dried dung, animated by restless horns and manes as animals champed to return to more familiar pastures.

Swallows, for me, were synonymous with books and summer. I was not a reader, but became instantly hooked on the smell of new or old pages when fetching or returning library books for my mother. Other than set works, I read my first book at Rhodes. Visiting swallows nested in the library veranda and I marvelled at the grace and ease with which those scimitar wings glided or tumbled through the twilight sky or sailed in and out to their inverted mud igloos stippled to the eaves. Miss Graham went about her business with meticulous care. When she had completed the process of signing out a book, she held it in both pale hands, as though gauging the weight of words and ideas and messages contained between the covers, and that hopefully, they would still be the there, on return.

Our postal address was P.O. Box 42, and the cluster of olive-green post-boxes, with tiny round glass windows, was set into the trimmed sandstone walls of the no-nonsense post office. It stood cheek-by-jowl with the severe, no-nonsense magistrate's court and offices. 'We're here to stay,' the stone façades of those Colonial buildings seemed to warn, 'and no contempt of court will be tolerated!'

Every morning one of us would walk or drive up town, over the iron bridge to the post office, to send or collect mail and telegrams. One entered through the obligatory 'Blanke' or 'Nie Blanke' entrance. Queues, be it bank, shop, municipal office or cinema, became an instant opportunity to chat; anything of interest or excitement that was too early for personnel on the telephone exchange to have dispersed (edification) or simple 'skinder'. Everybody knew everybody, sometimes better than anybody would have thought. City queues become boring and frustrating because of their impersonality. Here clerks would engage customers in lengthy conversation, enquiring about the health of a family member or pet, the performance of a new car, progress of a son at Agricultural College or a child at boarding school, while the rest of the queue chatted amongst themselves, (usually) oblivious to the speed of progress. Here, the smell of hot sealing-wax—that became shiny red flowers stamped onto registered mail (which we also collected)—pigeonholes stuffed with forms and documents, wads of labels, balls of twine, a clerk's cigarette sweating in a metal ashtray and a hint of Jeyes Fluid, could tell you, blindfolded, you were in the post office.

Under a corrugated tin roof and open wire-mesh sides, the market also stood above the stream. Here too, there would be lively customer participation with the market master, Ou Theunis—the town's most polite and friendly man—or amongst customers, as jokes, innuendos or friendly repartee were exchanged between the auctioned lots. In a good season there could be beetroot and carrots, freshly dug spuds or sweet potatoes and an assortment of pumpkins, squashes and melons. Firm cabbage and cauliflower, bunches of sweet 'kristal' grapes or punnets of fruit arranged on the long concrete tables. There could also be pure honey or segments of natural comb suspended in the amber nectar, fresh cream and glistening slabs of farm butter. I cannot recall who did our buying or whether we had a fixed order, which one of the drivers would collect, but on market days, every time one of the fridge doors was opened, the aroma of a newly turned garden mingled with biltong, bread, cookies and maturing cheddar in the pantry.

Beyond the hotel and stables stood the depot, with its high

207

loading stoep where larger parcels and heavy-duty goods were consigned. An industrial weighbridge trembled slightly when we stepped on it, and there was a loading bay for trucks. The office smell was similar to the post office's, but here, the shed's breath was filled with dried hides, baled wool and crates of live poultry. The opening or closing of those massive corrugated doors, rolling on steel tracks, sounded like distant thunder.

The railway station or Junction, about five miles out of town, had its peculiar bouquet of soot, livestock awaiting dispatch on the next goods train and on hot days, the smell of grease on signal wire pulleys and points. Fetching family or friends from Johannesburg was a daytime visit, while the Cape Town train came in after dark. We kids never grew tired of watching for the 'Jo'burg' train and seeing who would be the first to spot it. Our marker was a minute speck on the northern horizon—a large blue gum—and the first tentative signs would be a smudge of smoke and then the train came snaking around it, tiny as a newly hatched silkworm. It all blended so well with mirages dancing in the distance, that some days one could never be sure. The worm grew larger, until it finally came around the last bend and a thrill ran down my spine as those giant flywheels thundered by. I would edge to the back of the platform, near the red fire-buckets filled with sand and water (and a collection of dead moths and Christmas beetles) and couldn't understand how adults stood so close to the edge. I remember us fetching my mother one night and my father tripped over signal wires that we had to cross in the dark. He gashed his shin to the bone, which took a long time to heal and left a nasty chocolate coloured-scar on his sunless legs.

Colesberg had its seasonal breath. A pleasant pall of wood smoke hung over the location (township) during late autumn and winter afternoons, slowly drifting towards the hotel and blending with Antie Bee's frying hake or pot roasts. The sequel of odd winter rains was the smell of shoppers under damp 'Basuto' blankets or greatcoats; bean, barley or pea soup simmering in the kitchen and the smell of coal fires in lounges.

Summer released resins from pine, eucalyptus and pepper trees, while forging the taste of hot corrugated iron and softened tar. Algae and decaying organic material sent pleasant vapours to the surface of pools along the sloot, a reminder of primordial times when dragonflies were large as birds, and birds as large as dragons. It heightened not only 'laventel,' the old-world lavender perfume, but also the all-pervasive good, bad or lethal stench of sweat. Miemie and Anna were more tolerant in the shop, when during a stifling pre-Christmas-crush, one could dissect the pong and throw it out by the bucketful.

Many refused to recognise, or never thought about the fact that a tap could be up to a quarter mile from certain homes in the location, and they had no electricity. My mother was sympathetic, on the one hand. 'If I had to schlep buckets of icy water every day'—she, who bathed morning and evening in summer—'I don't think I'd wash too often either!' But when the smell became too overpowering in the Bottle Store, she would sometimes scribble figure-eights over the crowd with a can of air freshener; 'Flit' or 'Doom' in an emergency. And then there were some folk, who, in spite of all the facilities at their finger tips, could smell just as bad.

'Die Draai,' sometimes called 'Die Hoek,' was where the Coloured section of the location unofficially became the Black area. By way of myth or meddlesome mouths, it had been given rather sinister connotations. There were white kids who probably never knew of its existence and those that did, seldom ventured there. It was furthest from town, a jigsaw of small houses jumbled deep amongst Koppies and dongas. Water came from a solitary tap standing in a muddy pool, where people had set a mosaic of flat stones to keep their feet dry in winter. Our Black staff lived there, and my siblings and I were probably more comfortable visiting them, than they were, coming into town. Die Draai had its own heady mix of wood and coal smoke, grilled sheep intestines, samp and bean stew and the fresh smell of clothing—washed with ingots of cheap yellow or blue soap—drying on fences, stone walls or shrubs.

The original bridge over the Orange River was about 30 kilometres north, and occasionally my father or Boris, when he was older, would drive us there for a Sunday outing or picnic. There used to be a tiny house-cum-tearoom at the side of the road, where an elderly couple displayed a mouth-watering selection of goodies. While the adults had a pot of tea or 'moer koffie,' the kids trekked down the steep embankment to the riverside, and although we had older friends or family with us, that was about as 'benign' as neglect could get. Depending on the rainfall in the catchment areas, way up in 'Basuto Land' (Lesotho), the muddy brown water restlessly slid or rushed by, whispering or jabbering a story about the distant lands it came from. We collected amazing stones from the prolific 'Kimberlite pipes,' tumbled and polished to a silken sheen, while hoping to find an uncut diamond or two.

I have two sad associations with the river. On odd occasions, we found the remains of dogs on the rocks directly below the bridge; probably tossed over by travellers who had grown tired of sharing those long trans-Karoo journeys with a restless pet.

The other was more tragic. Two families, each with two young daughters, had gone on a picnic. The girls went off to play and when they were not back at the arranged hour, the parents became concerned and began searching. Then they heard that two girls had drowned further downstream and the tension became unbearable. The story goes that each family had initially prayed it would not be their children, but as uncertainty stretched the minutes, they began feeling remorse and silently pleaded: let it only be one of ours. As it happened, a younger sibling had slipped into the fast-flowing water, her sister went to the rescue and their bodies were snagged by driftwood in a gully much further down. The town was saddened and shocked and it would be my first lesson on the fickleness and impartiality of fate.

Chapter Twenty-one
FROM TIME, TO TIME...
Old Mister 'They come and they go'...and other memorable characters

Some of our Colesberg characters added colour and texture, while others '...were not always complimentary to the moral fibre of our town,' as old mister Perkins philosophised over his second, or fourth Limosin brandy. Mister 'they come and they go' as some of the younger men referred to him, when he was not around.

He popped in two or three evenings a week. Everyone knew his seat, at the far end next to the wall, and he would get pissed-off if some (non-regular) had taken it. Bad arthritis and a large, sagging tummy had slowed him and it took a while to hoist himself onto his barstool and find a comfortable position. 'When is it due, Oom Perky?' the men sometimes ragged him. After a few drinks, he would fold his arms philosophically on his paunch and the combination of a small beaked nose, high brows, and black-rimmed spectacles, gave him the appearance of a contented owl. 'Yep, they come, and they go,' he used to say, which I later learned, meant, amongst other things, the uncertainties of life.

Whenever he heard the younger men boasting about their physical abilities, he would summon me with a gnarled index finger. 'Little do they know,' he said, flicking eyes in their direction as he took me into his confidence, 'little do they know'. He told me he too was an athlete once, and as a young greenhorn, I couldn't equate old Mr Perkins with an athlete and my cynicism must have shown. He came in one day and handed me a scuffed manila envelope after I had served his drink. I recognised the well-built captain of a school first fifteen and athletics team, and the tousle-haired captain of the water polo trophy holders, flanked by coaches and his equally robust teammates.

211

I returned them, genuinely impressed, and told him so. 'I was at school in Natal' he said, 'we didn't have a pool deep enough, so we had to train in the river and it sometimes flowed faster than we could swim!' He took a sip and made the ritual of pursed lips, as if the taste did not quite agree with him. 'Yep, they come and they go,' he said, refolding his arms and twiddling knotty thumbs.

'Ag, I'll just have a aas cold Castle, please, my old friend,' Hennie Sieberhagen said in a heavy South African accent the first day he came into our pub. We soon learned he would be ready for his next beer, by the time he had scratched the label off the bottle with the thumbnail befitting a qualified fitter and turner. In winter, he switched to Oude Meester and when there was a convivial group sitting around the bar, he loved nothing better than a few games of 'matches,' to see who would buy the next round. The man had an uncanny knack of calling the right number more often than the rest.

On hot summer nights, when we sat on the veranda trying to catch a breeze, the low drone of the power station adding to the silence, we could clearly hear Hennie snoring across the road. He was a powerful man, well into his forties, and still playing a hard game of rugby for the town team.

He was a master craftsman at his metal lathe and there were few engine parts he could not turn or refashion from old bits when none were available. The concrete floor in his workshop was permanently adrift under the milky lubricant, glittering with tiny curls of steel, copper or brass, and the micrometer calliper looked even more fragile in his large hands, as he checked and re-checked measurements. 'In this business, if you cut too much, you're buggered, my old friend.' He put the 'purr' back into many old roadsters that had supposedly seen better days.

Visiting Colesberg in the early '70s, one of the backstays of my Station wagon had snapped en route and driving had been a nightmare. I told him in the pub that evening and he said I should bring it in next morning. His repair job was so good, that when I finally sold it, other than the engine, which could have done another circuit of the odometer, it was about the only functional body-part.

Years later, after he had retired along the coast, his daughter phoned to tell me he was in a Cape Town clinic, where he had had his second leg amputated. I went to the hospital, the sister gave me the ward he was in and I came back to tell her he was not there. 'Far bed on the left by the window,' she assured me and this time I realised the wizened old man was Hennie, slumbering under a white sheet hiding the hump of a cradle straddling his thighs. He opened his eyes as I approached and after a second or two, his face lit up. 'Ag my old friend, magtig, but it reely is good of you to come,' and it was the old Hennie speaking. We had a long chat about family and friends and then we were back in Colesberg. 'You know something, Oom Kappie was a very special person,' he said, before I left. 'I mean, he knew absolutely nothing about me or where I came from even, but he was the only one who helped me, and I don't just mean financially, when I decided to take a chance and buy the garage.'

Isaac van der Byl was a lanky farmer before age bent him. With a patrician forehead and forceful vocabulary, Oom Sakkie had a miniature wife with a forceful disposition. Six children she stoically bore him and although she could not drive, she most definitely held the reins. As if in perpetual mourning, she always dressed in black. Black gloves, shoes and a handbag, securely clutched under a dimpled arm. Her little black hats barely cleared the dashboard, as she imperially sat in the polished black Pontiac while Oom Sakkie rushed hither and thither, doing all the small purchases before driving out to the farm again. She had been an only child and it was said her wealth was immeasurable. She would scuttle into the shop, when she deigned to visit, to buy something for their workers. There was always a slight tightness around her nostrils, suggesting an overwhelming smell, which there well might have been, on occasion. I recall a dinner party at the hotel, where she sat bolt upright, like a perky little sparrow, attentively listening to the chatter but adding very little. I was tucking into left over savouries, one of my favourites, as the diners were leaving, and bit into a yellow jam-tomato that sent a stream of pips— reminding me of tracer shells from an ack-ack gun—splattering the back of her dress. In a state of fear for the next few days, I wondered if she would pin the pips on me, but fortunately, nothing came of it.

Oom Sakkie was having his usual 'just a quick one for the road' one day, while the good wife waited in the car. When it turned out to be not quick enough, she sent the wine steward to call him. The fellow waited politely for Oom Sakkie to finish his conversation with my father, before delivering his message. The old man turned to him, 'Now you go tell the missus...' he began, when the street door swung open and there stood the little sparrow, handbag tucked under an irritable wing. 'I'm finished, my treasure,' he said, changing pitch, flung the last of his Scotch back and hurried out.

It is strange how Bo, Bee and I loved taking our shoes to Ou Grappies du Toit. He and his assistant Thomas—Grappies refused to say 'Thamsanqa'—worked in the cluttered cobbler's shop, which stood next to his house. A flyblown globe hardly made a difference but enough light fell through the door and window for them to turn out some nifty leatherwork and repairs. He had a large collection of jokes, thanks to the well-thumbed pocket diaries he had filled with humour from the likes of Huisgenoot, Rooi Rose or Sarie magazines and occasionally having to refer to them in moments of crisis. In summer, a canvas water bottle hung from the ceiling by the open window and a thermos flask fed them sweet milky coffee in winter.

Their aprons were stiff from polish, wax and glue, and the smell of saddles, harnesses and the tacky adhesive filled the room. Folds of soft leather for uppers and squares of thick sole-leather hung from dowels suspended below the reed ceiling. An assortment of nails and tacks were stored in old fish-paste jars, and I was fascinated by the ease with which they clasped a prickle of tacks between their lips for easy access, while nailing on new heels. A collection of knives, their blades worn lean by constant honing, tongs, pliers and flat-head hammers, sets of wood and metal lasts, anvils and rolls of tough twine lay scattered around the place. Sunlight falling through the small window and burnishing the two cobblers turned it into another Dutch masterpiece.

Grappies was passionate about his fruit trees and paid his son, Thinus, a 'tickey' for every mousebird he shot. Before tossing it into the trash bin, each 'kill' was held up in the backlit doorway, so the old chap could take a stubby pencil off his ear, lick the tip and jot it in his notebook. Thinus was sharp as a tack. He plucked all but one of the long tail feathers of his first mouse bird of the day, and if they were not raiding regularly enough, mossies, the common house sparrow, were far more available and trusting. A tail feather would be inserted into the rear end (cloaca), the trophy casually displayed and tossed into the bin and old Grappies would notch up another 'tickey'.

Cannas, marigolds and asters seemed to be the flowers of choice for railway cottages. Lawns thrived and flowers bloomed during good seasons, but nothing was more desolate than a railway garden in the grip of drought. Gnarled peach trees rattled in the breeze, cannas withered and seared patches of lawn baked in the sun. Empty cigarette packets or chocolate wrappers, tossed from a passing train, added the only touch of colour.

Hendrik Labuschagne, the jocular stationmaster, could brighten the dourest of days. No matter how often he shaved, Ou Labbes, as he was affectionately known, sported blue jowls bulging over a starched collar and resting on his meticulous Windsor knot. In his neatly pressed shirts, sleeves hoisted by wire armbands, his hair slicked back and a green visor perched across his forehead, he resembled a nineteen-twenty Atlanta bookie, rather than a country stationmaster.

My parents always popped into his office while awaiting a train and he kept them amused with new jokes or the latest films he had read about. He and Ann were besotted film-boffins and I am certain had he entered a cinema quiz, he would have taken first prize. He could tell you every film James Stewart—et al—had acted in and who their leading ladies had been; likewise, every film Lana Turner—et al—had starred in and who their leading men had been. I was intrigued by the pink rubber thimble with which he niftily flicked through documents or inserted carbons, and the triple thuds that followed; twice as the official stamp struck the inkpad and once on the document.

When I was much younger, I sometimes accompanied Miemie to visit her friend Tant Koekie, after the kitchen had closed and all was quiet. A dressmaker by profession, she had gone from the hand, then the treadle, to a motorised Singer and would sometimes be finishing off a 'vinnige stuk lap,' her vernacular for an urgent dress. While Miemie and the rest of the family sat around chatting, I watched as loosely tacked or pinned lengths of material effortlessly slid under the old Singer's nodding needle and came out the other side perfectly aligned and stitched. I was fascinated by her dexterity as she re-threaded and loaded empty bobbins, snug in their mini-vaults beneath the cast iron flatbed, and my best 'trick' was the way she swung the large pair of scissors to the floor and deftly nipped up fallen pins with the delicacy of tweezers.

I liked her wonderful aura of zaniness. With a fierce explosion of hair, she was the only person I knew who could gossip without being malicious, curse without being vulgar, bad-mouth while sounding constructive and chain-smoke while doing all the above. I never saw her sewing without a cigarette either dangling from her lips—squinting through the smoke as it furled through her hair—or smouldering in an ashtray.

Her mother, Ouma Sarie, shuffled about in a pair of red woollen slippers with blue pompoms. She was the spitting image of Granny Mazawattee, right down to her wire-rimmed spectacles, grey hair snared in a loose net, toothless grin and a feisty glint in the eye. Seated by the fire, the old girl sliced biltong with a pocketknife and chewed on one translucent curl in the time it took one of us to finish an entire stick. She

216

enjoyed a juicy bit of skinder and had the rest of the family chastising her for innuendos stirred into the conversation with a mischievous puckering of her lips.

I would have rusks and coffee and later curl up on the lumpy couch, falling asleep to the pleasant drone of their voices. On winter nights, the splutter of embers invited 'Klaas Va'kie' (Willie Winky) into the room much sooner, but on our walks home, the icy air bit my ears and our breath glowed under the streetlights. Back in the kitchen, Miemie filled her hot water bottle from the pot simmering over the last coals; then she went to the office where my father served her a ginger brandy and ginger ale (or a beer shandy in summer). Finally she would be off to her room with 'The Friend' (Bloemfontein daily), her humungous bunch of keys and trusty old 'tortz,' to negotiate the long dark alleyway.

Jakhals van der Poel was our very own Davy Crocket: at one time he even sported a hat sewn from a wild cat pelt. He and Yster, the tracker, would rumble into town in his truck, a thick layer of dust camouflaging the original green. Often there were dried jackal, lynx or wildcat skins and once, the carcass of a male baboon, which had been marauding a farmer's orchards. It caused quite a stir, as, in his own words, it was 'the biggest bliksem I have ever seen'.

He would traipse into the shop to stock up on provisions, then Yster would watch over their goods, while Ou Jakhals came into the pub for a quick brandy or two. He laid his shapeless felt hat on the bar, dabbed a hankie to the top of his head—pale and vulnerable compared to his leather brown face—while some of the locals playfully ribbed the old will-of-the-wisp. His humourless smile showed teeth yellowed like an old Labrador, (a roll or two of chew tobacco was foremost on their shopping list), and he would patiently nod, like a parent humouring the children.

Any meat-eating animal was considered vermin and had a bounty on head or hide. Black-backed jackal, small spotted genet, African wildcat, Small spotted cat, (used to be the Black-

217

footed cat) and caracal, were trapped, shot or poisoned. This old trapper had earned his nickname by being wilier than his prey. I remember the time when farmers had been finding the butchered remains of sheep and calves and there were no known predators that could cause such wounds. Rumours circulated, suggesting it must be the work of one or more skelms, a 'tokoloshe' or worse still, some perverted lunatic, out for revenge. Farmers and the town council got together and called in Jakhals.

After nearly a week of silence, the truck rattled into town one afternoon. He and Yster hoisted the 'dierasie' (monster) onto the industrial scale that stood in front of our store and soon a large crowd had gathered. 'I neatly worked out his pattern and then we set our largest trap where we thought he would walk,' he told the onlookers. They were woken during the night by a frightening din, as the beast had nearly gnawed off a leg, in its attempt to escape. While Yster tried to steady the beam, Ou Jakhals barely had time to squeeze off a shot before it tore loose.

It turned out to be a Brown hyena, Hyaena brunnea. No hyenas had been documented in those vicinities, not in recorded history, and its journey that far south remains a mystery. They feed mostly on carrion and small mammals, but this one might have been desperate, or, in paradise. As it lay on the scale, shaggy mane bloodied and fangs glinting in the sunlight, it certainly looked a 'monster' to me. When he stepped into the pub that day, there was renewed respect for the wily old trapper and everyone vied to buy him a drink.

Oupa Ben earned that title not by acquiring years, but losing teeth. He was toothless before his thirtieth birthday. Short and paunchy, thinning hair and B.O. bordering on lethal, he was the young man who ran the power station until they built a more modern one on the way to the station.

The old power station crouched on solid foundations rooted into the base of a koppie. A metal door and small barred windows gave it a further air of immortality, but looks could be deceptive. Just as cicadas and crickets were part of the Karoo silence, so too was its low, reassuring but not always persistent thrum, as the coal-driven generator pumped out 220 volts of Direct Current. When it stopped, it meant trouble for business and the town at large, though ever more spectacular starry skies. We kids dashed out into the yard and lay on our backs, staring up at those winking trinkets and the edge of the Milky Way, bright as the steel filings on Hennie's workshop floor. We were still happily oblivious to the concept of endless space. Sometimes the beat would falter, sucking at the current and dimming lights, as drinks hovered halfway to lips and conversations stopped mid-sentence to see if it was another blackout or just a hiccough. Oupa Ben was the man who kept us going, though there were times when even his grease-stained fingers could not find the problem and they had to get a specialist in from 'Bloem' or De Aar.

If it was not too busy, I enjoyed listening to his yarns, in the slack-lipped-lisp of the toothless, or watching the way he sipped his brandy and coke while taking regular pulls at his Cavallas. Oupa Ben was never in a rush, which even a stranger could tell at a glance. From the measured way he took out a cigarette and firmed the tobacco with one or two thumps on the counter, to the slow strike of a match; the way he first studied his glass before folding his lips over the brim and the lackadaisical manner he brought his leg off the bar stool. He would finish the drink, wipe his mouth with the back of a hand, methodically collect his belongings on the counter and stroll out to attend to the emergency. As one old timer commented when the door slowly closed behind Oupa one afternoon, 'All I can say is thank God he's not our doctor!'

Luiperd le Roux was the quarry master. Close-set hazel eyes with a feline tilt, dark cropped hair with greying patches— hence the name luiperd—a sly moustache and thin, sunburned lips summed up exactly what he was; hard and vindictive. Always the first to champion the Immorality Act when it was discussed in the pub, he would threaten personal retribution to

219

any 'Kaffirnaaier' he ever caught.

On Summer evenings, when the main rush was over, some of the kitchen and room girls would sit on the steps, waiting for a breeze that might have come off the stream. This would also be the time, after family had held-back sufficiently, when we kids got our plate of food and would sit on the broad yard wall opposite the kitchen, enjoying din-dins in the dark. On a few occasions we witnessed White-on-Black soliciting, but there was one evening I remember in particular. Ou Luiperd slunk into the kitchen yard; drunk, randy and unaware of my presence on the wall, he first tried to canvas the shy Daisy by jingling change in his trouser pocket. When that did not have his desired effect, he became more forceful, grabbed her by the wrist and began pulling her towards the darkened bar yard.

Sanna, one of the older, streetwise Coloured staff members sternly told him to 'Voertsek! Go shove your dick up your arsehole,' she added as an afterthought and some of the other women began kicking up a rumpus. Like a thwarted leopard, he had to slink off again, tail between the legs, pennant still high, no doubt, but I'm sure he had murder in mind. I learned from Sanna that it was not his first foray, and she named a few other 'meidenaaiers'—her quote (White men who sleep with Black women)—who sometimes tried their luck. As I matured, I realised some of those men were the most vociferous pro-Immorality Act supporters. With permission from the Bard, I think those genitalmen protested a bit too much.

For me, the name Sophia Rothman conjures a peaches and cream, tastefully dressed, genteel lady, of British extraction. The latter probably did pertain, once, but that Rothman (of Pal Mal) had bedded with a Cavalla (of Colesberg). Put a grubby 'doek' on her head, a patched dress and scuffed shoes; add a few scars about the face, pare the name down to Sofie Rotman, as she referred to herself...and you have one of the most colourful linguists—expletivists—that frequented our Bottle Store. Her strident voice could still be heard, long after she had disappeared up the gravel road to the location.

220

Not many people could afford to buy a bottle of wine or spirits on their own, especially towards month's end and often, a combined effort was needed. To 'las,' in Afrikaans, means to join, and depending on how many people took part in a 'las,' it would be called a 'twee-uit' (two, out of the bottle) or 'drie-uit' (three) and so on and so on. That worked, if the Company had enough containers for equal division, but generally, it was a matter of trust...who drank first, second, third etcetera. They knew the halves, thirds and quarters of a sherry bottle down to the last cubic centimetre. The problem was it all depended on thirst or need, or who put in that extra penny or two. The first ones to quaff often overshot their allotted mark and that led to many nasty scraps. The more Sophia 'joined,' the looser her tongue became and I earned my E-Levels in expletives from her. She had the richest vocabulary in my experience.

After a 'two-out' went (more) sour one day, I saw her wind up an over arm, like a professional serve, and smash a full bottle of paraffin over the head of her co-imbiber. If that was not enough, she then stepped back and gave him a few anatomically-pertinent, maternally-derogative family secrets. He was more riled by the cuss than the cosh, which, theoretically, should have left him brain dead.

A flamboyant mix of suave, in-your-face bonhomie, a bubbly personality and the talent of a great raconteur made Gerrie Swanepoel a popular estate agent. He had a handsome set of teeth—one canine encased in gold—a natty moustache and thick black hair, streaked with silver, that swept back over his head in a frisky adolescent 'kuifie'. 'One of the reel woman's men,' as Wally once informed us. If anyone should have known about such things, it was Wally.

Gerrie's wife allegedly complained he was forever giving her backchat and making uncomplimentary remarks and accused him of being 'as stubborn as a donkey'. 'Well, what do you expect,' he said turning on her one day, 'If you keep shoving a stick up a donkey's arse, he's going to kick you!' He proudly related this sparkling bit of repartee in the pub one evening, to hoots of laughter. He lit up any occasion and was the heart and soul of a party. In a hurry to see a client one afternoon, he was caught up in a slow cortege to the cemetery. Turning to his assistant, he muttered, 'Christ! One would swear they're going to a fuckin' funeral!'

Colesberg sported two hairdressers, each had their loyal clan of hot-tong clientele and Ann, who could show no bias, supported both. But it was our barber, Vossie Vosloo, who was not just a colourful character, but one of the hubs that kept the wagon wheels rolling. In spite of being a man who thrived on chewing the fat, he was as lean as a stick of Springbok biltong. He led by example. Between clients, he combed his thinning hair in a two-handed back pass, the comb leading while the other followed low over the strands so no escapees sprang up in the slipstream.

Gaunt cheeks, a scraggy neck and black-framed glasses belied a gregarious personality. His spotless white crossover barber's tunic, with an assortment of combs in the breast pocket, added a little bulk to his frame. There was always a pencil nestling on his ear and a cigarette tweaked between his lips. I used to watch him in the rusted mirror, captivated by the way he managed to chatter on topics from rabies to babies and stud rams to governmental dams, while lengths of ash matured and dropped to the floor. A white shelf, where he kept scissors and combs in jars of disinfectant, resembled a piano keyboard, as cigarettes immolated themselves across the years. When Ou Vossie got on a roll, he could prattle about droughts, the cost of living, an illicit affair, income tax, how the town council should have handled an 'incident' or the hassles in finding a damned good pair of scissors these days!

He would step out onto the veranda during quiet spells, between the red-and-white spirals of the barber poles flanking his door, put one foot up on the low parapet and, resting his forearms across his knee, watch the main street going about its business. He returned greetings with a regal wave of nicotine-stained fingers and as the next client came off the street into the

222

salon, he deftly flicked the scorched filter over the wall into the gutter. 'Same as usual?' he levelled the rhetorical question while tucking in the cape, and 'Ag ja, Vossie,' would come the rhetorical reply.

I can see Sister Maine—'Nurse' Maine, as the townsfolk knew her—in her starched white uniform, stiff Sister's veil and white utility shoes, when she occasionally gave Doc Cooper a hand in his surgery. She did her training in Cape Town, having specialised in theatre and obstetrics, with many years experience. Like Doc Cooper, she cared for, and treated everyone equally, and between them they must have delivered half of Colesberg's crop of babies.

She played a big role in nursing Boris through his double pneumonia and Beryl, when she developed nephritis. From what I remember, and hearing about her in later years, she was a colourful character who never minced her words and had a wonderful sense of humour. There was a fire-scare at the hospital one day, and Ted, an elderly patient with his fractured leg in a 'Thomas Splint,' asked how he was going to get out with his leg and all. 'Och, I wouldn't worry, Ted,' she reassured the old boy, tongue-in-cheek, 'just tuck it under your arm and follow us out, dearie!'

Isaac Gordon, 'Ikey,' as he was fondly known by all, or Oom Izaak, in the farming community, was short, cocky and brimful of 'chutzpah'. There was an important court case once, the courtroom jam-packed and Ikey came in, his trusty shooting stick—so he could comfortably seat himself at any venue— bang-banging on the floor as he entered. 'Silence in court!' boomed the magistrate. 'Kush mier in toches!' Ikey boomed right back. The magistrate obviously thought his 'kiss my arse' was an apology, otherwise he would have been held in contempt...or an overnight cell.

Even now, as I picture Koos Terblanche, he epitomises mischief and someone who enjoyed more than a morsel of good-natured humour. The mole on his chin, smiling blue eyes and a rugged complexion gave the old man a sense of boyish

223

charm. Whenever he and his wife came into the shop, a look of contained bemusement pleated the corners of his mouth, like someone waiting to spring a prank; his wife (under her hat and severe grey bun), held an anxious expression, as if afraid he would spring one on Miemie.

The popular Nasionale Toneelspele were in town. One night stands, they were, simple flats and props went up in the afternoon, show time that evening and by next morning; no one would have suspected a comedy or drama had unfolded there the night before. This particular thrilling drama had been cleverly advertised, not a vacant seat in the hall or gallery. Koos and his wife were amongst those in the front row. To add tension to the publicised blurb, a phone starts ringing insistently as the lights dim and before the curtains part. It continues jangling when they do—which, I remember thinking was a clever ploy—revealing a 1950s lounge with a black Bakelite phone shrilling on a small table at the edge of the stage.

Better than any Hitchcock movie that would follow in later years, the audience were breathless with excitement and between each 'tring,' one could hear the metaphorical pin clatter to the floor. At the height of expectancy, Koos suddenly leaps from his chair—a second before the hero enters backstage—picks it off the cradle, turns and casually leans against the stage, (oblivious of the hero heading for the phone with a somewhat bewildered look), levels a beatific grin on his audience and bellows: 'Ja, demit? Kry nou klaar met jou bleddie rumoer!' (Get done with your racketing already). I will say one thing for those thespians; they were honed for any kind of emergency. With the crowd literally rolling in the aisles, the fellow must have seen the humour and allowed Koos' scene to play itself out, a good five or ten minutes, before he relinquished the instrument. The actor suggested they start all over again, but the damage was done and odd titters still bubbled to the surface. The moment had been lost and the only drama that night must have been the cuff Koos collected when they got to the car.

Chapter Twenty-two
MAKE UP FOR LAST TIME...
Boarders without borders; from ethanolic epicures to gin rummy for lonely hearts

B oarders played a big role in country hotels. Some were transient, while others remained long enough to become friends and add texture to our lives. Some preferred their privacy, but most were good mixers and friendly, and a warm camaraderie developed between them, commercial travellers and the bunch of regulars. The latter were generally a jovial lot and needed very little encouragement for a party.

Before my professional era of petty pilfering set in—age four or five—my mother found a large cluster of change in my pocket one day and asked me where I got it. I told her I earned it, which she could not believe, and confiscated the lot. How could a three or four year-old earn that kind of money?

We had a relief Postmaster at the time, 'Joebbie,' who supposedly was to stay for a couple of weeks, which turned into months and he became part of the family; after a good 'gob' (telling off) from Ann. He had been instantly captivated by my repertoire of succulent Karoo expletives and she discovered my lucrative occupation a Sunday or two later, giving him a blast for his money. 'It's bad enough encouraging my son to swear, Joebbie, but on a Sunday? Your holy day; you should be ashamed of yourself!' 'But Antie Annie,' he tried to explain with his endearing smile, 'I've never heard anyone this age vloek so nicely.'

When he was at a loose end, he would ask me to 'swear a little bit' and began paying me coppers and tickeys, depending on the length and speed of my renditions. If I got on a roll and gave him the equivalent of a royal flush, he coughed up a sixpence, which was a lot of money. It could buy twenty-four toffees or twelve bulls-eyes. For two pennies more, it bought a ticket to the bioscope. I only have a vague image of Joebbie, who apparently had a great sense of humour, was always smiling and full of fun, so Ann couldn't remain angry for long. It might have been at the time I developed a transient stutter, which would vanish when I cursed. 'I have never known a child,' he told my mother before he left, 'who can swear better than he can talk!'

Ansie was booked for a month but stayed more than a year. She was a clerk of the court, in her late forties and attractive in an old-world kind of way. She had a heavy lower body—'iets om aan vas te vat' (something to latch onto), as Oupa Ben told the men in the pub one evening—thick wavy hair and scarlet lips, which reminded me a little of Miss Berman, the commercial traveller. Ansie was quiet and introspective, uncertain, as if she knew there might never be someone waiting for her hand. Rumour had it that her extended stay was due to an anticipated liaison, with a married man from one of the neighbouring towns. A man did call on her sporadically for a few weeks, but those rare visits finally fizzled out and she spent many summer evenings knitting on the stoep, or in the lounge in winter, possibly waiting for him to return and rekindle a flame.

She tried to teach this card-blunt idiot gin rummy, probably as her fruitless vigil became unbearable. When Louwtjie, the barman, heard I was having lessons in her room, a malicious grin stitched his earlobes. 'Give it to her, ou pal, she wants it,' he advised. 'And has your little bird ever been into a nest, hm?' Petrus, his giant counterpart asked. This double-whammy ignited an instant blush and Louwtjie shuffled off.

Going on thirteen, thoughts like that were often on my mind but not yet on my agenda. After my uninhibited 'housie-housie' games during my single-figure years—my brother sometimes reminds me of those exploratory forays he happened to come across—I went through a long period of shy insecurity, not made any easier by a gangling growth spurt.

Ansie allowed me to win game after game so she could anoint me with praises. One evening she suddenly leaned forward and gave me what was to be my first 'French' kiss.

226

Her initial forays filled me with a thrill of excitement; finally, I was in the big-league. It soon changed to uncertainty, when her tongue began venturing beyond the bounds of hospitality, or should I say, comfort. I don't know who the person was who taught Ansie, but by the time it was nearing my 'little tongue'— and threatening to block off my air intake—I thought my sensitive gag-reflex might kick in, and those were tricky seconds, trying to disengage without making an arse of myself or damaging her fragile self-image.

She seemed more startled by her 'Gallic osculation' (as someone later brought me up to date), than I was, because she immediately apologised as if she had accidentally belted me, and it was not mentioned again. She left a few months later and no one knew where or what became of her. I remain a card-blunt, and for many years, I associated gin rummy with a lonely woman.

An ancient English gent, Mr Morgan, arrived annually from the coast to take advantage of the dry air for a month or more. In late autumn, his stately black Rover pulled up to the kerb, his uniformed chauffeur would step out and open the door for his young nurse, and they would help the old man to his bedroom on the ground floor.

A neat white moustache, inquisitive blue eyes, large shiny forehead and a heraldic agate on his pinkie, gave him a kind of military elegance, in spite of gaunt cheeks and a pinched blue nose moulded by, what must have been, asthma and emphysema. He would question me in his polished accent about school, our latest hobbies, my birds and aviary, which he once came to inspect. His neck and shoulder muscles emphasised every laboured breath or word he spoke, and like mister Rozovsky, he had a genuine interest in what went on around him.

During the day, his nurse, a not unattractive woman, would bring him to the veranda, and sit him in one of the wickers, a soft tartan rug across his knees, his cap at a jaunty angle and a thick scarf draped around his neck. Some evenings I joined them by the fire in one of the lounges, where he soon dozed off, listening to our chatter or while she read beside him. Occasionally she lowered the book and stared at the embers, her thoughts tantalisingly mysterious. Then, one year, the Rover did not appear, and the hotel felt and missed him. It took a good couple of autumns before comments about Mr Morgan's absence slowly began to fade.

There was an unusual threesome. A middle-aged couple and her brother, who stayed a few months. The wife, delicate, sweet-natured and pale as a Ming vase, (I imagined), had the haunted look of someone expecting bad tidings. She was polite and not very communicative and, like a film star going incognito, wore the largest dark glasses Colesberg had ever seen; the few times Colesberg got a chance to view her.

Her husband was not only swarthy and surly, but a Hitler-like moustache definitely won him no kudos with the Kaplan clan. His nose and cheeks were finely tattooed by alcohol, and a growth of coarse hair carpeted his knuckles and forearms. He reminded me of a baddie in those Humphrey Bogart films, with a permanent sneer as if he was raging at life or inner demons, perhaps?

'She damma (darem) deserves a better chappie than that one,' my mother would say, and he brought out the worst in my father. 'Aych mir a mensh, ah pianetze un ah poyer.' Not a nice person, a drunkard and a peasant.

Her brother was a gentle, timid man with short curly hair and an oily skin. His finger-nails were dirtied from constantly emptying, packing or tamping his pipe with exact movements, a supply of new and used pipe-cleaners stored in his lapel pocket. He would slowly play his lighter over the bowl, sucking at his pipe as he stared at nothing in particular with closely-set eyes. 'I'll make you a preposition...' he used to say, until my sister led him in the right direction one day, so subtly, he hardly realised she had done it. He enjoyed one or two Viceroy brandies in the evening and would occasionally comment how some of the local lads were 'making up for last time,' but what he possibly meant, was lost time.

Miemie had warned my father from the start, but he was too tactful to turn them down 'without a proper reason'. He paid upfront without any qualms. He told my father he was a businessman ('ganif un ligner'...a crook and liar), taking a break ('probably on the run')—on this occasion, even I could see through the farce—but no one knew where they came from or their next port of call, when they left. It was rather sudden and he left a few outstanding bills. Not much can be hidden in a small hotel. His drunken binges, in the confines of their bedroom, were not too difficult to spot, and the bitter charade of the dark glasses was soon apparent; so too, the nervous ritual of the pipe smoker, who must have been trapped in a domestic pincer from hell.

Old 'BC'—as the cumbersome Bartholomew Chamberlain had been whittled away and compressed by his friends—was a permanent boarder for as long as I could remember. He reversed his car from the garage every morning with such deafening revs and gear gnashing, that a blissful silence, that is the only way to describe it, followed his departure. Long retired and well into his eighties, he was fastidiously neat and still wore a jacket and tie every day except Sundays, when slacks and an open-neck shirt, showing a ruff of virile grey hairs cascading over the second button, was considered mufti.

Extremely hard of hearing, hence, all that revving, requests or conversations were generally barked. When his hearing aid sometimes failed—it was a convoluted contraption that reminded me of an embryo, after I went to medical school—he would cup a hand behind his ear and bark even louder: 'Whah? Speak up, man! I can't bloody hear you!' Other times he would turn up the volume until it screeched like a cicada, drowning out all other conversation. He seemed oblivious to that as well and if it happened in the dining room, one of the waitresses would go through a set pantomime of home-baked sign language; bold screwing motions, ear tapping and palm lowering.

229

He was another avid reader, including the tabloids, a dull glow slowly chewing the paper of a cigarette dangling from his lips and leaving a curl of ash, sometimes more than an inch long, before it dropped to his lap. While our 'ritual pipe smoker' cleaned his after every wad, Old BC would forget to clean his briar or meerschaum and it sometimes rattled louder than the last drops of milkshake we slurped at the Palace Café. All there was to show that there once was a garden fence, were the two brick gateposts, standing in the middle of nowhere, as it were. Old BC's eyesight was also waning and after the second time he took one down, Natie decided to throw in the trowel, while he was still ahead, and had the twin removed at the same time.

I vaguely remember another couple with a young daughter staying with us for an extended period. According to Bo, who had a room opposite theirs at the time, she was probably twelve or thirteen, 'and a real Lolita,' he informed me many years later. ('I heard this giggling, one afternoon, which suddenly changed to annoyance,' he told me, 'when you tickled her fanny too roughly with a turkey feather...') She was a pretty, precocious young coquette who divided her attentions between being seductress to him (sixteen)—I'll omit his erotic graphic descriptions—and instructress to me (six), on how to play 'housie-housie' when her parents were out. I recall the father being a large man and the mind buckles to think what he would have done to the accommodating Lolita, an eager Nabokov or the gullible Tom Thumb, had he caught them bed-handed.

We learned many things in the hotel trade, especially in the bar, some almost instinctively, others by trial and error. I never became a kenner (expert) or epicure, in the drinks department—as many aspired to be—because not only did I serve time at two universities, but I learned that most purists of the spirit, were as good as their first drink and often only if they were in sight of the label. We had customers who only drank a certain brand and who supposedly could tell if it was not theirs. There were many busy nights, when a brand ran out, no time to dash to the

230

storerooms and we simply carried on with another. I cannot recall any aficionado ever being aware of the fact, especially if they were in the lounges.

Old Wynand, who had been drinking with his cronies in the lounge all evening, came into the pub for a final 'neem my huistoe' (take me home). In the rush that evening, we had run out of Hague, his dedicated drink, and too busy to go to the storeroom, I had served him another brand. Now, as he stood at the bar, he was still astute enough to see me go for the other bottle. 'Jy weet ek drink nie daai kak nie,' he said, quite belligerently and I just had to lie and tell him we had only that very minute, run out of Hague. 'Good then,' he said, appeased, 'I suppose I will then just have to drink that shit'.

A special point in case was Herman. He was a young bank teller, whose relief post lasted nearly a year with us. Herman was popular with the regulars and made it very clear from the outset that 'I only drink Oude Meester 'n Coke, nothing else.' He constantly reminded his mates and us (the barmen) that he could differentiate it from all other brands. Something else I learned, was that after the fifth or sixth drink, it sometimes became difficult to assess how much brandy, if any, was with the Coke.

My father had a basic and inflexible code of ethics. He made many overnight-enemies by adamantly refusing to serve them another drink when he felt they had overstepped the limit; but they would invariably return next evening, a little sheepish, apologise and thank him for what he had done. He also taught me how to appease more prominent revellers without embarrassing them, by keeping a strict tally of the 'duds,' as he called drinks where only a mixer such as ginger ale, ginger beer or Coca Cola had been served. At the next visit, the customer would be refunded.

And so it was another busy Saturday and the boys were well into the spirit of the evening. For the next few rounds, I poured Herman a different brand to test his powers of detection. He drank them with his usual smacking of lips, followed by a deep

231

draw on his ciggy, before dashing on with his yarn or lurching into another. Finally, the others called it a night, Herman decided to press on and I decided to press home Natie's ploy, serving him four neat Cokes before he finally retired.

He came down for Sunday lunch, pale in the gills, and ordered his usual 'beer to jerk me right'. He did not believe my alien-tots story and when I told him his last four drinks were pure Coke—at one-and-six a tot, I owed him six shillings—he told me I was trying to trick him and refused to take the money. That soured our friendship and from then on he would watch me like a hawk, right up to his final going-away bash the men gave him some months later. I used it on other revellers when they were 'sprinting for the opposite (try) line'—a Mr Perkins metaphor—but they were grateful for the credit on their next visit. I suppose playing tricks depends on how seriously the game is taken and telling the truth is not always wise. It goes to show that sometimes a lack of alcohol can also cause a bit of 'fariebel' (discord).

When the new prison was being built, a young fellow, who worked for the Prison's Department, came from Pretoria for a few months. He was very much aware of his good looks and was smitten by my sister, home on vacation, for a while. Henry Harrington told us his father came from a posh, moneyed family in England, 'but that was a long, long time ago'. He was a textbook briber of younger brothers and my sister soon let me know that I was not to accept any more cash offers, and not leave her alone with him.

One Sunday afternoon, the adults were on a farm, Bee holding the fort and the three of us were in the lounge. Henry, with a few drinks under the belt, opened the bid at a sixpence…then a shilling…and finally raised the stakes to two shillings! I was drooling and ready to go for it, when I saw her murderous look. Henry, smiling broadly, got up in a playful mode and started wrestling me, my head soon in a muscular arm lock and I realised his beaming smile—directed at my sister— was directly proportional to the pressure he was applying. I had

232

a flash vision of a watermelon that once fell from the school bus, in the Parkie, and in desperation, I instinctively went for this heel's Achilles and grabbed him by the goobers. He let me go, trying to play down his discomfort and left the lounge, also with a murderous look. When I first heard the L.P. from 'My Fair Lady,' it reminded me, in a roundabout way, of that incident. For two shillings, 'enry 'arrington nearly 'ad my 'ead.

There was a backslapping pack of friendly engineers, quantity surveyors and builders, when roads, bridges or dams were being constructed in the vicinity. Many blended with the season of their visit, while one or two left some kind of mark. I remember a large fellow who only drank neat double Mellowood brandies. He could drain between one and one-and-a-half bottles on a good run—'stayed at the crease the whole innings,' was his way of describing a good party or a romp under the blankets—and no one would have suspected it. He never sat on a barstool but stood, one shoe on the rail, knocking back the drinks while his fellow imbibers dropped out along the way.

'Men, if I have one more drink I'll get tipsy,' he would announce to the barman, then stride out of the pub and up the stairs to his room. He never appeared to suffer from hangovers and next morning, after a hearty breakfast, he was off to the job.

The voracious appetites of many gourmands, men and women, often left us spellbound, but one of the engineers, while laying the Colesberg bypass, had an appetite I have not come across since. He was not a particularly big fellow, but he could have two helpings of each main course, and those days you got a 'bord kos,' before rounding off with pudding. Loin lamb chops are not particularly large, but during the course of a barbeque, he once demolished twenty-one, plus other eats he must have had.

'Ah gezundte fresser,' (a healthy glutton) my mother said. 'Gargantuan,' Beryl called it, fresh into Rabelais's classic, and Miemie's summation was more down to earth and one of her more severe criticisms, 'Hy vreet ne's 'n verdomde vark!' (He

233

scoffs like a damned pig). She did not take kindly to waste or overindulgence. 'A person must know when a person has had enough, long before a person feels bloated,' and she always led by example.

Then there was a lanky electrical engineer at the time of the Verwoerd Dam, his face cratered by childhood acne or chickenpox, who did a fair amount of travelling between sites. I gleaned some good advice hearing him chat to some of the locals one evening. 'There are three things you watch on the road,' he said and ticked them off on his fingers: 'your petrol gauge, your heat gauge and the second car ahead of you.' 'Why not the car directly ahead of you?' someone wanted to know. 'If he suddenly slams on brakes, you're deep in the shit and already halfway to the morgue!'

Terse, but sage advice, which often alerted me to trouble on the road ahead. A pity one could not always apply that bit of wisdom to the path of life.

Chapter Twenty-three
TIME, WAS THE ESSENCE...
Karoo surfing and some other simple pleasures

I remember when the sun rose over Kiep-Kiep and slowly crawled down towards our hotel, on the first morning of the 'Krismis' holidays; it felt as though an endless jamboree lay ahead of us. Days and days and weeks and weeks of 'vakansie'; to do and play, explore or build, trap or collect...with nary a thought to homework, school or any other major impediments. Six whole weeks. It felt like a lifetime.

I recall another anecdote sometime towards the end of the war. My mother is darning socks in their bedroom—inserting a small calabash into toes and heels to facilitate the curves—her tatty old wicker sewing basket on the bed beside her. Certain foodstuffs and other commodities are in short supply and my brother comes home from school one day with a balloon.

Delirious with excitement, I watch as he blows it up, Bee secures it with a length of wool and he hands me this bright yellow bubble. He could be quite a thoughtful blighter when he wanted to. I waft my first precious balloon into the air and it fills me with indescribable wonder as it effortlessly drifts across the room and settles on one of the sharp wicker ribs. The explosion not only scares the shits out of me, but I howled like a lunatic at the loss of my short-lived treasure.

Many of our toys we knocked together, scavenged from storerooms or throwaways from the shop. Slender wooden frames supporting rolls of material made (flimsy) ladders. Empty polish tins were turned into wheels for wire or wooden cars. Notched cotton reels, a disc of soap (or candle), an elastic band and a sugar stick made wind-up 'crawlers'. A sturdy cardboard box could make one or two slaloms down a steep ravine, while whiskey crates, wire mesh and a length of cane became birdcages. Scraps of machinery, like my friend Jasper used to collect, gave us hours of delight.

235

We cut catapult frames from 'Taaibos' (Rhus pyroides or common Wild currant), two thin strips of bicycle tubing, a piece of leather to hold the missile and we were in business. A supply of pebbles or lead 'ammo,' which we made by melting grids from old car batteries, were kept in a tobacco pouch. We always had a 'kettie' and pocketknife when setting off into the countryside. There were serious competitions. Koerie was the champ in our group. He had a good eye and steady hands and would aim along the taut rubber bands for quite a while, tensing and relaxing them before releasing the missile with the ease of an archer. He had his father's blood, and thinking back now, I can picture him sighting along a slim arrow.

In keeping with the age of 'benign innocence,' we shot at doves, birds, dassies and 'bloukopkoggelmanders'. The male Agama rock lizards tauntingly nodded their bright blue heads or did vigorous push-ups to warn off other males and entice a loitering female into their rocky lairs. They are apparently related to chameleons, in that they blend quite rapidly with their surroundings when threatened. Due to another myth, we were petrified of them, as they were supposed to be extremely poisonous and their bite 'could kill sheep or cattle'. (Certain poisons were dispensed in beautiful deep blue, long-necked bottles...could that have been the tie?) Even the retiring little gecko, that surefooted, nocturnal wall climber, was cast in the same villain's role.

Came the first real spring day—on Ann's weather chart—and after weeks of persistent badgering she gave the green light. Going barefoot felt like a new lease on life, as I ran outside and stomped about in one of the stagnant drainage furrows behind the taproom. Shards of glass lay waiting in the mud, and that is where we often cut our feet.

For the better part of the year we went about barefoot and there were times mine were so hard and calloused that only larger thorns, 'duveltjies,' made any impression. I never had the courage to dig them out with a pin or darning needle, as Ziems and Koerie did, and would rather walk on tiptoe or favouring a heel until they festered out. The Coloured kids called that thickened skin, plus a few layers of imbedded dirt, 'magolies,' and Miemie would tell me 'Jou pote lyk al weer ne's 'n skilpad s'n'. (Your paws again look like a tortoise's). When it got too embarrassing, my mother got Boris and Beryl to collar me in the bath and give my feet a good rasping. According to them, it took at least three assaults, on three different occasions, to get my 'tortoise feet' looking anywhere near human.

Very interesting, those duveltjies. 'Tribulus terrestris,' as they are called in botanical circles, are a common weed, also known as the 'puncture vine,' which caused most of our bicycle flat tyres. And it becomes more interesting. It is also a 'dietary supplement,' according to the blurb, allegedly increasing the production of natural testosterone in men and women, with all those horny and zesty side effects. Little did they know, in days of yore, when referring to a lady's man as being a bit of a 'Doring,' just how close to the bone they were? Ou Pens, a much larger version of my friend Pensie, could have done with some. When they used to rag the tubby widower if he still managed to get it up, he told them: 'Easy! I just splint the old chap with a teaspoon and some insulation tape and I'm ready all night!'

Our games were usually communal affairs. 'Kennetjie,' 'kat in die kring,' 'wegkruipers'—hide-and-seek—and 'blok-blok' were unisex games where everyone joined in. On summer nights or winter evenings, we gathered with the Plaatjies children, Jasper, and kids from the 'maroon house' further down the road, to play beneath the tall pepper trees in the back road. Our shadows elongated and shrank under the street lights as we dashed to get to the 'blok,' while whoever was 'on,' turned their back to count.

The excitement as we searched for new hiding places in the dark—not near enough to be caught first and not too far from the safety of others—was electrifying. Most of us were scared of 'spoke' (ghosts) and formless creatures that haunted our

237

stories. There were also 'tokoloshes,' who in Xhosa culture are tiny, wizened old men who come out after dark to cause mischief and abduct naughty children and beautiful young maidens, which made our games all the more delectably frightening.

Playing hide-and-seek one afternoon, I snuck into my parents' bedroom, which was out of bounds for such games. Crouched behind the bed, I saw a glass of water on the pedestal and gulped it down. Only when the sediments came sliding into my mouth did I realise I had polished off my mother's glass of 'Steradent'. 'Wat nie dood maak nie, maak vet' (what does not kill, fattens), went the old adage, but it can make you bloody bilious.

It was my runaway imagination that turned the 'maroon house' into a ghost house. It was a corrugated iron homestead with steep pitched roof, the paint blistered and baked to a dull maroon. It stood far back from the road, partially shaded by Casuarinas, and creepers clambering up broken balustrades added to the gloom. The father seemed a jovial fellow when he popped in for a 'Ship Sherry,' but I have no recollection of his wife. It was the old, ebony-skinned woman who sometimes sat on the veranda, shelling a basin of peas or peeling potatoes that scared me most. She could have been his mother, her toothless mouth folded in like an empty purse and grey hair tucked under a wide brimmed hat.

There were four serious-looking children; two older boys and twin girls who joined our regular evening games. But it was only the latter, who seemed so shy, who came to our more adventurous get-togethers, when a small group, including some of the younger Plaatjies girls, played a souped-up version of 'huis-huis' in their garden. Eight or nine years old we could have been, some a little older and there would be much indiscriminate clutching but pointed rolling around in the shrubbery and beds of lucerne, (meant for my father's horses); as we tried to copy what we had seen or heard from older kids and those commercial drivers. Heady evenings they were, as wakening hormones and graphic tutorials got our fantasies racing ahead. Although my parents never objected to where or with whom I played, they might have had second thoughts had they realised the scope and intimacy of our innocent attempts.

It was only when I was much older, that I began rethinking those days. I cannot remember hearing racist remarks from Miemie or my parents. As one of a handful of Jews in a predominately Nationalist little town, I am sure my father may have felt uncomfortable or possibly threatened, by his children's close association with the Black and Coloured community, beyond the accepted age of fraternising. But there were never any overt sanctions or limitations as far as I can recall. He did get rather uptight and edgy once, when my sister walked around the hotel with a Black baby on her hip—bathed and freshly swaddled—as the mother was too poor to take better care of it. Many farm children also enjoyed childhood friendships with labourers' kids, usually up to an acceptable age, and, although there were the exceptions, there generally appeared to be boundaries and protocols beyond which they did not.

Hopscotch, rope-skipping and 'klip-klippie' were usually girl's games. Kleilat, as Gerhardus, the bank manger's son enlightened us, was now a real boy's game. We went down to the stream where we cut a few flexible Willow switches, and each would knead a lump of black clay, heavy and charged with a kind of tacky energy. Many peoples, including the San, must have used those clay banks over the centuries. Up in the koppies we split into two groups and faced each other from the safety of our rock forts. A small ball of clay, tightly moulded to the tip of a switch and deftly flicked with an over arm or sideways snap, whizzed across no-man's-land to hopefully strike an opponent. Contacts were fortunately rare, but a direct hit was painful. Some of the more reckless amongst the older boys stuck a pebble in, which was 'Nisht kosher, exectly,' as my father would say.

Simon, whose mother once worked for us—and who later came to work in the hotel—sometimes invited me on stick

239

fights or 'induku'. Although they were nowhere near as serious as their initiation bouts and we were basically only playing, those boys were too slick, and a painful ankle or knuckle was usually my reward in spite of wrapping cloths around our blocking hands.

Some of our games were seasonal and blowing bubbles was an early summer delight in our younger days. A mug of water, some lye soap and a tubular section of crisp pumpkin runner— cut from vines that occasionally rambled around our otherwise barren kitchen yard—were good enough. I used to watch Beryl and her friends scrape off the prickly spines and blow chains of small or large solitary bubbles, intrigued by their delicacy as they elongated and wobbled at the end of the stalk before effortlessly floating up and away. Occasionally Bo deigned to join us. If he had cadged a 'Cavalla' from one of the hotel boys or zipped one from the shop, he would blow smoke into them, and we waited for those silent explosions with great expectation.

We either notched our spinning tops to make them sing or sharpened their points to facilitate splitting the opponent's during top-fights. Sias, who we hero-worshipped, three or four years our senior, who besides marbles and tops, was also an athletics champion. So accurate and deadly was his aim in top-fights, he had the audacity, the 'chutzpah' to turn some of his prize 'singers' into 'fighters'. It was awesome the way he deftly scooped a top off the ground, between splayed middle and ring fingers and onto his palm. 'Listen now how this mister, sings,' he told us, bringing it close to our ear and then with a burning sting, allowed the notches to nip our lobes. He would give an innocent, white-toothed smile and his victims would rather have lost an ear than wince in Sias's presence.

He had won enough marbles and 'ironies'; marble-sized ball bearings, to fill two cake tins, and those days a cake tin could comfortably house a new 'homburg.' His 'goen' collection was legendary. Goens were large industrial ball bearings, shiny and reassuringly solid in ones pocket—while ours were still

240

developing—and every kid's prize possession. They could be bought or bartered and for those who literally had-the-balls, could be won (usually lost) by playing 'lê-lê'. Challengers would have to toss their goen quite a distance towards a target drawn in the sand and the one who lay closest, two out of three times, was the winner, and the winner took all. Possible ties were measured off with our feet; 'fractions' marked with a licked finger on a dusty foot, and acrimonious re-measures were often called for.

There are many 'essences' in my past; the crystallisation of moments in time, preserved like insects in amber, from another era. The delicate perfume of aandblomme, (wild freesias) was the essence of Autumn. We would set out for Platberg, a little more than a 'kleilat's' throw from the hotel and much closer than Spitskop, another range of much higher hills beyond town. Their blooming depended on the amount and time of rainfall, and if we were too early, it could be weeks of fruitless searching.

Then, on a day, we would catch the first scent, tantalizingly subtle, and like bloodhounds, we lifted our noses and the hunt was on. On one of our outings we came across a rusty Condensed Milk tin and we were about to lob rocks at it, when a bird flew up. We found a neat 'Tink-tinkie' nest inside, with four tiny sky-blue eggs. What carefree marauders we were; dividing the trophies amongst ourselves, we continued with our search. Could it have been the equivalent of a geologist stumbling on the Cullinan and not pocketing that 3,106.75-carat trinket?

We collected aloes and yellow (berg), white (skerpioen) and pink (hongerdoring) vygies. Some of the miraculous so called 'resurrection' plants in those areas were the uitdroogvaring (Ceterach cordatum), a small fern that grew on cliffs or amongst rocky outcrops, which after the first rain suddenly changed from brittle grey stalks into a cluster of fresh green fronds. Also mosses (Saleginella dregei), which changed from dusty clumps, to puffy green pillows, with a drop of moisture.

241

Darkened by decayed organic residues and the oxides of manganese, the banks of the sloot yielded a never-ending supply of clay that turned jet black and released a tang of long buried sediments, when mixed with water. Ziems, Koerie and I shaped oxen, horses and cowboys, wagons and cars. Sometimes we exploited poetic license and with much ribald giggling and encouragement, our male and female figures became over endowed.

Soetbessie and taaibos remind me of other smells, the heady cocktail of our 'adrenaline' games, which were equal portions of fear and pleasure. Chatting to Bee a few days ago, she reminded me how we used to careen down steep sandstone runnels in the koppies, balanced on old motor tyres, a flattened cardboard box or sections of corrugated iron. Either singly or in groups, we invariably ended up in a tangle at the bottom, often with scuffed knees and elbows. It was definitely not as soft nor user-friendly as snow, but I suppose that could be the equivalent of Platteland Tobogganing.

At the end of a rope tied to one of the tall willows along the sloot, we sometimes swung from embankments over pools of stagnant slime, which were not kosher even by our unsophisticated standards. One had to time the swing to bring you back either onto the embankment—not quite as easy as Tarzan made it look—or to the opposite bank; what we did not want, was to be left dangling. Few things were worse than plummeting into that fermenting, lukewarm, pea-green broth.

Those escapades were quick and relatively safe, but when scaling a cliff face at Kraaikop, searching for hawk and crow nests, or leaning out between the crown branches of trees in the park; I was very aware of everything, including the sharp smell of fear in a young boy's sweat. Pepper trees that grew between an eruption of dolerite boulders next to the Plaatjies house, had dropped a thick carpet of dried leaves and 'corns' over the decades. Not even weeds grew in that hostile environment. Those trees were another surprise, as I always associated them with small Karoo towns or dreary railway sidings. 'Schinus molle,' also known as the Californian pepper tree, are indigenous to Mexico and the northern parts of South America. No matter where they were carted around the world, they soon peppered their adoptive lands.

Going for a bird nest one day, Koerie slipped and fell onto one of the rocks, blood instantly spurting from a scalp wound. Ouma Siena put some concoction on the deep cut and finally staunched the bleeding with 'twakblaar,' the pungent wild tobacco leaf, and then Ma gave him a few smacks for good measure. From the height he fell, it is miraculous he did not break any bones or kill himself. Thinking about it now, our search for young birds or eggs was not only ecologically unfriendly, but dangerous at times.

Another 'adrenalin' game was lobbing clods or stones at wasp nests under the overhang next to the dining room. This large protected slab was an ideal surface where perdebye or paper wasps (vespid family), slung their paper-like mini-hives. We would form a circle below and take turns shying at them, and the first to run would be a meisie (sissy) or bang-gat (coward). They were large wasps, with needle-thin waists and unlike honeybees, the blighters could sting to their angry little hearts' content. Not only was it extremely painful, but many a time we ended up with swollen lips, eyes or hands and I remember on one occasion having to go to school with one takkie taped under my foot, which looked like a shiny pink melon. Belatedly I learned, that a dab of Reckitt's Blue, was a sure antidote! Honeybees have barbed stings and the first jab anchors it in its prey, although the little venom sac keeps pumping away for quite a while. And wasps don't have little hearts, but a kind of modified vein, that pumps their haemolymph along.

Our school celebrated the annual watermelon feast in Die Parkie. We gorged ourselves, until finally stuffed, we could not resist the sweet, pip-less hearts and chomped until juice dripped from our elbows. It ended with a watermelon 'fight,' everyone chasing and daubing each other with the skins, sometimes

243

liberally dusted in sand, and afterwards we stripped to our undies or cossies and jumped into the cement reservoir.

This park was a short distance out of town and served as a picnic and parking spot, shaded by tall pines and blue gums, and quince hedges bearing loads of the tart fruits in summer. There were two reservoirs and it was the smaller dam, fed by a windmill further up the kloof, which served as a swimming pool. Through the long summers, algae formed on the surface, with tendrils dangling below and we shared this amenity with a collection of frogs, tadpoles and dragonflies. As far as I remember, none of us contracted any creepy crawlies or weird diseases.

Another blissful moment—akin to kicking off our shoes each spring—was a visit to Die parkie on the first warm day of summer and jumping into the pool. We revelled in the buoyancy of the sweet water, diving and gambolling in its post-winter clarity; doing handstands, somersaults and carefree bomb-drops. Finally, our skin puckered and shivering, we went to lie on the cement paving, as sparks of sunlight danced on the surface. After all our horse-play and yells reverberating off the surrounding hills, a stillness finally settled. That was the essence of summer: our first swim, the slap of water under the coping, crows cawing and the steely scratch of cicadas.

There was a small cement dam behind the pepper trees next to the Plaatjies. Built in a protected corner between a shed and garage, it warmed earlier than Die Parkie dam each year and late afternoon sun released the subtle fragrance of well-water and the respirations of algae. This is where Jasper, Ziems, Koerie and I learned to be waterborne, each in our own ways. Afterwards, we would lie on the narrow dam wall, the only place to dry, and where miere (ants) could not bite us. The sound of bees foraging amongst pear blossoms, birds racketing for new mulberries and dassies calling across the stream, as the sun slid behind the koppies, was the essence of a carefree spring afternoon. Speaking of ants, I apparently told my brother once that 'the walls did bite me!' 'Muur,' means wall and 'mier,' is an ant. The perennial linguist... yet.

'Do you remember how exciting it was searching for old pieces of China in the sloot?' Bee reminded me not so long ago, 'and if it had flowers or a pattern, it became an instant treasure.' There was a momentary silence on the line, 'They were such simple pleasures,' she said. That was part of the magic of those times. The simplicity of our games or interests and the way we could entertain ourselves for hours, days, weeks...months. Our lives seemed to be so elementary and uncomplicated.

The veld was an Eden for succulents, cacti and eintjies (wild bulbs). A few of the latter were edible and one of the (succulent) vetplante, locally known as 'Hasieballas,' had small, round furry leaves, hence the name 'rabbit-balls,' and had a sweet-sour flavour. Rock gardens in the Karoo were as common as rose gardens in Kent. Prickly pears, Turksvy in Afrikaans, 'itolofiya' in Xhosa, are delicious to eat but a nightmare to pick and clean. We used a length of hooked wire to tug them from their broad, leaf-like stems and in spite of giving them a good drubbing with Karoo bushes and sand, we invariably ended up with a rash of fine hairs between our fingers and around our lips. They could irritate for days, until my mother or sister tried to locate and pluck them with tweezers.

The klipspringer (Oreotragus oreotragus), is one of our smallest antelope. Amongst other characteristics, they mate for life, walk on the tips of their hooves like ballerinas and prefer the hills, where they bound with great ease from rock to rock. If one qualifies the first and omits the second, we were similar, though not quite as adept. With agility and the lack of concern that goes hand in hand with youth, we literally leapt up and down those koppies.

On one of her bolder boulder leaps, my sister gathered too much momentum and was about to become airborne, when a prickly pear bush put a stop to her fall. Days of painstaking and painful thorn plucking followed, not to mention clothing snagging on unseen barbs and many sleepless nights. She used

245

to wonder which would have been the better option, the cactus or a crash landing. My brother claims to have suffered a similar 'cactastrophy' coming down 'Kiep-Kiep' one day. Someone once described a hangover as having 'hairy-eyeballs,' but I think Bo took it a step further, when a cloud of fine hairs blew into his eyes, also causing him much grief and pussy eyes for many days.

We had our own form of 'Karoo surfing' as we nimbly rode empty forty-four gallon paraffin drums. We raced some fifty yards across 'the garden,' the large parking area next to the hotel. Sometimes we could be three or four abreast; our bare feet arched and ready to fly out of sync any second. Two ribs near the middle of the barrels allowed us not only forward and backward motion, but we learned to move to either end, and steer their course. Some incredibly surefooted athletes came to ride our drums but there were also plenty of spills and grazes galore.

My brother and sister remember a time when this parking area was a real garden—hence the name stuck—with fruit trees and grape arbours, but by my time, only three hardy lilac trees survived at the far end. One of the yard boys helped Bee fence them off so she could have her own little garden. Remnants of the cement furrows that once channelled municipal water were all that remained, and she had to lug bucketfuls from our bathroom. She went off to boarding school and came home to find that Miemie had turned it into a chicken coop, with hens roosting in her precious lilac trees. It put her in a foul mood for quite a while and later the poultry were moved to the Plaatjies' back yard.

In one of our discussions, I mentioned that, while working in the UK, English lilacs seemed almost odourless when compared to a single bunch in our bedroom, which permeated the entire flat. She agreed, having had similar sentiments about the Toucy flowers in France. Could our icy winters and hot dry summers—with plenty of chicken manure—have distilled a more concentrated perfume? And for some inexplicable reason,

246

they sometimes bloomed twice within a year and bunches seemed disproportionably large for the size of the stunted trees.

The forgotten Eden. Miemie, Boris, Beryl and the surviving lilac trees (1934)

Every spring we suffered the consequences of gorging unripe fruit. We couldn't resist the first green peaches, plums, apricots or clusters of sour grapes and would raid the back garden before they had a chance to blush. Bad cramps, the 'trots' and worst of all, the thought of more castor oil, curbed our zeal long enough for the remainder of the crop to ripen.

Bo remembers a large Alberta peach, the last fruit tree in the garden, whose branches cascaded over the dividing stable wall at the far end. It was so large; he and his mates would climb into the upper reaches, find a comfy spot and guzzle to their heart's content. Should the need overtake them, he mentioned, they simply slipped off their shorts and further fertilised the paddock below! How much more carefree could country life get?

On this (final) scatological note, there was very little that could beat a good old vlaktekak. Having wandered in the veld all day, a group of friends find a protected spot, lower their shorts and go down on their haunches. With arms resting comfortably across their knees, they enjoy the pleasure of an ecological country-crap, while chatting and perusing their next avenue of exploration. One or two oval stones rounded-off ablutions. When the sun baked and glinted off the rocks, we placed them in our shadows, while on brisk days we first tried to warm them in our hands. Many years later, I would have chosen them instead of the pre-cut squares of 'grease-proof' paper we would get at boarding school.

Chapter Twenty-four
PLAY, WITH TIME IN ABUNDANCE...
Dog doesn't eat dog...but children can. Some of our
four and two legged friends

We grew up with Nature as part of our everyday lives. Gerhardus, the bank manager's son and one of our slightly older, more streetwise pals, once remarked: 'There is always copulating (animals) in the vicinity.' 'Twee-kop honde' (two-headed dogs), as he described their post-mating samba; the courtship chase of roosters, the quick flurry of doves and the cacophonous coupling of cats were as common as a passing car.

My first encounter with the four-legged world was our dog 'Blackie'. He was a mutt of indeterminate parentage and I thought the two of us were good friends. Relaxing on the front stoep after lunch one Sunday, I sat beside him while he gnawed on a mutton bone I had brought from the kitchen. Someone told me to move him out of the way and as I tried to take it, he bit me. More out of anger and betrayal, than the pain, I grabbed a hind leg and (unwittingly) bit his Achilles tendon, the only place narrow enough for my teeth to do maximal injury. He ran off yelping to the yard and left me with a mouth full of hair. He never bit the hand that fed him again and the supposed antidote to a hangover, hair of the dog that bit you, still reminds me of old Blackie.

There were scores of hotel cats feeding, fighting or fornicating around the place and we woke to early morning rooster sirens, quacking ducks and turkey hens chirruping submissively to the argumentative gobble of the cocks. No matter how fast the dowdy hens ran, their glossy suitors always managed to pin 'em down and the rooster's smugness was in sharp contrast to the hen's startled looks—as they tetchily rearranged their plumage.

We watched many ferocious rooster or turkey fights and they could be bloody and prolonged. Turkey cocks, with eyes like mean old men looking down their noses, went into bitter clashes for mates and territory. Miemie learned the hard way, before she realised it was better to have only one 'gobbler' to a harem. Their normally pink wattles turned deep crimson as they strutted about, scraping wing feathers on the ground with convulsive snaps, hissing and gasping and tail feathers fanned out like Native American headdress. If this show of prowess did not deter one or the other, the fight began in earnest. The loser usually scuttled off, but if evenly matched, a ferocious battle raged in the noonday sun. They would get into neck-locks, stubby beaks latched onto the opponent's throat or wattles, bleeding profusely but refusing to give in. The victor finally trampled and pecked the other, and if we did not intervene or if it could not get away in time, the loser sometimes died from shock or heat exhaustion. I remember Miemie once sending one of the yard boys to pour water over a young male who had taken a Turkey KO.

Someone told us that tucking a chicken's head under its wing, laying it on the ground and drawing a circle around it, hypnotises the bird. It probably has a calming effect or induces a catnap for a minute or two; the circle was simply part of the myth. Ziems and Koerie helped me catch half a dozen of Miemie's chickens one day, which we 'hypnotised' and laid on their sides in the back yard. I went to tell her the chickens were dead and she came stomping down the kitchen steps, pale with fright, and must have noticed the rings and their strange but similar attitudes. Just then the first one came out of its slumber, got to its feet and toddled off, followed by the rest, and our grins completed the circuit of her reckoning. My getaway was quick, but not fast enough for the wet cloth that painfully stung the back of my legs before I could pass her.

One Sunday, after another fine luncheon, the adults were settled on the stoep, and I was hunting for goggas (insects) in one of the tap recesses under the stoep. I found one, cupped it in my palms and proudly went to show my trophy. As everyone lunged toward me, I instinctively closed my hand and the scorpion stung me. My hand swelled, like a rubber glove filled with water, and throbbed for a few days, but that sting did not dull my quest for creepy crawlies or other creatures. I carried the tiny spot on the heel of my right palm for many years.

Kids in the location came with animals they had found or trapped. Baby dassies, hares, tortoises, meerkats, birds, doves or field mice. One of the dassies became so tame, he would perch himself on my bare feet, providing warmth for both of us on a biting winters morning. They brought a wild cat 'kitten' once, quite similar to some our 'banded' domestic cats, which I put in a cage, where it hissed and spat when I fed it bits of raw meat, scrounged from Antie Bee's off-cuts. I had made slight progress easing our mutual fears and uncertainty, when someone in the council got to hear about it and they took it away. Anything other than livestock was considered vermin and there was no chance of a second chance.

Up-country rains occasionally brought geelvis fingerlings down to larger pools along our sluggish old stream. We must have been seven or eight when Ziems and I went to trap fish some distance beyond the washhouse one day. Too busy herding them into shallower corners where we could scoop them up with bits of fly-screen, we didn't realise the day had turned violet and tongues of lightning licked the hills behind us. The thunderstorm overtook us on our way home and we began to sprint, clutching canned fruit jars flashing wide-eyed minnows as lightning and thunder exploded. Then hail pelted down and with nowhere to take shelter, we were fortunate they weren't the large stones that occasionally caused major damage, but forceful enough to sting us. Ziems was almost as pale as I was when we got home. No one had noticed our absence in this storm, or we would have been given some handy-reprimands.

A few fish survived and in spite of Ou Willem telling us ponds had to be sealed and given time to set, we quickly dug a shallow hole in the yard, lined it with stones and some cement we found in one of the sheds and managed to fill it with cans of water before nightfall. Up with the birds to inspect our

251

surviving trophies, the pond was, needless to say, empty and cats had feasted on the fingerlings. It has taken me many years to remember that impatience is a vice.

A farmer once brought my brother two blue crane chicks he found wandering on his fields. They grew up amongst Miemie's menagerie, which must have left their parental imprints, as they remained there until fully-grown. They were quite tame and played a kind of ball game with mealies or small stones, tossing them around and running after them with much wing-flapping and loud ridiculing. Then came a day when instinct overrode emotion or devotion. They took off with slow determined flaps, stick-legs trailing as they crossed the sloot and followed their amazing C(rane)PS to join a migratory clan and start a new life somewhere.

Between my brother and me, we built a spacious walk-in aviary under the overhang of the first floor below the dining room windows. I remember my excitement, when I discovered the wild birds were nesting in the jam tins, and the first heartwood crumbs on the aviary floor indicated that the budgerigars were burrowing nests in the garingboom trunks, 'Agave Americana'. Like the pepper trees, I always thought them offspring of the Karoo—they have become as typical to our landscapes as the koppies—but also hail from Mexico. We sawed the trunks into short sections, sealed the ends with canned fruit tin lids, then cut them so that the upper sections could be lifted, allowing us to inspect eggs or chicks. Some memorable moments were watching the clutch of pale white eggs slowly darken through the brooding process, and the thrill and excitement of seeing those minute, pop-eyed, round-bellied little clots of life. Pink, featherless and defenceless, they slowly matured into inquisitive, clumsy chicks, which were soon fully-grown and whirring about with the rest.

In my varsity years, it became a bind to clean and repair the cage when I came on vacation, so I decided it was time to sell up: lock, stock and budgies. There must have been in excess of fifty mixed birds and I wrestled my conscience for days as to what would be a fair price. Jaapie, one of the regulars, was a jovial, paunchy young man with a round smiling face and a mop of fair hair. He had often intimated interest in the birds and the next time he popped in for a 'brênie 'n coke,' I tentatively broached the price.

'Twee Rand?!' I add the exclamation mark to indicate the way his eyebrows almost disappeared under his slicked curl and he spluttered on the mouthful of brandy he had just taken. I was about to drop my price by fifty cents when a sparkle leapt into his eyes and to my relief, he accepted. The deal was sealed. Proudly I took my Two Rand note to show my father, who happened to be talking to Miemie in the shop, and gave them the 'Church Street' scoop of the year.

'Two Rand?!' This one indicates how close Natie came to popping a vessel.

'Not just the birds, Dad, also the aviary,' I tried minimising my avarice and when that disclaimer made him look even more gob-smacked, I threw in: 'And the ten pound bag of bird seed!' Miemie used to order seed through the shop, and that bag had only recently been delivered. He shook his head, as if my words had physically struck him. 'Oy veyh! Mine zuhn the businessman!' was all he managed and the rest was simply too embarrassing for words. In my defence, that was in the early sixties, and a Rand bought a hell of a lot more than it does today. But, I admit...my price was, maybe...a bit too ridiculous. Even Miemie, who seldom had a bad word to say, blinked her lazy eye two or three times, also shook her head and said: 'Our heavens child, are you then mad in your head?' Her eye blinked a few more times: 'Just the seed cost more!'

After 'Blackie' passed on, my mother bought me a pup from 'Big Eyes' (one of the taproom troopers), for half a crown. He told her the little mite's name was 'Dogs,' which she immediately softened to 'Doxie,' who became a legend in the town. Had I been more adventurous, he could have become a 'Dox of the Karoo'. He was pure, pedigreed mongrel and must have had a generous mix of Jack Russell, Fox Terrier, Staffie,

253

Scottie and a long line of proud but scruffy 'pavement specials'. Small but tough and tenacious as 'blousool'—the thick leather used for soling a velskoen—he was a dogged little fighter with a good few titles behind his name.

He would be my childhood and adolescent pal and loyal companion. He survived innumerable car accidents on the busy main street, until he became street-wise. He once had a hind leg in plaster of Paris, which gave us no end of amusement when he cocked the wrong one. Hit with a full bottle of paraffin across his back—they didn't only ignite fires, but sometimes extinguished confrontations: a Karoo-cosh—he was almost paralysed for a few days and we thought that would be the end of him, but the spunky little fellow pulled through. He survived an attack of billiary fever and had his neck and chest dissected by an Alsatian in one of his innumerable skirmishes. If a cat supposedly has nine lives, Doxie must have had nineteen. He was not just a pretty face. He soon learned the rhythm of our school bus and would walk me to the stop in the morning and fetch me at one thirty on-the-dot. Not only did he pine for days when I went to boarding school, but he perked up when they got my bedroom ready for the holidays.

Other than horses, Natie was not an animal-person. He had a strong dislike for cats ever since one leaped through an open window onto his chest one night. He was not a dog-lover and showed very little interest when we first got Doxie. It was only after I went to boarding school that he slowly grew attached to him and would not go to bed until Doxie came in from his interminable pre-nocturnal ambles and piddles. Near the paraffin heater, on its three bandy-clawed-legs, he dozed on the couch next to Natie and did not budge until he heard the 'Time! Gentlemen' call. I had him put down when he developed a tumour in his fifteenth year. It was ironic that the young man, who kindly took him out into the veld, would one day also die by an unsuspected bullet, very close to that spot.

Besides all the other fauna we collected, we relished the thrill of turning over rocks and searching for scorpions, which

254

we would goad into fights or feed grasshoppers. In the absence of toy planes, we tied a piece of fine cotton to the hind leg of scarabs or Christmas beetles and let them fly in circles. It was tricky untying the knots, but we always let them go again; regrettably, minus a leg, occasionally.

Bird eggs were one of our non-ecological collectibles. To prevent rotting, we blew out the contents by drilling a tiny hole at either end and storing them in a shoebox lined with cotton wool. Occasionally it was a rotten one, crumbling against our lips, and the putrid taste seemed to last forever.

Another no-no was trying to hand-rear fledgling chicks we sometimes came across in nests. If they were too young and we over-'shtupt' them with soggy bread crumbs, many passed to that great flight path in the sky before feeling the wind beneath their wings.

Little did I realise, wading calf deep in green sludge, that 'Platannas' we caught in the sloot would one day be presented to me in waxed dissecting trays for zoology practicals, as Xenopus laevis, the common African Clawed Frog. They laid endless gelatinous bands of black-beaded eggs and those that ended up in shallow rock puddles would either dry out or fry, and flutters of tadpoles baked in that hot soup. No one can be as fanatically dedicated—or cheerfully unconcerned—as children, and we spent untold hours trying to ferry newly hatched tadpoles to deeper water, only to learn much later that platannas dined on their young.

Back in 1933, Lancelot Hogben discovered that a pregnant woman's urine caused female frogs to ovulate, and that would be the pregnancy test long before quick colour strips indicated joy or sorrow, sleepless nights or Bacchanalian celebrations of relief.

We caught doves and birds in various ways. The commonest were homemade traps using bicycle rims covered with a dome of wire netting. It could function 'automatically' or 'manually,' depending on how we set them up. They were almost infallible, unless one of Miemie's escapee chickens scampered in to relish

255

the bait. We also used the 'fishing' technique for doves and pigeons. A piece of sturdy 'sheen' (cotton) was tied to a mealie seed by drilling a tiny hole through the kernel. Anchored to a peg in the ground, they were scattered with the rest of the feed and as soon as one was gobbled, we dashed in, grabbed the bird and removed the seed before it regurgitated. Birdlime, must be the tackiest man-made concoction ever invented and was another method of trapping. The song of caged 'Black Heads' or 'Cape Canaries' lured others to a sticky end of freedom. We needed a small container of paraffin or turpentine to clean fingers, then feathers and then fingers again, which was one hell of a schlep.

Silkworm season arrived with the ancient Mulberry tree coming into leaf. Day after day, my sister would open the shoebox and inspect the harvest of motionless cocoons. Then, with their precise timing mechanism, they all seemed to come to life. (The mature nymphs of the '17-year (cycle) cicada' all surface within a couple of nights of each other). The cocoons would twitch as moths chewed their way out. We watched the constant flutter of stubby wings as they manoeuvred into coupling positions. After the final parting, absolutely spent, the males began dying, while females fluttered about, depositing batches of tiny pale-grey full stops, before making their pre-coded exit.

By the time those minute black 'commas' emerged, about two weeks later, a diet of fresh Mulberry leaves rapidly transformed them into thick, porcelain-white 'Michelin' worms, who, no matter how hot the day, always felt cool and vulnerably soft. Summer, was the pleasant musty smell of their droppings and dried mulberry leaves. The older kids cut cardboard squares, circles, rhomboids and hearts, which they pinned to corks, and let the worms spin thick carpets of silk before utilising the rest to incarcerate themselves for another season in their golden sarcophagi. Beetroot leaves lent a pink tinge to the strands and those mini silk carpets served as bookmarks, gifts or barter.

We spent untold hours up the mulberry tree in the back garden behind the Plaatjies. Barefooted we shimmied amongst the branches, protected from the hot sun by a thick canopy of leaves, our lips, hands and clothing stained deep purple. Male cicadas sang by the stream below, trying to attract a sympathetic ear in all that dinning and life was sweet and carefree. We took home loads of berries for Miemie and Ann, but Natie found that the seeds got stuck under his dentures.

On one of my trips home from varsity, I came across a large mountain tortoise (Geocholone pardalis) crossing the N1 between Laingsburg and Beaufort West. His dome must have stood 35 to 40 cms above the tarmac and it was the first and only one I encountered in the wild. He was already an old fellow when we were kids and must have been a frisky youngster when Tolstoy (finally) published War and Peace, after six years (1869) and the Impressionists weren't making an impression in France. After giving my Anglia a measured once-over—Hells bells, he must have mused, I thought I was big!—he slowly paddled his way across the road, an extra hour or two would make no difference to his journey. Continuing on mine, I imagined our excitement had we found it on one of our outings, but on second thoughts, it would have needed at least ten of us to cart it home.

Then there was 'Hansie,' a Merino lamb a farmer gave me. In Afrikaans, hanslam means a hand (bottle) reared orphan sheep. They form a strong bond with foster parents and like dogs, follow them around, but unlike dogs, one could not train them to sit, lie or wait. He became quite a nuisance as he matured and followed me around the hotel—dropping tiny pellets at the most inopportune moments—but was a great hit with tourists, who could come nose to nose with a live Karoo lamb.

Natie finally put his foot down and Hansie was banished to the chicken run, where he could 'noedge' (irritate) other farmyard animals for a couple of weeks. Miemie had purchased a few sheep in the interim and they were all railed to her father's farm at Anysberg. It is comforting to think, that somewhere on the vlaktes of the Little Karoo, there are sheep that once had an ancestor who not only had free access to a flat, corn in the shop and lemonade in a pub, but could boast of having crapped in the 'foi-yee' of the Colesberg Hotel.

Chapter Twenty-five
ONCE, THERE WAS A TIME...
Holidays in the Little Karoo and Cape Town

In the late seventies, we took the kids to Eight Bells Holiday Farm, between Mossel Bay and Oudtshoorn. On one of the visits, I met an old farmer and his wife, who invited us to their cottage. Camel thorn embers in the little stove, (a distinctive aroma), braising lamb, black coffee and reed ceilings instantly transported me to Anysberg.

My siblings and I were shaped by the Great and Little Karoos, where we spent our early childhood holidays. First, it was my brother's turn to accompany Miemie on her annual vacation to her father's farm, and when my sister was old enough, the two of them would go with her. The last time they were there together, Boris found an old airgun in the barn and the absence of pellets was no deterrent; the crafty assassin found an endless supply of peppercorns dangling from a tree. Only he would know why he told her 'You better run for your life, I'm going to shoot you,' and with that, she dashed for the cottage. Struck in the back of her neck, she allegedly screamed, 'I'm dead! I'm dead!' and hearing those chilling words, he dropped the gun and ran off in the opposite direction. It took skill and patience for Miemie to remove embedded seeds from the squirming girl who thought she would die. When he finally came home, ashen with fear and remorse, his joy at seeing his sister alive was short-lived, instantly terminated by a hiding he would long remember.

I began going with Miemie from a very young age. Although I was much older when my mother took me on her Cape Town vacations, I seem to remember the train trips with Miemie more vividly. The best would be her wicker picnic basket, packed with segments of roast chicken, frikkadels, hardboiled eggs, brown bread sandwiches, a twist of greaseproof paper filled with salt and pepper, the ubiquitous jammer lappie (damp cloth), and a thermos of sweet milky coffee. She was never one for chitter-chatter, but if there had been good rains, she would gaze at the countryside. 'The world is darem (indeed) very beautiful,' or during periods of drought, 'Ai! but the old world is indeed very grey and dry.'

She forbade my father to purchase bedding or meal tickets at the station, in spite of 'Ou Labbes' cajoling her, 'Don't be silly, Miemie, old Kappie is paying.' 'Why waste all that money?' she asked, as if expecting a revealing answer, 'Our food and bedding is as good as theirs, if not better.' Seated in our coupé, I tucked into the goodies as soon as she set the hamper on the fold-down table. I savoured every morsel as the veld stretched motionless to the horizon, only the occasional sweet thorn or stagger of rocks whizzing by in the foreground. Lulled by the rhythm of wheels and rock cuttings slamming the clatter back at us, that was as good as heaven. Miemie would slowly peusel (nibble) at her food as though it was just another job to complete. She was not one who lived to eat, and never ate to live, in excess.

We had to detrain at Touwsrivier in the bleak morning hours and porters took our luggage to the 'Slegs Blankes' waiting room, where we joined a motley crowd patiently waiting for other connections. Regulation-brown paint added to the gloom and the chimney pipe of a regulation-SAR coal stove disappeared through a halo of soot in the ceiling. Her portly roll of blankets and pillows, bound with rug straps, would be spread on the wooden benches. I fell asleep as I put my head down, while she fitfully dozed to the sound of shunting engines, clanging bogies and the short, cheeky whistles or mournful hoots as trains came or left this busy junction.

Sometime after sunrise our antiquated little locomotive, dubbed 'Makkadas' by the locals, stoically hauled us towards Anysberg, squealing to a halt at every siding to load or unload cans of milk, goods or passengers, until we finally reached our destination, the forlorn little siding at Kareevlakte.

Her youngest half-brother, Dolf, would be waiting under

some Acacias, next to 'Gryspens' and 'Hans' tethered to a small cart, their heads lowered to the sun. I was never sure why donkeys were called stupid. As far as I can remember, they might have looked bored or indifferent, and 'davke' at times—challengingly aloof—but seemed to do exactly what they wanted and at their own pace. Between missions—threshing dried bean or pea pods on the small cement floor next to the outhouses, taking the family to visit her sister at 'Sandplaas or to the hamlet, to purchase heavier supplies—they seemed to be in deep contemplation behind lowered lids and long lashes. No matter how often I went with Miemie, each time we crested 'Die Hoogte,' I experienced the same rush of excitement as cornfields, small orchards and vineyards stretched below us. Then their thatched cottage came into view, beside the majestic 'Kameeldoring,' a twirl of smoke lifting from the chimney and further in the distance, the tiny hamlet of Anysberg.

There was one outhouse where bunches of onions and garlic hung from the rafters, lending their tang to sheets of cured leather and raw thongs; the dusty smell of dried bean and pea pods mingling with the earthy aroma of freshly harvested potatoes. Bags of walnuts and almonds and old milk cans filled with dried peaches, pears or apricots, stood against the thick stuccoed walls and wind-dried racks of sheep ribs and beef biltong hung from the ceiling. The smell of milk, cream and yesterday's whey, lingered in the separating room next door.

Wooden beams, reed ceilings and thatched roofing lowered their fragrance on the mud and dung coated floors below. If one did not grow up with dung floors, they must have been an acquired taste. A sloppy mixture of wood ash, sand and cow pats was regularly spread by hand on the kitchen and barn floors, then left to dry for a couple of hours. It did not help the fly problem, but once one got used to the smell, it added a warm, homely flavour.

Other delights awaited us in the solder (loft), reached by a wooden staircase attached to the side of the outhouse. Miemie's father, Oupa Faan, made a variety of crossbows: small ineffectual ones for children, slightly more potent ones for older boys and large bows that Izaak and I could not set, no matter how hard we pressed our feet to the bow and pulled back on the gut. Hand-made wooden furniture, ousted by a few characterless chrome and Formica kitchen chairs that Miemie must have purchased over the years, lent their subtle nose. Petrified they would settle on our heads and gobble our hair—another myth—we were in awe of the common bat's ability to outsmart our attempts to swat them, as they whirred back and forth in the gloom. I often wondered where the 'blind as a bat' story came from.

Tucked under my patchwork blanket at night, I could see the light of paraffin lamps casting wavering shadows on the passage wall, while adults chatted around the voorhuis table. 'Voorhuis,' was an entrance room, cum sitting room, cum dining area in most old homes. The haunting call of jackal, in search of prey, filled me with a kind of fear and comfort, knowing I was safe in Miemie's house, with Miemie's people.

The farm was a child's paradise. Izaak and I played on the white sand beside the farmhouse, where a river must have coursed in past millennia or up at the spring, 'die oog' (eye), where water siphoned out of the earth, filling a crystal pool surrounded by fern, bracken and arum lilies. Sometimes we played under the wide swathe of shade that the sun sketched with the old Camel thorn as it moved across a cloudless sky, or collected tortoises in the veld. Early morning we went into the vineyards and lay on our backs under vines sagging with dew-spangled Hanepoot, biting off grapes by simply lowering bunches to our teeth. How we did not drown or choke—or 'grow goat horns'—is another miracle.

Izaak was Barnard the shepherd's son, and taught me to chew or suck Acacia resin and to use their ivory white thorns as horns for the cattle that we shaped with clay found near the spring. The cement press, where nagmaal (communion) wine and mos (grape juice, before or during fermentation) were made by crushing grapes with our bare feet, became our fort, while the redundant old ox-wagon, now mired under the tree, could be a house or boat or anything else we desired. There was great excitement when they cleaned and scrubbed the parskuip (wine press) before dumping in baskets of grapes for crushing. Dolf, Barnard, Izaak and I, occasionally the women folk or neighbours, would take off our velskoens, (I'm not sure if we always gave a preliminary wash or not!), climb up the ladder and feel the fruit squelch and burst under our toes.

Sitting in a London departmental store once, I watched locals and visitors strolling by, to the throb of shop-till-you-drop music. An elderly couple walked in and their Afrikaans confirmed the origin of his T-shirt, knee-length sky-blue socks and comfortable suede boots, which reminded me of my first pair of handmade velskoens.

On my first visit to Anysberg, I noticed everyone in velskoens and begged for a pair. Although we sold them in the shop, factory-made were never quite the same as handmade ones. Dolf selected a sheet of blou soolleer (thick squares of bluish leather for soling shoes), laid it on the ground and told me to stand on it, as he carefully traced each foot. He cut them out with his pocketknife, and, after careful selection, cut uppers from a suitable piece of soft leather. A few days later, after being soaked in a tub of water overnight, they were ready.

That was the easy bit. First, he wet and lathered my feet with soap and told me to lie on my back, under the Camel thorn. Then began the process of getting them on. The amount of tugging, pushing and painful slaps on my soles seemed to go on forever, much to the mirth of the bystanders. Finally both were on and the thong laces tied. 'Now you go with Barnard and Izaak to fetch the sheep,' he said and we loped off into the veld, my shoes feeling tight and very uncomfortable. Barnard promised they would come right. By the time we returned towards sunset, the flock of Persies swinging their fat-laden tails in a halo of dust, they had dried and shaped exactly to each foot. After a day or two, they fitted like a sock.

Any other time, I would have gone with Miemie to the tiny
263

hamlet. It was an hour's walk along the gravel road and then a shortcut through some fields. The small cluster of thatched cottages nestled amongst eucalyptus, oak and sweet thorn, where a tributary of the Touws River ran by. One of the houses doubled as post office and another, near the riverbank, as general dealer, with a fair stock of sweets…

There was the night when the river roared; 'toe die rivier gebrul het'. It usually lapped over and between the rounded stones, but a flash flood came swirling past one night and folk spoke about it sounding 'ne's 'n gedierte' (just like a wild beast). The farm was too far from the village, but we came the next morning for provisions and I went to join some of the burghers who were viewing the banks that had been badly mauled by the torrent. Large Acacias were uprooted and toppled and the air was filled with the raw, pungent odour of their exposed roots and damp vegetation; an elixir I will always remember. Frightening too, were the gaping wounds in the red earth, which were not far from the little shop.

Now, Dolf was going to slaughter a pig and she urged me to come with her. 'You mag miskien (might perhaps) be sorry,' she put a choice to me, but I was adamant and keen to watch the spectacle. They led the porker, with some difficulty, into a shallow depression scooped in the soft river sand, and it was restrained by Barnard and one of the neighbours. I should have listened to Miemie; she always gave good advice. The pig moved just as Dolf fired the shot and, badly wounded, began a wild stampede around the farmyard, storming at those who had come to watch. Everyone scattered. Izaak and I scampered in panic until we found safety on the wagon and I have never been as petrified as when the boar charged at us and I could have sworn its mean little eyes were searching for me. Weak and exhausted, it finally lay down and Dolf delivered the 'doodskoot' (coup de grâce).

She also warned me to stay away from the pigsty, unless one of the adults was with me. I plucked some lucerne, added potato skins and carrot tops and went to feed them early one morning. Climbing onto an empty tub, I leaned over the wall and one of the Landrace boars loomed up from the trough, opened a drooling mouth and snapped it shut over my entire forearm. Wagter, their German Shepherd, had fortunately accompanied me and as I yelled, he leaped snarling onto the wall and the pig fled. Those fellows could weigh 350 kilograms or more.

Miemie came running out in her dressing gown, found me writhing on the ground and I was lucky not to receive the gratis hiding. She did give me a good dressing down on the way back to the house, reminding me that 'Pigs have been known to 'vreet' (devour) small children! Did you know that?' I got the (usual) flannel-lappie-steeped-in-vinegar and was told to 'go sit on that chair now and stay away from the verdomde pigs!' My arm had only been temporarily entombed, but I had nasty abrasions and bruises that slowly went through the colour spectrum, reminding me to give pigs a wide berth. Those incidents went a long way in consolidating my pact with the covenant; forbidding us eating swine, but The Old Man's rules obviously did not apply to the porker.

There was the story about the local harridan standing at the bus stop clutching a goose under her arm, when a local walks by and asks, 'Where you going with that pig?' 'Can't you see it's a bloody goose, you stupid idiot?' she snarls. 'I know,' he replies, 'I was talking to the goose'.

It reminds me of what happened when we got home after the holidays and I proudly told my parents the pig-feeding saga. 'Kakker,' my father said with his reserved smile, 'tell me, vos weiss a chazzer foen lokshen?' What does a pig know about noodles? goes the Yiddish saying, or, what does a lout know about culture / something good? Thinking about it many years later, the goose joke reminded me that Natie may have been referring to the pig!

Then there was Hendrina. 'Driennie,' in her simple sun-bleached dresses, who brought with her a mix of healthy perspiration, a touch of wood smoke and soap. She and her

265

parents occasionally visited the farm and that was when she taught me a game she called 'Groot mense' (Grownups), which we played on the sand under the thorn tree. While the adults chatted in the voorhuis of an evening, she directed this game with an amazing feel for tension and delectable expectation. With only an old travelling rug as a real prop—our 'bed'—I would play the role of someone in need of a place to sleep, and each time I came knocking at the imaginary door of her imaginary house, she would politely turn me away, telling me to 'try a little later'. Amazing!

When she finally allowed me in and patted the rug beside her, before cocooning us from moon and stars flickering between the Acacia branches, it felt as if my chest would burst with excitement. I was ten, she could have been twelve and although we only cuddled, as far as she was concerned, we were 'big people'.

*

Everyone used to refer to us as 'Miemie se kinders 'and being the youngest, the name strung along with me. My wife had heard our childhood stories so often, that I decided to include a detour into memory land, one, I had been pining to do for more than fifty years. I wanted to return to the place of Miemie's birth, and where I had spent so many memorable holidays: Anysberg.

At the turn of the century, after a journey into the heart of the Little Karoo, we arrived at the farm gate mid-afternoon and I drove down the road that once bisected rolling wheat fields. I expected to find the homestead with its whitewashed walls, thatched roof, a friendly smear of smoke rising from the chimney and the old wagon standing under the large thorn tree. I had also told her about the vineyards, fruit trees and the outhouses that stood on the periphery; the smell of lucerne, Acacia and wood smoke that was part of the country air we breathed.

266

Instead we found an unfriendly looking nineteen-sixties' homestead—bricked veranda, corrugated iron roof and metal windows—which seemed to avoid making eye contact with me—standing where the stately Camel thorn once spread its welcome shade. Everything else seemed to have vanished. Distraught, almost disorientated, I got out of the station wagon and began sniffing the air for some clue, anything that would somehow rekindle, even for a fleeting moment, a hint of those wonderful childhood memories.

A familiar old road leading to a strange new house.
What used to be the Anysberg farm (1999)

'Gutted,' as they say in the UK, we drove to the tiny hamlet and here too, things had changed. The towering blue gums and quaint thatched cottages were gone. The house I was looking for seemed smaller, standing in the middle of a vast open ground, but retained its small wooden windows and quiet, homely dignity. A gardener, in khaki trousers and a patched shirt, was patiently turning soil in a small vegetable patch. I walked over and greeted him, then enquired if anyone was

267

home. He leaned the fork against his thigh, unhurriedly removed his hat and seemed to consider how much information he should give this stranger. He stared in the direction of the tiny cemetery beyond our car, then courteously lowered his eyes, saw my wife in the passenger seat—no 'Bonnie and Clyde' stories to taint this man's memory—and decided it was okay. 'The Old Missus is inside,' he said, running a hand across his hair, 'mister can but go and knock'.

I rapped on the door. 'Who is that?' a hesitant voice came from the end of a passage. I gave her my full name.

'Who?'

'I used to come with Miemie de Wit, from Colesberg,' I told her. Silence. I heard her shuffle closer until late afternoon sun fell on a pair of worn slippers, climbed up her apron and hovered below her face, partly shrouded by a 'kappie,' one of those floppy turn of the last century bonnets. It was difficult to recognise Ant Tina, but the best was still to come.

The screen-door complainingly opened and she narrowed her eyes to the glare. Still not sure, her train of thought must have shunted back and forth; coupling or uncoupling vague memories while trying to contract the vast time span. How to make sense of this tall, bearded (and scruffy looking) man compared with that little skinny boy.

'You're as thin as a crow,' Miemie, and everyone else genially scolded me. 'Nothing but skin and bones,' my mother confirmed, trying to encourage me to eat, and I only began filling-out and shooting up post-puberty.

Then it all finally fell into place and there was an instant change. 'My gracious me, but you must then be Miemie's child?' she said and held onto my hand while muttering: 'My world, my dear world; the very same Ivan, can you now believe that?' My name had initially been Ivan, but at the age of five or six, for the royal sum of two shillings and sixpence—half a crown—my mother had the registry office in Pretoria change it to Evan, in memory of her mother, Eva Traub.

Ant Tina se huis (Die ou poskantoor) Anysberg (1999)

Ant Tina must have realised her breach of protocol and looked enquiringly at Ferdi. 'This is now my wife, Fernanda,' I said, and she wanted us to come in for coffee and a little something to savour, perhaps, but it was getting late and we were well off the beaten track in rotten-road territory. The sun balanced on a koppie, elongating shadows of the simple graves, where the handful of Anysberg burghers lay behind a low mud and brick wall topped with iron palings. I remembered the names of some of the wonderful old men and women who had plied us with almonds and walnuts, fresh and dried fruits, Boerekos, rusks and mugs of coffee, sometimes sweetened with condensed milk. Country hospitality that had shaped our youth.

I felt a flush of heat in the corner of my eye. Glad I had the opportunity to capture this moment and tremendous sadness, realising I was standing on the fading brink of a wonderful, irrevocable past.

*

As we became more independent, the same routine now applied going with Ann on her annual vacations to Cape Town. Having grown up in Colesberg and only known the Great and Little Karoo, my first trip with her was an exciting collection of firsts. Much like a treasure hunt, only these were not hidden but jumped at me whichever way I turned.

We dined in the saloon car and that was the first novelty. Seated at a table decked with starched white linen and silver cutlery where we could sit and watch the countryside sliding by while White 'waiters' served our delicious meals. Next morning I woke to my second 'first': the Hex River valley with the lofty Hex River Mountains, part of the Cape Fold Belt Mountain Chain, rising steeply to our right and my first encounter with the Western Cape. Endless vineyards, vast orchards, trees and grass as far as I could see. The extent of greenery was unbelievable.

Even in the 'fifties, Cape Town's endless suburban sprawl was staggering for a country bumpkin; then we rumbled into the cavernous station and what looked like hundreds of platforms under one roof. Porters, in faded khaki caps and uniforms, trundled barrows beneath the famous 'station clock' with its instantly recognisable but impersonal face. It was a well-known landmark where old friends met, life long relationships were first sealed or hearts broken by someone not turning up for a date.

Into the sunshine and new delights. The perfume of flower sellers and fruit vendors mingled with hot macadam and the mechanised breath of the city. Buses, trams (trolley busses)— with twin arms that clacked and sparked as they crossed overhead points—cars, trucks, pantechnicons and horse drawn carts; visitors, shoppers, hawkers and the purposeful stride of the working brigade. Traffic officers were smartly directing endless streams of cars with long white-gloved arms. (With them around, one rarely saw a traffic jam those days.)

On our way to Sea Point, I craned my neck through the open window and was agog at the tall buildings rushing above us, while Ann struck up a friendly conversation with the cabbie. As we came around Signal Hill along the foreshore, I got my first tentative whiff of the ocean—somewhere on the air, like those elusive aandblomme (wild freesias)—and then we were on Beach Road, the navy blue sea sparkling endlessly into the distance and our taxi suddenly filling with fresh ocean air. 'Kavlotik!' as a Greek friend would say, many years later; orgasmic!

In an age where industry, change of habitat and global warming has altered so many of the natural dynamics and rhythms around us, it is difficult to relive many of our childhood smells…and tastes. Very occasionally, when my wife and I walk the dogs on the Sea Point promenade, I catch a hint, a poignant reminder of what the English referred to as 'the ozone' and what our oldies simply called 'yam luft,' (sea air). The raw, brisk and energising smell of salt, iodine, washed up kelp and drying shellfish.

A neat turn left into the circular driveway of the old Bordeaux Hotel and the marble fountain, where a naked marble cherub clasped a large carp, both etched by the trickle of time and water. Here was a real garden with local and exotic trees. Geometric Norfolk Pine, Royal palms, magnolia and oleander. Flowerbeds, trellises interwoven with honeysuckle and shaded benches; a gazebo, where quartets entertained guests enjoying sundowners, and scallops of coloured lights undulated at night.

Bordeaux Hotel,
Sea Point

Across the road, the original 'Graaf's Pool' had become a men's-only swimming pool, before it turned into a men's-only 'swinging pool,' many years later. Behind its solid concrete walls, firmly anchored to the five hundred and fifty million year old Malmesbury shale which Cape Town rests on, elderly gentlemen used to bathe, winter and summer, often nude, in the icy waters that must have reminded them of their central European origins. The ferocious Atlantic fury could not budge those walls, which have only recently been levelled to prevent modern-day hanky-handy-panky.

This fine old hotel had different smells from ours. Sliced white shop bread, tangy broths or consommés, leather furniture, wood panelling and plush but ageing carpets that mingled with sea and garden. Some nights a north-westerly brought the crashing of waves into our bedroom and at other times, it was only a distant murmur. It was my first introduction to Melba Toast and Pepsi Cola served in a tall glass with ice, a slice of lemon and a straw! Every bedroom had a telephone, one could order a cool drink at the other end of the garden and it had its own tennis courts.

We took a 'lectric train to visit friends of my mother in Muizenberg, who had a daughter about two years older than me. The proverbial scarecrow, I was all knees and elbows in my scratchy woollen bathing trunks as I ventured into the sea for the first time. Literally bowled over by the surge of waves and their relentless constancy, I alternated between being buoyant or dumped on the sandy bottom. By the end of the day, I was bodysurfing with the rest of the bathers and hooked on 'la mer'.

Muizenberg served my first hamburger, first hotdog and my first peek at the 'snake pit,' where hundreds of 'cool' boys and girls baked on the hot sand from morning 'till late afternoon, in the pleasant aroma of vanilla ice-cream wrappers, tanning lotion and hair lacquer. It was my first exposure to bikinis and my eyes must have popped. It was not always easy for someone with my spatial-dyslexia, to find my way back to the group again, and on numerous occasions I found myself settling down in a tiny space on the periphery of a crowd, only to realise I had been off-target by about ten degrees. One had to have the homing instincts of an Adele Penguin finding its chick in a breeding colony.

'Maybe you two will hit it off,' Ann told me on the train, another of her favourite expressions, and I began building sand castles in the sky, thinking about this 'shiddach' (matchmaking) with the daughter. But her body language was loud enough for even a hillbilly like me to hear. Not happy that she had to chaperone her parent's skeletal country-connection, she soon ditched me to join her mates in the 'snake pit,' and how they found me again, in the equivalent of a Durban sardine run, remains another benign mystery. Exhausted and famished—'That's what the yam luft does for one,' Ann would explain year after year when we holidayed at the Cape—we got back to the hotel in time for me to shovel down my food and then slept like a dog.

The smell of fresh Alberta peaches, Satsumo plums, Royal apricots, nectarines and Hanepoot grapes drifted from every café and kiosk. Ann, ever dilly about flowers, happily chatted to the flower sellers on Adderley Street, in their colourful dresses and 'doeke,' under striped umbrellas; a current of familiarity fizzing amongst tubs and buckets jammed with protea, pincushions, hydrangea and any other flowers she could possibly think of.

The perennial naturalist, I have no idea how many rock cod, painstakingly trapped and brought back to the hotel in my bucket, ended belly-up in the hotel fountain, or how many chameleons escaped from our bedroom into the carpeted interior of the sedate old establishment.

On a trip through the Namib Desert, when my brother visited us sometime in the nineteen-eighties, we came across a large chameleon crossing our track. 'Just as well those buggers you brought into my bedroom weren't this size; I would have turfed you out with them!' he joked.

He was referring to the time my parents sent me to spend a

273

couple of weeks with him and my sister in Cape Town. He had a room in the old Balmoral Hotel on Main Road, Sea Point, where dwarf chameleons (Bradypodion family), thrived in the hedges bordering the walkway to the front veranda. I was intrigued by the turret-eyed, slow-footed showmen that could coil their tails and turn from dusty chalk to rust, and from green, to black, when angry. He had come home that first night and nearly had a heart attack. A tangle of reptiles were hissing on a branch, suspended from the picture rail, almost on the light switch. Livid, to put it decently, he ordered me to take them to the hedge, 'Right this bloody minute!' 'But it's dark...' I whinged. His reply...is superfluous.

That was not the end of my expeditions. Another evening he found dead and dying rock cod floating in his washbasin and that had caused another late-night eviction. In my ignorance, I still had not realised their need for salt water. On my steep learning curve, came another early first...that a washbasin could stand-in as a urinal and I told him 'that was very naughty!' Politely translated, he told me to mind my own business and that he was not prepared to amble along miles of corridor in the middle of the night to ease the sensitivities of a silly little twit like me, and fiercely barred me from bringing any other animals to his room.

In the city one day, I stumbled on my first pet shop and I could have (should have) spent the rest of my vac right there. After scrutinising the amazing collection of birds, parrots, fish, terrapins, rabbits, white rats, guinea pigs and hamsters, I realised I had just enough money to buy a rather fat little white mouse and catch a bus home with my trophy. In the early morning hours, Bo woke to unusual scuffling, switched on the light and realised the commotion was coming from a strange shoebox on his wardrobe. Inside he found pink sextuplets suckling at mammy's milk bar, and that had done little to heal a teetering détente-tion. Luckily, they were not evicted there and then, but next day I had to take them to my sister, who was staying at the King David Hotel, right next door. It was too much even for her generous spirit and so it was back to town, back to the pet shop, but no money back. Once, no-businessman, always, no-businessman.

If all that was not enough, and just when he thought it was safe to go into the bedroom again, I put my foot in it, in the dining room, where he and Harvey, a good pal, shared a table. (One of their 'klabberjass' games lasted a few months and scores filled an exercise book. Could it have been a Guinness record?)

Those were still very staid and refined days. One evening I asked Harvey in my loud peri-pubertal croak, if he had ever doodled a girl? Every knife, fork and spoon fell silent; all conversation ceased and every head was cocked in our direction. Then his Adams Apple bobbed once or twice and my brother gave me a 'lummy' under the table—an exquisitely painful knuckle-punch on a muscle—that rattled the cutlery and had me limping for a few days. It taught me another good lesson, that it was not always wise to take too great an interest in someone else's well-being.

Chapter Twenty-six
YE HAVE DWELT LONG ENOUGH IN THIS (KOPPIE) MOUNT ...
Thus saith Deuteronomy, and so it came to pass, I was off to masters and pastures new

A time for learning and a time for yearning...

Approaching my eleventh birthday, there was no rabbi to teach and prepare me for my passage into manhood, my 'bar mitzvah' in two year's time. I was still a 'pisher' (wet behind the ears) and a 'poyer' (peasant), who was a bit of a 'goy' (gentile) at heart with very little knowledge of 'Yiddishkeit' (Jewish faith/ customs), as Natie sometimes described me. Although Mister Stern was a 'chochem' (knowledgeable person), he was already getting on in years.

He could have tutored me, but I think the consensus was that either way, a stint away from home could do me no harm. My parents decided to send me to Grahamstown, where the 'shul' would shore up leaking 'Yiddishkeit,' the school would try and inculcate academic growth, and the two might turn me into 'ah balabatisher mentsh,' a person of substance. My new school would be Kingswood College in The City of Saints and Sinners and that is where Kasper drove my mother and me in January 1951. He had been monitored, cajoled and threatened with his life, to remain sober.

We stayed at the Stone Crescent Hotel, tucked away in the scenic Howisonspoort. It was a short distance out of town and owned by very good friends of the family, Elias and Daisy Cohen, who ran this popular and idyllic venue for many years. I was struck by the mix of sandstone flooring, polished antique furniture and my first breath of the lush Eastern Cape bush.

Muirheads supplied my uniforms, where polite middle-aged assistants quietly went about their business of assessing size and shape of head, body and foot without the need for tape measures

276

or unnecessary familiarity. In the muggy heat of starched clothing, cardboard boxes and black leather 'B.G.' shoes, they fitted me out with untold stiff or scratchy items, each one throwing me into further panic as they were neatly wrapped in brown paper and tied with string. Then up High Street to 'Stirks,' for takkies, tennis racquet, rugby boots, cricket bat and other sporting kit. (Only a signed medical certificate or bilateral above-knee amputations got you off sport.)

On my last day of freedom, we drove to school. My ribbed trunk was schlepped up the gloomy, ornate staircase in Jacque's House, where sunlight falling through stained-glass saints and angels cast ruddy shades on Kasper, who looked like he badly needed a drink. The old Neo-Gothic Jacque's House was also referred to as 'Jack's House'. I was fortunate to have Jack Slater as House Master in Prep School and then as Head Master when he took over from Captain 'Cappy' Rich in 1954.

On our way out, we bumped into three lads in uniforms and 'bashers' (boaters), who reminded me of a picture from the 'William' books by Richmal Crompton. I found it so incongruous, me, dressed like that? One of the trio turned out to be Jason, whose parents owned the hotel in a nearby village and who came to Colesberg for Jewish High Holy days. He introduced his two mates and when Ann, with her usual largesse invited them to join us for lunch at the 'Palmerston Café,' their over-polite, helpful manner only sharpened my feeling of entrapment. That turned out to be a long and trying afternoon and when we were dropped at school, it almost came as a relief.

They were my age, but 'old boys' and invited me to join them and two other 'oldies' to the sixth bed across the narrow wall of the cavernously long Second Dorm. Two days into term, one of the trio, in a burst of exuberance, hoofed his bed towards mine as I was bending down to find my shoes and my bony hips were caught between the rims of the cast-iron frames. That led to a serious scrap and cuts from the head prefect.

Boarding school rudely dished out some other 'firsts'. Impersonal dormitories, cold showers and lumpy porridge; the

277

smell of locker rooms and sweaty togs, Brylcreem, linseed oil, Jeyes Fluid and the proverbial cabbage and stale bread. Being in the Eastern Cape, a King-pine cost a penny at the market, and we had pineapple in various guises for breakfast, lunch and supper. There were rows of toilets with neat packets of toilet paper, each symmetrical sheet so stiff and waxy—one could wrap sandwiches in them—we had to crumple a few at a time to soften and get them reasonably absorbent, skid-proof and user friendly. In the tuck-shop, redolent of cream soda, ring doughnuts and Cornish Pasties, the ever patient 'Auntie,' a cigarette dangling from her lips, served the clamouring masses with unbelievable patience. The smell of newly-cut grass drifted in from the playing fields on summer afternoons, to the measured thwack of 'leather on willow'. (What would my old Colesberg mates have thought about this lot?)

It was a quantum leap from the intimate warmth of Mrs Van's class, to the strict austerity of an all-boys 'English' boarding school and it took me a full term, if not longer, to come to terms with the real world. I scribbled off nine-page letters on my blue 'Croxley' pad, with matching envelopes, which ran out in the first week. I pleaded to come home, promising to be good, while firing other emotional missiles I could dig from my skimpy arsenal. Was I professional? I drew rings around the occasional tear that splashed to the page, with a large arrow, 'tears of sadness,' for good measure. Thankfully, to no avail. As Odysseus's men lashed him to the mast to thwart the sirens, so Miemie and my father must have stilled Ann's pen from calling it a day and recalling me to kith and kin. In spite of knowing the exact day term ended, it was only when we fetched our trunks from the storage shed, that 'going home' became a reality. It gave me some insight into why Ann would bring her cases into the bedroom weeks and weeks before going on holiday. Depending on our budgeting during term, we could withdraw any outstanding balance of pocket money on the last day and at the station that first departure evening, my euphoria was indescribable.

Pupils were divided into 'drips,' 'weeds' or 'moegoes,' while prefects, the machos with flair, and sporting champs were revered and reigned supreme on their lofty pedestals. I clocked in somewhere between...drip, actually. Friendships were either casual or best mates, what we called 'bok-pals' and Larry, another old boy, took me and two other newies under his wing for a time. The four of us were eleven years old, but he was way ahead of us in maturity, street-wise savvy and his fluent patter honed in Durban. He walked with a 'Durbs' swagger that sometimes bordered on a kind of prowl and he had the vocabulary of a seventeen-year-old.

At the station one night, he noticed an adolescent girl in a rather low-cut dress, leaning from a carriage window. He swaggered over. 'Lady,' he said in his muffled, rolling voice, as if he had a large wad of gum in his mouth, 'You better be careful or you could fall clean outa that dress.' The three of us blushed more than she did, but Larry carried on walking, hands deep in his trouser pockets, casually lifting his chin over his shoulder for us to follow.

Our singing teacher was beautiful; tanned, blonde hair, possibly two or three years out of Training College, and everyone had a crush on Miss Benson. She would lean, what we thought of as seductively, against the front bench, when arranging our harmonising sequences. At the beginning of a new term, Larry informed us, 'You can smell if a woman's had sex recently.' That pricked up our ears, inter alia, but when he said he was going to test her the next day, we couldn't wait for our singing class to begin. The four of us usually sat in one of the back rows, but we got there early and slid towards the centre of the front bench. She raised an eyebrow and commented on his—not our—presence in the front. 'And to what do we owe this honour, Harris?' I think she might have had a soft spot for Larry; that was how my mother described something more than just a liking.

She sat at the piano as we went through her repertoire of love or love-lost songs and Larry was beginning to fret that all would be in vain. Finally, she came over to select the harmonising layers for 'The Bells of St. Mary's'. Lady Luck was (momentarily) with him, as her thighs pressed against the bench and she leaned over us. In his scientific or exploratory zeal, and not wanting to miss this perfect opportunity, he gave a robust sniff, and lady-luck instantly deserted him. 'Harris!' she gasped, jumping back, 'What are you doing?' A moment of bewildered indecision followed and then she rushed out of the room. No one knows how she explained this pantomime to the headmaster, she must have watered it down, to leave a 'modesty' of decorum, but that sniff earned him the rank of full Naval Captain with four neat stripes across the poop.

During the week we took morning showers, often tepid or cold by the time 'cops' (prefects) and house-monitors had squandered the supply. Plebs had to literally dash through on winter mornings. Sunday evenings we lined up in two rows for our weekly bath. Mrs Thomas, who timed our dunks in two tubs, standing side-by-side on their ball-and-claws, monitored the use of soap and shampoo. I think deep down, the buxom, no-bullshit matron was a kindly old soul. Three or more pairs sometimes bathed in a tub before they were drained and fresh water run in. Such was my luck that during my three years in prep school, no matter how I timed it, I never once found myself in line for a 'freshy'.

For a non-pugnacious chap, I somehow found myself on the boxing squad. Our fights were usually much of a muchness, but two, one actually, I clearly remember. There was Fletcher—today I can describe him as Neanderthal—who was not only in a higher age division, but a strapping lad at that. On the evening of our competition, his opponent 'didn't feel well,' and our boxing coach seconded me. Fortunately I did not have to quake too long in my takkies. Thinking I would make him run around a bit, I ran into his long-armed right glove while the chime of the bell was still in my ears...and then there were stars in my eyes.

The other fight was against Jason, and we had become

reasonably good friends. He came up to me in the change room and put an arm around my shoulder. 'Listen Kappie, we're good friends and Jewish and all that; we shouldn't be bashing each other about. Why don't we just take it easy and sort of, you know, spar around a little? Okay?'

I was still trying to work out how one went about something like that, when it was our turn. No sooner had we touched gloves than he came at me like a thresher in full harvest, a whirl of arms and gloves and it took a while for the penny to drop, fortunately before I did. It was so explosive, that only in our third and final round did I manage to catch up and overtake his points. 'What's your case, hey Jace?' I asked, back in the change room and a look of bewilderment couldn't hide his embarrassment. 'C'mon man, I told you, we were just going to, you know, spar, didn't I?'

Geography was one of my favourites. Once a week we had a reading period, when we studied a set topic and the teacher got on with some of his work. Still fresh out of Colesberg, I put up my hand. 'Yes, Kaplan?' (You-again tone). 'What does in-di-genious mean, Sir?' The entire class guffawed and I realised I had asked a silly question. To save face, I further buried myself. 'Does it mean easily digestible, Sir?' Louder guffaws. (I still blush).

At 'cheder' classes, studying for my bar mitzvah, for some inexplicable reason, I one day asked our old Rabbi whether it was true that putting an apple in a suckling pig's mouth made it kosher? (No wonder my father sometimes called me a peasant.) I had been his star pupil: polite, diligent, helpful and 'a voice like an angel' (his assessment). As in Snakes and Ladders, that question dropped me to the bottom rung, plus penalties with his ruler, fortunately, only a twelve-incher.

Grahamstown had a warm and hospitable Jewish community, who would have us (school kids) for the festival meals or breaking of the fast. I recall one occasion, when, for some reason or other, everyone thought I had been invited—the equivalent of too many fielders calling 'leave it to me!'—and

281

the drip dropped between the families. Finally, I was alone with the Rabbi. 'Nu, come, Dovid,' he said, 'you will break the fast with me,' and we walked across town to where the old man lived. His maid had set aside three hardboiled eggs, a few pieces of fried fish, bread and butter. The little house was clean and depressingly austere, and he was not a talkative man. After what I thought was a decent interval, plus the litany of pre and post prandial prayers only a Rabbi could intone, I thanked him, said goodnight and left.

The fickleness of youth. All I could think of, wending my long way back to school through the quiet streets, was the banquet of delights my fellow brethren were enjoying in the respective homes they had been invited. Looking back now, I remember that frugal meal, the candles, a handful of dark-framed family portraits and the old Rabbi, with more clarity than any of the other sumptuous dinners I've had.

Then came my bar mitzvah and I only learned the same morning, that my parents (Ann, who else!) had invited Mr and Mrs Slater. If that mortally embarrassed me, I was shattered when he was asked to make a speech at the reception. Poor man. Trapped amongst the fawning 'vibeleh' (wives/women) and plates of 'kichel' (sweet home made crackers), 'gehakte leber' (chopped liver), 'perogen' (tiny minced meat pies) and blintzes (cheese pancakes), what else could he have said? Most of those very kind attributes and predictions did not come true or rather, I didn't live up to them, but were enough for Ann to 'klayb' enough 'naches' to last her a 'hundret un tsvantsik yor'. (To receive pleasure from someone else's achievements, to last 120 years).

In senior school we learned to chant that old favourite: 'Latin is a language, as dead as dead can be, It killed the ancient Romans, and now it's killing me.' Two lies and a truth! In spite of my cursing and pilfering youth boding delinquency, I only cribbed once and as fate would have it, I couldn't have chosen a better day. I used to sit next to the class boffin in Latin and Mr Slater sprang a test on us one morning. I had not prepared, so I peeked at PD's paper, word-for-word. After class, some of the lesser boffins came to consult the oracle, and on his first and only venture into the underworld, Orpheus had chosen the one bloody day that PD came a cropper.

It worried me. No, it gnawed at me all day. That afternoon we had net-practice with Jack. (He still coached more senior rugby teams and often he would not have had time to change into his tracksuit. He must have been well into his sixties, when I remember the 1928 Springbok winger, having taken off his suit jacket, he would demonstrate how to run full-tilt, bend at the waist and scoop up the ball in one hand—without changing stride or pace.) At the end of our session, I finally plucked up the courage and went to tell him my sad story. He put his arm around my shoulder, told me that stress and peer-pressure can sometimes make us do strange things, and that he was sure I would never do it again. 'Now get going, Kappie, you don't want to miss the bell.'

There was a wonderful (if potentially fatal) incident with PD (Patrick Dorrington), who was also my chemistry partner. We were going to liberate oxygen from a potassium chlorate and manganese dioxide mixture, 'a nice, simple experiment,' Mr Peters, our science master added. PD went to fetch the relevant apparatus and set them up. I left him for a few seconds—his elbow on the bench, chin cupped in a studious palm, and gazing with scientific wonder through his bottle-end spectacles, at a Bunsen burner licking the bottom of the flask—when there was a deafening explosion.

Dust and smoke filled the air and as it began to clear, there stood PD, spitting out bits of glass and oxygen producing chemicals, his eyebrows and hairline singed, face blackened and his tie smouldering. Mr Peters bounded over, extinguished his tie and PD was rushed to the sanatorium, (where he made a rapid and complete recovery). Our teacher was flummoxed. 'I've never seen this in my thirty-five years of teaching,' the old chap kept mumbling, as he sifted through the debris like those aircraft-accident sleuths. Then he discovered the cause. Voila!

Instead of using a connecting glass tube, PD had used a glass rod.

Northern and Southern Rhodesian kids on their long train journey through Botswana, sometimes arrived with an assortment of small mammals, reptiles and birds, bought or bartered from children along the way.

In senior school, a chap called Brightman once arrived with a baby python, well over a metre long and almost as thick as a wrist; not bad for an infant. He kept 'Adolph' in a wooden box under his bed and for the first couple of weeks it somehow went undetected. Sunday evenings, after church, he fed it a white mouse, purchased at the pet shop on Saturday mornings, and we crowded around to watch this macabre dinner.

One night, the box was empty. Twenty-two boys leaping onto the central row of lockers caused enough commotion to bring the prefects from their study and after Brightman assured them it would cause no major harm, they called for a search. Adolph, coiled round a toilet base, got a ticket to a snake park, Brightman was gated for a month and the incident did for toilets what Hitchcock's 'Psycho' would one day do for showers.

Pre-puberty, I was lean as a thong, useless at ball games, but could hold my own in track events. In my first term, running in takkies against the under twelve champ—whose 'spikes' I thought were black takkies—I managed to pass him by a nose. The next year my pituitary gland decided to wake from its slumber one spring morning and make up for lost time. I became gangly, awkward and pimply. I remember Natie complaining about having to pay for new uniforms, raincoats, shoes, rugby boots or takkies almost every second term. Fortunately, I did not become a 'pituitary giant,' but I was like the cartoon duck, the clumsy one who fell over his own feet, and, I was immature and shy.

I managed to scrape together enough marks, in matric, to earn a study, which I shared with Mac, a fellow from Northern Rhodesia. Our matric dance was not far off. In spite of gallant attempts by well-meaning friends, all dates telephonically

284

organised for me, suddenly developed chronic ailments or had to visit dying grannies, when they met their prospective partner. Those introductory meetings took place on Sunday afternoons and I marvelled at the ease with which my sponsors introduced and tried to sell me, while chatting up the chicks. 'You look ridiculous in a cap, your head's too small, borrow a basher,' Mac, ever subtle, suggested. Even that did not turn me into a Maurice Chevalier, although I had picked up a little rhythm watching my brother during those fiery lessons.

Some of the blind dates, who turned me down, weren't 'Miss Proms,' exactly, but then I was no heartthrob either. At the last second, literally, a date was found. She really was a sweet, shy little lass, built like a sugar cube—and, Jewish...my old mum would have been so proud—whose name I sadly no longer remember, though the saying 'two left feet' springs to mind. Neither of us had had much bargaining power and we made a fine yin-yang pair; the only difference was the vast distance between our heads.

I had an angelic voice, until it crashed, in conjunction with my physique, and sang in the Methodist Church choir. On holiday once, I was putting some oomph into 'Onward Christian soldiers,' when Natie asked me what that was. 'Methodist hymns,' I proudly told him. 'Oi veyh!' he muttered, 'Those you can sing, kakker, but from your own you know kadoches' (nothing!).

It's (a) high time...

When his older son showed no interest in the hotel business, Natie levelled his sights on the younger, but he had long set his on medicine. In Standard 9, one of the chaps was giving us career titbits after lights out one night. 'Geez Kaplan, you gotto be a bloody genius to do medicine. Maybe you should rather do something simple like pharmacy!' There I had it, straight from the Oracle of Dormitories and changed my mind in two seconds. Who needed career counselling or professional guidance?

Syria and Egypt put their heads together and their gripes aside and formed the United Arab Republic on February 1st 1958—which my father thought 'could be a problem for Israel'—and I enrolled a week later to do 'simple pharmacy' at Rhodes. He was right but my erudite adviser was way off.

That year can be summed up by four 'V's: Volare, Vodka, Vertigo and Vacuity. It turned out to be a great year socially, but abysmal, if that is the strongest condemnation, academically. Having grown up in the hotel, other than the odd cigarette I pilfered from our shop or dry horse manure Koerie, Ziems and I tried to smoke in homemade reed pipes at the stables—I was a non-smoker, a non-drinker, had never voluntarily read a book and, uhm, so on...

'Volare' was all the rage and had everyone crooning. Getting ready to go to a varsity 'hop' or drinking spree—somewhere, a radio or turntable spilled that beautiful song into the quadrangles where it scampered up and down the walls and slid through our bedroom windows. Vodka was in vogue and parties ran out of mixers long before alcohol did. There were no such things as 24/7 cafés, which resulted in neat 'shorts' by the end of every jamboree, long before quick 'shots' became the in-thing. We swilled insane amounts of vodka for the pure joy of adult freedom (getting drunk) and vertigo released rollercoaster beds that persisted in slamming me against the wall or being bucked to the floor. Voluminous 'ejections' of Russia's only honest export ended up in the washbasin and all over the place. (And I had had the temerity to tell my brother he was 'naughty' for peeing into his!) It took us many months to learn that what went down too fast came up the same way, but near year's end, I'm glad to report, nothing had changed. I suffered blockbusting hangovers that now and again made death seem attractive.

Those were the days of curfews, when 'Slegs Blankes' were allowed on the streets after 9 p.m. and police vans sometimes did a bit of snooping. We were coming back from another Russian-blitzkrieg, raucous and totally out of control, when they picked up a bunch of comrades that had strayed from the pack and took them to the gulag for the night. It is ironic, to think, that had we been a little less rowdy, hooligans like us had free access to the streets after dark, while law-abiding citizens of Colour did not have the same rights.

I initially siphoned into a clique of half a dozen shy, nerdy kind of fellows from various departments, who seemed to socialise much easier after a few warm-up drinks. What a psychology textbook would refer to as 'getting a flying start'— although some of us found it hard to titrate, as we did in chemistry, the optimum point before crashing. Suddenly we were 'gantser knakkers' (big shots) blowing plumes of smoke through pursed lips, discussing 'the meaning of life' while stifling a cough. The closest I got to being an apothecary was the potent pineapple beer we brewed. With all that yeast— some lunatics added pure alcohol snitched from the chemistry lab—bottles regularly exploded like detonators.

Chemistry was our last Saturday class in the G.L.T. (Great Lecture Theatre), which supposedly ended at 11 a.m. The professor invariably overshot the mark, sometimes by up to fifteen minutes, which was akin to stealing time from the poor (revellers). The older 'repeats'—and there were some—decided we should all bring our alarm clocks the following Saturday and teach him a lesson. One went off a little early and the prof looked up and over his half-moon specs. 'Whoever was responsible will kindly leave my class.' Ditto when another went off a few seconds later and then all the clocks sprang to life at five past eleven. Before he could utter another word, everyone packed up and left and his lectures ended punctually a few minutes to eleven thereafter.

Through a (brush) stroke of luck, I met someone in the Fine Arts department, who introduced me to some wild and spontaneous parties, which further eased my slide to ruin. I got hooked on the smell of linseed oil, drying canvases and natural

287

turpentine, blending with joss-sticks and perfume worn by the 'arty' girls. They somehow seemed so much sassier and had plenty of 'chein'; the spark that sets some girls apart from others. The only academic up-side, was my baptism into literature—at the deep end, one could say—by one of them, who persuaded me to read her set works. I have never been a fast reader and made heavy weather of chaps like Kafka, Balzac and Faulkner, the few I recall. I found Louis L'Amour much simpler.

Porn magazines and blue movies lay on the distant horizon, and as adult and newly liberated as we thought we were, it was in essence still the age of innocence. To entice as many students as possible, our zoology prof advertised a Saturday morning lecture as: 'A film about rough black males mating with smooth white females.' A successful production of Othello had recently been staged by the English Dramatic Department and everyone was raring to come. (It was to demonstrate Mendel's laws of genetics; crossing coarse-furred black male rabbits with smooth-furred white females and their progeny.)

The G.L.T. was packed to capacity. Voyeurs came in droves from geology, law, accountancy, music, art, you name it, when halfway through the film one of the top rear doors opened, silhouetting two inebriated young men peering into the gloom. We had all been silenced by a woman in labour, the full-Monty, as they would have said today. Legs spread, knees up and feet in stirrups, with the baby about to crown, it must have taken the latecomers a moment or two to adjust to the dark. What was meant to be an awestruck whisper, came as a hoarse bark. 'Christ! That's a cunt!' The days of innocence, indeed.

From the bawdry to the tragic. My physics partner, who I'm sure had a touch of the Savant, was incredibly bright and could often mentally calculate lower logs faster than I could look them up. 'I d-don't know, I just c-can' was his reply to my silly question. Painfully shy, (he made me seem like an extrovert), covered with angry adolescent acne, brimful of low self-esteem and a stutter that did not help matters, he was a perfect foil for varsity jocks. I cannot remember his name, but his face, vividly. 'I-I'll do all the cuh-calculations if you d-do the experiments?' he tested the situation that first day we entered the lab and had to choose partners. 'I-I'm not v-very good with muh-my hands,' he added and the expectation of rejection showed in the small creases gathering around his eyes. During the few months we worked together, he began relaxing and a dry, self-deprecatory sense of humour came to the surface, which slowly allowed other pieces of wit and clever quips to slip out into the precise atmosphere of a physics prac. lab. We managed to coax him out a few evenings, where he seemed to enjoy himself, without sinking to our level.

Early one Saturday morning a few senior men collared him in his room, stripped and put him in an industrial laundry basket, carried it to a women's res, rang the bell and gallantly dashed off. That little prank must have played a large role in precipitating a 'nervous breakdown' and he was sent home, where, we later learned, he took his life. I don't know what method he chose, but his hands must have been good enough to put such a fine brain away.

Serving my time...

There was A Year in Tibet, A Year in Provence, and 1959 was A Year in Colesberg. 'You had your chance, now you come into the hotel,' Natie told me, furious at the money and time wasted at Rhodes. Even though I was far from being anywhere near a brain box, it nevertheless came as a shock to Ann and Miemie when I failed all four subjects. 'Dear Lord in heaven, what did you then do there?' Miemie wanted to know, and I saved her a stroke by not divulging. Ann shook her head, 'Not even one subject?' To which I honestly replied, 'No, ma'. Then she sadly tut-tutted until the shock wore off, but happy that I had now joined the family again.

That year I was fully blooded into reception, bars, Bottle Store and shop; handling customer and staff problems, sorting out inter-staff relationships as well as their many domestic and everyday difficulties. But as my aviary-enterprise had proven, I was not cut out for the business world and now, more than ever, wanted to do medicine. I had allowed Rhodes to spoil me. From the strict regimentation of boarding school, into the carefree headlong plummet into wonderland, I was much too immature for the reality of independence and had paid the price. All Rhodes unfortunately led to Home.

I wheedled, whinged and begged most of that year, and probably with enough emotional input from Ann and a few practical words from Miemie, the old man finally relented. There was a condition, and it only sharpened my resolve. If I failed first year, he had warned me, not looking at all happy, it was 'Oys nit mer' (No more!).

Better luck next time...

In nineteen-sixty—the year Harold Macmillan's 'Winds of Change' blew in Sharpeville—I enrolled at Stellenbosch University to do medicine.

Initiation at Rhodes had been a two-week lark that we were aware of, but did not really experience. Stellenbosch was something else. Fortunately, on the first introductory night a few of the 'ou manne,' salted seniors, were taken by this 'Boere-Jood's' repertoire of jokes and amusing anecdotes, something I had honed for more than a year in the pub. There are no rules in those rites of passage and it was a 'Catch 22' situation; punished for telling clean jokes and punished for telling lewd ones, but as the evening progressed, I was only penalised for clean ones, which made life much simpler.

Those chaps turned out to be my guardian angels during the hell-nights that were to follow. They mainly tried to minimise the hardcore attacks on body and mind—although there were occasions when a shark or two slipped through the nets—other times managing to terminate my sessions a bit earlier than most. Pulling pillowcases over our heads, our tormentors, screaming or commanding in high-pitched voices, remained anonymous, but the following year I recognised them and they were mostly the tyrants I had suspected. That they abused fellow students to such a degree, simply because they could, came as another jolt.

In the showers after those grillings, the physical abuse tattooed across some of the 'poephols' was frightening. (We were called, and had to refer to ourselves as 'arsehole' at all times during the initiation period). After one particularly hectic night, a huge chap—who, in the real world, could have taken on his tormentors three at a time and would later become a fine Springbok forward—had tears of frustration brimming in his eyes. 'If I only can get my hands on them, I'll kill the fucking bastards,' he said, trying to restore his Nugget-Blackened genitalia to befit a 'Slegs Blanke'; his body criss-crossed with angry red welts and older bruises. Another fellow, who would be a fine Springbok scrumhalf, had the same sentiments.

My only confrontation with anti-Semitism at Stellenbosch was sudden and unexpected. A couple of us were chatting in someone's room, as we often did, and the conversation turned to greed. A fellow I had considered a good friend, began steering it to Jews, and I thought he was having me on. The uncomfortable looks and body language of the others made me realise this was no joke. There was a ray of light when he discovered his gaff. Genuine regret, endless apologising and repeated attempts, for many weeks, to make amends. 'That's what we heard at home!' he said, sadly shaking his head, shattered by the myth that 'you could recognise them anywhere'. Whether or not his Teutonic surname had any bearing on it, I cannot say, but like aids or syphilis—or the common cold, for that matter—anti-Semitism and racism have no bounds and often appear from unsuspecting quarters. We always dine out on the lame old cliché, and one he also used: 'But you're, different!'

It would also be at Stellenbosch that I learned we cannot

always blame our parents, our home or upbringing. My roommate in our second year came from a staunch Nationalistic home—'Blerrie verkrampt (narrow-minded and bigoted), and an even more opregte Boereskool'—his words. This lad was more universal and uncluttered in his considerations and deeds, than many supposed 'liberals' I would later meet, and taught me a thing or two about cross-colour behaviour and relationships. 'Only the good die young,' my mother said whenever she heard of a tragic death or read the obits. A year later, all those incredible sentiments and 'ubuntu' were erased, at a poorly signposted level crossing.

On a lighter note. There was a gentleman's agreement that university students could only sit in the gallery of the Plaza Cinema and did not mingle with the staid burghers in the stalls. We were watching a Western one night, where the hero and heroine are madly in love but her stepfather, the obnoxious, blue-stubble-beard-baddy, thwarts their ardour at every opportunity. Finally the big showdown: 'Bluebeard' and his henchmen take on the town. Baddies pitch from rooftops, Bluebeard takes a bullet and the heroine escapes across the dusty street. One can hear and sense sighs of relief in the gallery, but, alas, the baddy squeezes off a dying shot, meant for the hero, which strikes her and she slumps back, dead in her lover's embrace. In the stunned silence, a voice thunders from the balcony: 'Bonk her while she's warm!' Not in good taste, but how crisply it lifted the gloom that could have hung about our shoulders for the next few days. (That anecdote might help explain the reason for the gentlemen's agreement.)

At Medical School, there was a brilliant Gynaecologist, who was fiery and short on humour and that old stickler, bedside-manner. Our group was learning how to interrogate gynaecological patients and this woman seemed to be complaining about everything but 'female problems'. Things were not looking good. He glanced up from her folder:

'Tell me, Mrs X,' he asked in a cynically controlled voice, 'do you get a pain in your neck when you pee?'

292

'Yes Doctor!' she said, in a tone indicating he had struck the very root of or her ailment.

'Sister!' he shouted, 'Get this woman out of here before I strangle her!'

We had an elderly Orthopaedic Surgeon, who had retained his braw Scottish brogue. Stellenbosch University had only opened a medical school in 1963, and he was invited as a part-time consultant. Our fifth year tutorial group was standing in a decorous semicircle behind his chair, while he was interrogating a large Tannie, with back problems. Finally, he wrote out his prescription, handed it to the Sister and advised the woman: 'Mefrow, you moet krai 'n stywe matroos'. The patient nearly fell off her chair and we had a hard time keeping a straight face. Instead of telling her she needed a firm mattress, he had told her to get a stiff sailor.

Little time, for play...

I did a six-month house job at the old Woodstock Hospital in Cape Town, where we were only two housemen, working alternate nights and weekends and having to cover all departments. We learned discipline, as well as having to 'watch all the pots without any boiling over,' as a feisty old medical officer put it to me in casualty one night.

He was brimful of Irish blood. Burn wounds were common, and the number of patients dusted or smeared with a variety of spices, condiments and other household ingredients, was legion. When a particularly badly burnt toddler came in one night, covered in Currie powder—one of the favourites—he blew his top. 'Jesus Christ!' he bellowed at the bewildered parents, 'Why the hell didn't you add a little vinegar and masala, you could have marinated him at the same time!'

A fisherman, who had been badly flensed at a night club, was drunk and obnoxious as I did some 'cosmetic' sutures, which a young 'plastics' registrar had taught me at Karl Bremer Hospital. (They were not meant for this type of case.) As I was cleaning up afterwards, he sat hunched over, maudlin sobbing replacing his aggression. The nurse told me he wanted to give me a present and when I got to him, he held out a fist and dropped something into my hand. We get used to many strange things, but it took some nifty juggling before I finally held the catch, a little squeamishly, and insisted he put his glass eye back where it belonged.

My next six months of general medicine at Livingston Hospital in Port Elizabeth, taught us how to handle most emergencies in our field, through sheer numbers. Our registrars were often too busy themselves or simply left all initial treatment and clerking to us.

There are good memories of those times and dark ones. The Medical Superintendent summoned me to his office one day. 'I think I should warn you, you're playing with fire.' I was shocked, thinking he might be intimating malpractice or some other sinister shenanigans and my look of concern prompted him. 'It has been brought to my notice that you are fraternising with non-white staff.' We did socialise over weekends, especially amongst the Black, Coloured and White doctors.

Although we grew up with apartheid, it was only at the Livingston that I was reminded even Chinese were classified 'non-white'. During quiet spells on weekend call, my registrar and I would sit and chat somewhere secluded in the hospital or in the housemen's quarters. She was pretty and bright and too principled and reserved to scuffle with a houseman, but some Good Samaritan must have snitched on us. The moral of that episode was that Black, Coloured and Chinese were good enough to teach us, good enough to work with us, but not good enough to socialise with us.

As new housemen, we were introduced to Luckie's, a Chinese restaurant in the Coloured Township near the hospital. When a group of us went there for our first meal, which turned out to be a banquet, it made me think of old Bert Goodall, from Port Elizabeth, a commercial traveller for motor spares and accessories, who had many years earlier told us about this well

294

known Chinese restaurant in P.E. A born raconteur, he occasionally referred to the large Chinese community and the incredible food they made, describing with great enthusiasm the volume and variety five Rand could get you. None of us had ever seen a Chinese person, let alone eaten Chinese food, and to me it conjured a kind of mystery and romance.

Returning home after a trip, so another of his anecdotes went, he came across a car outside Middelburg (Cape), bonnet up and a man leaning over the engine. It was a Chinese couple with an elderly father and when Bert offered assistance and told them he was heading for the windy city, they graciously accepted a lift for the old man.

Entering the city, he proudly announced that he had improved on his best time by five minutes. The man told him they had better spend the next half hour very carefully, as those five minutes had put them in 'borrowed time'. We were all very impressed, but on reflection, there might have been the whiff of an oriental 'time-warp,' lightly stir-fried in yellow bean sauce.

Time (and surgeons) works wonders...

I had wanted to be a GP, like my mentor, Bill Cooper. Unfortunately, my first twelve-month contract, that I managed to reduce to six—with a great deal of animosity and aspersions regarding my integrity—was in a one-man practice in the city. I need not go into details, but it was so blatantly alien to what I had witnessed and formulated as good general practice, that it put me off, completely.

Disillusioned, I applied for a medical registrar's post at Groote Schuur Hospital (G.S.H.). If I could not be a GP, then I would be a physician. I enrolled January 1968, a month after Professor Chris Barnard exchanged Denise Darvall's vibrant young heart for Louis Washkansky's ailing one, making world headlines and becoming an international celebrity.

Foreign registrars and consultants applied for posts or

popped in for informal visits, while reporters, photographers and visitors swarmed around the place. On call, I was going up to see a patient on the sixth floor late one Saturday afternoon, when Prof. Barnard and Peter Sellers stepped into the lift as the doors were closing. He greeted me, but didn't introduce Mr Sellers, who looked a little preoccupied. It might have been a 'low key' professional visit, as the actor was known to have had cardiac disease, and died in 1980, only 54-years-old, from a heart attack. A healthy mix of strange languages and accents, sometimes difficult to interpret, filled the wards. Outwardly, the old hospital on the hill gazed unperturbed across the Cape Flats towards the Hottentots Holland range, as though it was just another day in the surgical suites, and blissfully unaware of the celebrity manning them.

There were many brilliant and highly thought of lecturers and professors at 'Grooties,' as the old hospital was fondly known. I was fortunate to have had both Prof. John Brock and Prof. Frank 'Frankie' Foreman, possibly two of the most brilliant minds at the time. 'Frankie' was extremely modest and polite. He never entered or left a ward until he had proffered everyone through, down to the last medical student. It could be awkward at times: 'After you...,' 'No, you, Sir...,' 'I insist...' and so on, his physician's palm, a fine-tuned detector, not budging until we embarrassedly slunk through innumerable corridors and doorways, the Prof. always bringing up the rear.

In my two years as a Med. Reg., I had the dubious privilege of being 'on intake' (call) on two occasions, when senior staff member's wives were brought in; O.D. One was a cardiologist's wife, and Prof. Barnard unexpectedly stepped in behind the curtains, in casualty—to see how she was doing, in solidarity to his colleague—as the senior registrar on duty with me was trying to pass a gastric tube (stomach pump). The patient had been resisting, and at that moment I put protocol aside, squeezed her nostrils, she opened her mouth and he got it down, possibly remembering my caster oil incident with Ann.

The Prof. didn't stay long, as we flushed out the goodies, but

296

seemed satisfied with her condition and our administrations.

During my six-month stint in cardiology, it was interesting to watch the subtle and sometimes not so subtle interplay between the cardiologists, led by the diffident, slightly bashful Professor Val Schrire, a stethoscope casually dangling around his neck, and the cardiothoracic surgeons, with the gallant, boyish Prof. Barnard brandishing his scalpel at the helm. There was plenty of good-natured ribbing. The former saw the latter as 'showmen' or 'prima donnas,' while the latter viewed the others as 'a bunch of staid old faahts,' a playful remark Barnard once made on one of his impromptu visits to our dour cardiac clinic meetings. He would sometimes pop in, unannounced, in a swirl of restless energy and vitality that temporarily lit up the show. 'Wen aah you boys going to get us another case (recipient)?' he would ask, an elbow irreverently propped on a bookcase crammed with hefty textbooks and journals. Prof. Schrire and 'his bundle' of cardiologists would humour him, as one did an overeager schoolboy, while Barnard almost goaded them for not coming up with more recipients, itching for another 'traahnsplaahnt,' while constantly flashing that disarming toothy smile.

Almost to a month later, Dr Philip Blaaiberg became the second recipient.

The Grand Ward Round, ('a bloody circus,' as someone referred to it) went on tour, when the entire cardiothoracic and cardiology departments reviewed medical as well as pre, peri- and post-cardiac surgical cases. Professors, consultants, registrars, housemen and students; matrons, sisters, nurses, ward secretaries and a 'flutter' of foreign medicos—an endless white-coated entourage—systematically wound its way through wards and corridors. Sometimes the head of this medical snake would be leaving a ward, while the tail was still slithering in.

The Prof. was meticulous and a perfectionist who expected no less from his staff than what he himself put in. On one of those 'circuses,' some time later, he flung the endless ribbon of E.C.G. tracings at one of his registrars. 'How do you expect me

297

to operate on this bloody flabby haaht?' he asked, and stomped out of the ward. Someone had overlooked or failed to delve into the patient's 'ethanolic' habits! (Ethanol or Ethyl Alcohol: C2H5Oh, is the chemical name for alcohol, which sounds better in a patient's folder.)

Some months later, I was working with the Renal Unit, where our duties included dialysing patients in renal failure. Those old machines, 'as big and complicated as Boeings,' as a fellow registrar described them, took ages to set up. On call one night, I was summoned in the early morning hours to the surgical intensive care where a 'dilemma' had occurred with a renal transplant patient and I was a little apprehensive about possibly having to dialyse her.

Prof. Barnard had done his first kidney transplant in October of '67 (on Edith Black), and although others, like Dr John Ackerman were now doing them, he still retained a keen interest. But it was pure chance, on this occasion—he paced the wards and corridors at any odd hour—that we arrived at the unit almost simultaneously. The room bristled with equipment, monitors flashing and beeping, tubes and drains, and the night Matron already there, when the King and I entered. He had jokingly raised his eyebrows, 'You or me,' but went straight to her bedside when he heard the problem. The patient was a bright bubbly young teacher, and even a layman could tell at a glance, that this was no medical or surgical emergency. In spite of her condition, she was livid. 'I refuse to drink my urine! Call the doctor!' she had screamed at the duty nurse.

Post transplant patients were put on strict fluid intake and output charts, which had to be followed to a 'T'. Her daily allowance had read: 'X cc of water, plus half the previous day's renal output.' The nurse had unfortunately followed these instructions to a 'P'. Amongst the battery of tests potential transplant patients were put through, a thorough psychological (and IQ) assessment was mandatory...for this very reason. He was furious when he heard the cause of this furore, and after giving the patient some calming words and restoring her faith in

298

medical care, he told the Matron to get a proper nurse. 'How the bloody yal did that goon get in here?'

We had some entertainingly quirky and moderately eccentric professors and consultants gracing the wards. One of my senior consultants in the General Medical wards did not take fools lightly. Serious, precise and an inveterate pipe smoker, he had a droll sense of humour. He listened attentively as I briefed him on patients to be seen on the round one morning, while sucking on his briar. As we entered the ward, he ritually shoved it into the breast pocket of his white coat, but on this occasion, a cloud of smoke started spiralling halfway through the round. In an instant, the sister doused it with a patient's drinking cup and while it might have extinguished the fire, it lit his short fuse. He gave her a verbal belting for being 'much too bloomin' precipitous!'

An elderly female patient with a chronic—rather than a life threatening—disorder, had more than once blurted on this consultant's rounds, 'I'm dying, doctor, I know I'm dying!' One morning, sitting up in bed and watching his approach, she did it again. 'So die!' he boomed, 'I want you to die, now!' The ward, normally silent during rounds, was deathly still and the patient looked at him, flabbergasted.

'So? Die now,' he said less fiercely.

'What do you mean, doctor?' she stuttered, looking to the other patients for help, 'I, I can't just, die?'

'That's what I've been trying to tell you!' he snapped, moving on to the next bed. She was discharged a week later, much improved, but mortally embarrassed.

There was a senior registrar—who is probably an 'eccentric' consultant today—who brought his dog along when doing his Sunday morning rounds. The hound was intelligent and well-behaved and about the only thing it couldn't do, was diagnose. But it brought smiles and cheer to many patients, which was often more than we managed to achieve. With subsequent discoveries of both the therapeutic and calming effects dolphins, dogs, Rhesus monkeys and other animals can have on humans, generally, and those with psychological / mental disorders, specifically, I am sure he inadvertently brought more soothing and consolation—plus bucking up their immune systems—than he was aware of.

I had a junior consultant, a very bright and promising young fellow, who everyone said was going to go far. He told his wife he was going to a congress in Johannesburg, but unfortunately, he didn't go far enough. Unaware of a low parapet in the small seaside hotel, where he was spending a 'cosy weekend,' he ended up in hospital with a broken leg. I imagine the moral of that little snippet, must be, make sure you have a fall-proof alibi, when going out on a limb.

Approaching the end of my second year medical registrar-ship, it dawned on me I was not seeing much of my young family. More important, I still had not learned that subtle art of being empathetic, without becoming too involved with patients and their families. I often tried to nap on a spare gurney in casualty, surrounded by the moaning, mumbling or the moribund, instead of going to the doctor's bungalow if there was a lull during 'call'. I was letting off steam to a colleague in the X-Ray department, while waiting for a patient to be x-rayed one night, when he suggested: 'Why not radiology?'

The following year, 1970, three other young medics and I enrolled as junior registrars and I was sent to the 'neuro' block. The Prof. of neuroradiology was on sabbatical, and one of the senior registrars, standing in for him, very smartly brought me up to prick, as they needed extra hands to do arteriography and AEGs; (air encephalography). There were times, during those first weeks, that I felt like a chimp who has learned new tricks, but still has to come to grips with the 'science' behind them. Most of those rather tricky and potentially dangerous 'direct' arterial punctures and AEGs—'invasive,' and, we had to wait for the radiographers to develop each set of films, before we could carry on with the rest of the examination—are now obsolete; replaced by speedy CAT scans and 'textbook clear' MRI. studies.

I was doing an A.E.G. on a patient that both the neurologists and cardiologists had an interest in. The young woman had had TB meningitis as a child and now, possible TB of the pericardium, the sac that surrounds the heart. I was unaware that Prof. Barnard also had an interest in her. (After his stint as a GP, he returned to G.S.H., and, long before he became a 'cutter-and-planter,' he had received a Doctorate in the treatment of tuberculous meningitis, in 1953.) I was a little surprised but bloody terrified when he and one of his registrars popped in during the examination. Fortunately, it all went well and he was pleased with the results. Before they left, he asked 'Ah you related to the Kaplans who owned the Royal Hotel' (in Beaufort West)? I told him no, but my mother and uncles grew up there. He didn't know them—they had left Beaufort while he was still wearing a kortbroek (short pants)—but seemed quite chuffed with the connection. (Could it have been a subtle hint that that was the direction I should have taken?)

One of our senior consultants was a loveable character who had served in the medical core in North Africa. He could tell a fine story and during my eight years in the X-Ray department, he captivated us with some wonderful yarns. His radiological knowledge was legion and heads of all departments came for his advice.

We had a young consultant, who was hoping to emigrate to Australia, and needed a letter to one of the hospitals. He was a pleasant fellow and competent radiologist, but, a little, how shall I put it, labour-compromised?

'I was at wit's end what to say and not spoil his chances,' the consultant told us and after wracking his brain overnight, he included the young man's strong points, ending with 'Any department who can get Dr X to work for them, can consider themselves extremely fortunate.' He looked up at us with his disarming grin, 'Well...I wasn't lying, was I?'

The professor of radiology was doing a barium meal on a farm labourer from Paarl one day. That was before the era of hi-tech T.V. monitors, and screening rooms had to be in almost

301

total darkness. Patients had to be undressed and gowned and the Prof. noticed that the man still had his trousers on. He instructed the patient: 'Trek af jou broek'. The fellow didn't respond, so he repeated the instruction. Still no response. In a loud, irritable voice, he asked the man if he was deaf? 'Oh! Noo, doctor,' came his laconic reply, 'I thought doctor was talking to the nurse' (radiographer).

More Modern Times...

By 1978, I realised that even a Junior Consultant's bonus was battling to keep up with the bourgeoisie; I was the only one in our group of friends who was not self-employed. By word of mouth, I got an assistant's post with a well established one-man firm in Cape Town. The radiologist had a thriving practice in the city, with a small satellite set of rooms in Sea Point, and a barely thriving practice in Goodwood, with other satellite rooms in Athlone. I was to run the latter two, but first I had to do a six-week probation test with the old chap, 'to get rid of all those bloody bad habits they teach you in hospitals and show you how a good practice should be maintained'. 'The Chief,' as the girls (typists and radiographers) referred to him, was much larger than life in all sense of the phrase. Tall, strapping, assertive, outgoing and, 'I take no shit,' he told me, with his unblinking stare. He had a fiery temper and his language, in vintner's blurb, was sharply colloquial, with a hit of chilli and Cape spice. He served it to anyone who crossed him or 'crapped up'. Written contracts were superfluous, his word was his honour. New staff either left within the hour or stayed for years and his 'girls' were loyal and loving and knew how to handle 'the old tiger's' cursing. 'Don't worry, it's all hot air,' they tried to ease my fears those first few days.

Shortly after I began my test run, there was one hell of a commotion one morning. An acquaintance of his had been referred for a Barium Meal, which the patient had not been keen on having. Afterwards, when he had been given the bill and a

302

negative report, he came storming to the reporting area, yelling how much he had paid for something he didn't want or need 'and a negative report!'. I thought the chief was going to belt him, but looming over the patient, he bellowed even louder, 'Would your fucking money have been better spent if I told you that you had bloody cancer of the stomach?' The furore was instantly silenced, the waiting room began to twitter again, and the penitent patient returned next morning to apologise.

'You go and speak to every patient, and I mean, every patient, and examine any injuries, no matter how small. A lot of GPs are too busy and sometimes give you any old crap for history!' He was adamant about good film quality. 'Don't be stingy with films like some of my colleagues. You can only give a proper report on a decent X-ray!' My only truck with him was the fact of his lengthy and extremely detailed reports, which often ran well into two or three pages, as he commented on both the positive and negative findings. 'Every chest, or lumbar spine or even a fucking pinkie, has a set routine. Stick to that and you won't crap up!'

We got on well and the old chap seemed to like me. He came in one Monday morning, limping more than usual. He had bad osteoarthritis of the hips. 'Ah, nothing much,' he said, when I asked him if something had triggered it. He told me they got back to their car, which he had parked near the old Colosseum cinema, Saturday night, to find someone in a Fiat had parked them in. To summarise, rather than give it verbatim, he got so terribly cross, that he darn well began angrily rocking the encroaching vehicle, until its silly old tail end was almost at a jolly right angle to the blinking kerb. 'I would have had the fucker in the middle of St Georges (street) if my wife and the couple with us didn't stop me!'

Satisfied with my work, I went to run his Goodwood practice, which I bought some years later. I stuck to all his 'principles,' but as the practice grew, I began shortening the reports. One soon learned that clinicians and GPs weren't interested in negative findings—unless they may have been part of a 'differential diagnosis'—and mainly wanted the nitty-gritty.

Many years before, I had met an Italian stonemason, Signor Lorenzi, and it turned into a warm friendship. I would regularly visit him and his wife, in their old rambling house in Woodstock, where rabbits, doves and chickens went about their business amongst the massive granite and sandstone sculptures the ninety-year-old had carved in his spare time. Short and sturdy and even at that age, he was unbelievably strong. I asked him once how he moved those massive stones. 'Dottore, all stone have his walking spot, you yoos have-ah to help him, a leetle!' (I cannot explain it more scientifically than that.) On some of my visits, I would sit with him in his kitchen, over a carafe of wine and home-cured olives, or under the overhang of his shed, where his forge and bellows stood. I enjoyed watching him anneal his chisels, or mine, which I sometimes brought, and our conversations would be punctuated by the old leather bellows, breathing life into the charcoal.

Over the years, he told me about his youth, growing up in extreme poverty on the outskirts of Caprino, a small town in the mountains of northern Italy; his father, grandfather and as far back as he could remember, working the marble quarries. One winter morning, cold and hungry, he got onto the kitchen table to cut a tiny piece of salami, and his mother reminded him it was Friday. That was when he decided he would remain a good Catholic, 'in here,' he said, pointing to his heart, but would no longer listen to those who look after the holy books, 'with the full stomaco'.

He spoke bitterly about how poorly led, armed and fed they were, as soldiers in the First World War He once threatened a senior officer, in their small mountain camp, that if they didn't stop taking the best food for themselves, he would personally deal with him. At a station one day, a pregnant woman in the queue of refugees in front of him, was barred from getting onto the train by a soldier on the landing, who told her the train was full. The stonemason told her to get onto the first step and turn

304

sideways, then he gripped the handrails on either side and pressured his way up and into the carriage. 'I give-ah the man a punch, find ah seat for the woman and-ah look after her till she get off the train.'

He sketched the voyages, third class or deck passenger, as he worked his way to Sydney. He was one of the (two hundred and fifty Australian, Scottish and Italian) stonemasons who cut and trimmed the massive rocks for the piers of the Sydney Harbour Bridge. Foremen used to arrange competitions amongst their teams, hefty bets being laid on the outcome. 'Dottore, I not-ah lie, when I feenish the sekkond (side of the block), they still on the furst!' he would say, beaming a smile that crinkled his rugged face and lit up the room. The bridge would only open 19th March 1932, six years after work had begun, but he had 'collected a few pounds' and having heard, via the stone man's vine, that good money was to be made in South Africa, he decided to try his luck. In 1930, aboard the Themistocles, a Greek vessel almost as old as the Athenian statesman, he set sail for South Africa, reaching Durban on 27th December, and Cape Town five days later.

I have taken this detour to North Italy and halfway round the globe for two reasons. Although his name is carved into many of Cape Town's marble, granite or sandstone facades, untold tombstones and his sculptures, I would like him to be remembered for the man he was. For me, Signor Lorenzi was a fine example of mankind: humble and honest, warm, generous and talented, and used his tremendous power only for bettering the world around him.

Down the passage from my rooms in Goodwood, Theunis Stofberg had his physiotherapy suite and he would refer patients or occasionally pop in himself for rugger injuries. Locked and bent with severe backache one day, I took off a few moments to see him. As the hefty flank-captain ('Springboks' 1980-1984) tried to iron out those pesky knots along my spine, our conversation was rather one sided and my replies reminded me of my mason friend's bellows, as my breath left me in

305

prolonged wheezes. But, I walked out of Theunis' suite feeling very much better and well enough to knotlessly tie myself to the yoke again.

Shortly before his release from prison, Nelson Mandela was referred to the rooms. While two well-dressed men stood at the doors, I went in to greet him, shook his hand and asked the questions I would of any other patient, and quietly and politely, he answered them and thanked me, just like any other patient. I wished him well, realising that in the not too distant future he would never be 'just another patient' again, but like most of us, not quite realising to what heights he would ascend. Then he was escorted back to whence he had come.

Having amalgamated with a large firm of radiologists, I finally retired from private practice in 2002 and did locums in the UK until 2007. On my return to Cape Town, the old practice asked me to do the odd locums for them, but I was done with the Sturm und Drang of the private sector. 'Vot voz, voz!' as Mr Jackson, the Commercial Traveller, used to say, and I opted to do general reporting for the embattled 'Day Hospitals' instead. My small remuneration literally comes with the territory; they are spread across the vast, industrialised Cape Flats and look after the medical and social welfare of some of the poorest of the poor.

Chapter Twenty-seven
IN THE FULLNESS OF TIME...
A late visit to Ladismith

When my parents sold the hotel in 1964 and moved to Cape Town, they asked Miemie to come and stay with them but there was no way she would have survived in a Sea Point flat. Dolf and her father had passed on, the farm had been sold and so she bought a house in Ladismith. It had a large rambling garden stretching to the next road, with rows of fruit trees, a pale old white-fig and a few grape arbours. Depending on her needs, she planted potatoes or sweet potatoes, carrots, cabbage, onions and garlic or rambling vines that dotted the rich red soil with squash, pumpkin and sweet melon. Her poultry foraged in old flower or veggie beds by day and were coaxed and clucked into a large coop at night.

Once or twice a year she caught the old SAR passenger bus and we went to fetch her at the Cape Town station. Ever cautiously, she would come down the steps and then we hopped in to collect her small suitcase and a large assortment of packages, tins and jars that were awaited with great excitement. Preserved peach, orange or apricots; dried peaches or pears; a tin of homemade rusks and another of ginger biscuits, a packet of fresh almonds or walnuts and a small wheel of sweet-milk cheese from their local factory. While those items were either-ors, a fixture, was the old 'Royal Baking Powder' tin of freshly roasted and coarsely ground coffee beans, referred to as 'moerkoffie,' which left a thick residue at the bottom of the flannel bag, which was suspended in the coffeepot, by its wire rim.

We also used to visit her and later took our children, where they enjoyed playing in the garden or helping her gather chicken eggs. As she had done with us, so she introduced our kids from an early age to homemade bread and jam, mealie meal porridge or a braised lamb-neck bone to teethe on.

307

Her sister-in-law, Miems, came to live with her until she passed away a few years before Miemie. Like a fine Millet study, they would sit for hours under the pergola, straw hats casting dappled shadows about their shoulders, an enamel basin resting on their laps as they peeled, sliced or de-stoned fruit. They discussed the scandalous cost of staples these days, who was ill, births and deaths ('what a shame, he was still so young'), the best place to procure firewood, what to prepare for dinner and 'did iemand (someone) perchance buy candles?'

Their preserved green figs glowed in syrup; peach and grape jams were legendary, each berry was skinned, halved and de-pipped! Apricots, peeled Kakamas or Alberta peaches and occasionally pears were set out to dry on mesh racks. The heady scent of gardenia mingled with the foul sulphide preparation, aptly nicknamed 'poep' (fart), that was placed inside milk cans to deter weevils and other unwanted insects. It was a time when chores were love-intensive.

They rolled sheets of fig, peach or apricot 'tameletjie,' hung cuts of beef biltong to dry and rendered lard from the fat tails of Blackhead Persian sheep. These 'Swartkoppersie' were ideal for tough, dry conditions and because they have hair, could tolerate the heat far better than their woolly brethren. Momentarily forgetting about fatty acids and long and short chains, it still takes a lot to beat 'Persie' lard mixed with Golden Syrup and spread on a thick slice of home-baked bread. Roasted coffee beans, braised lamb and newly-baked rusks were part of the 'Koningstraat' redolence.

I would go with her to visit Tant Lena Crafford, a few houses up from Miemie, a good friend and distantly related by marriage. It was Lena's son, Stanley, who put the lights on Elandsberg, the mountain in front of Towerkop. 'I put my first wind-driven light up, 31st of May, 1963, on the peak of Elandsberg. I am telling you, climb wise, it's higher than Towerkop (also known as 'Toornkop'), but the strong North winds smashed everything to pieces.' Later he brought it halfway down, protected under a krantz, and those are water driven bicycle dynamos, mainly fed by snow-melt, which, he says, is getting less and less each year.

In my youth, I would go with Miemie to visit the other Craffords, who lived between Anysberg and Ladismith. The road ran past their quaint thatched old homes and barns at the base of a low hill, where enormous Oak and Wild Fig grew so dense and high on either side, the stretch of road was cool and gloomy on the hottest summer day. I remember their kids would climb into a tree on one side, where their thick bows interlaced, and came down a tree on the opposite side! The film, 'Green Mansions,' based on the 1904 book by William Henry Hudson, would one day remind me of those antics. When I took Ferdi on that trip a few years back, I nearly missed the spot. The remains of one or two mud-brick houses were slowly bleeding into the earth and there was not a tree in sight.

All those years, my siblings and I often pondered the Natie-Miemie relationship during their 'smousing' years. As it turned out, it would be on my last visit to Miemie, before ill health and frailty necessitated her being placed in a comfortable home, that I plucked up the courage. Frost lay thick on her bare winter garden and the two of us were sitting in the kitchen, clutching enamel mugs of coffee and dunking rusks. The little wood stove spluttered and hissed and breathed its pleasant warmth around our legs and I thought about popping the question.

Finally, there was a pause during our chat and then a thought suddenly struck me; how does one phrase such a question, to someone who could have been the Afrikaner equivalent of a Mother Theresa? More time passed and then I heard myself ask: 'Sê vir my Miemie, doorie jare toe jy en my pa so rondgery het, het julle ooit...?' and that was when she looked at me, steadfast, as ever, waiting for my question, 'was julle, ooit...intiem?' (Were you ever intimate?)

I felt instantly relieved but terribly disloyal. Sullied, might be more suitable, but the words were out and nothing could ever cancel them again. I suppose I might have been expecting something dramatic, life changing, like: 'Well, if you want to know, Boris is really our child!' or, 'Actually, we put three children up for adoption,' but like a good poker player or as honest as they come, she never blinked or took her eyes off me.

'Nee wat,' she said and to my relief, in a rather matter-of-fact tone, 'hoe kon ons, hy was dan my baas?' She did not seem surprised and there was no groping for words. A simple: 'Not at all, how could we have, he was, after all, my boss?' That sealed it for me. It was the very essence, the ethos of Miemie de Wit.

She never believed in slippers and next morning it was business as usual when I heard her clomping down the linoleum passage in her utility shoes, warmly wrapped in her winter 'goan'. She came into my room and put the mug of coffee and a few rusks on my bedside table. 'Here is your coffee, my child,' and when she got to the door, 'Put your jacket and a jersey on, it's devilish cold this morning.'

Chapter Twenty-eight
MERCY FLIGHT
Cape Town…and the closing of time

'Coffee?' I must have dozed a few seconds and the tail end of a dream merged with the male nurse's offer. I nodded and he handed me a paper cup poured from his thermos.

'We better have it now,' the pilot said over his shoulder, twin horizons flashing off his Raybans, which must have seen many sky-miles and acute cases, 'We'll soon hit the Hexrivier range and funny things can happen.'

Fortunately, we didn't hit the mountains, but funny things did happen, although they were far from funny. Pilots speak endearingly of their 'kites' and this mercy flight had taught me why. Massive cumulous clouds were stacked overhead, foamy and passive, but those thermals that raise them there, and not to mention crosswinds, were anything but. The plane slid and shuddered or dropped and levitated like a plastic packet on a breeze.

My father became restless and for a moment or two I thought he would come out of his slumber, but on the physician's instructions, Dok Dupie had given him a splendid cocktail. There was more turbulence as we seemed to rollercoaster across ominous dark shadows filling kloofs and highlighting sunlit craggy peaks, then we were over the mountains, with fertile valleys spreading to the distance.

Sleep-deprived and jittery, we landed at Ysterplaat, where a waiting ambulance whisked us off to the Volk's Hospital. There were no CT, MRI or Doppler scans in those days but the consensus was that it might have been severe spasm or a partial blockage of one of my father's carotid arteries. Starched nurses fussed around him as he lay heavily sedated, while further tests were carried out.

He did not speak for two or three days after he came round and the team called in a psychiatrist. Long before cell phones,

311

this man suffered from, or rather, exulted in what is known as SMS, small-man-syndrome.

Cocky, self-assured and opinionated, he briskly quizzed my mother and me for family details and dates to interrogate my father and check lucidity.

I will never forget the morning we all trailed into the private ward, three of my medical lecturers, the ward sister, my mother and I, and the psychiatrist, centre stage at the foot end of the bed. Each question, intoned with practical professionalism and a hint of boredom, produced no answer. He tried dates, places, family names, even pointing to my mother and me, wanting to know who we were. Stony silence.

Finally he made his way to my father's side and took his hand. 'Tell me, Mr Kaplan,' he asked, 'Do you know who I am?'

After some seconds, my father licked his dry lips and we all strained forward: 'Yes,' he huskily replied. There was a murmur of surprise and, much encouraged, the psychiatrist now took my father's hand in both of his.

Turning to his audience with a knowing smile but addressing my father, he asked, 'And, do you know what I am, Mr Kaplan?'

Natie let the question hang for a decent moment or two: 'You're a poephol!' he said without malice, but I sensed a hint of satisfaction in his tone. Titters ran around the room, as court reporters used to say, and I was terribly embarrassed, but my three mentors found it hilarious and it soon did the medical rounds.

My father never quite fully recovered, but was well enough for him and my mother to move into a flat. Soon there would follow a relay of day and night nurses, until he became too ill to manage at home and we placed him in Highlands House, where he died of Parkinson's slow complications and pneumonia.

No one would have recognised the shrunken, wizened man as the once robust publican, who enjoyed his weekly flutter on the fillies, a drink or two with friends and occasionally airing

312

the Anniversary Waltz, as he had seen the Great Caruso do. And who, when the smoke yellowed bar clock registered ten pm: would step to his post and announce in the sternest tone he could muster: 'Time! Gentlemen, time.'

Epilogue
86 Temple Fortune Lane, London. February 2007.

The rattling of the latch brought me from my reverie. 'They're home!' the little artist enlightened me and began stacking her busy output as they trooped in, pink-cheeked, proudly dishevelled and accompanied by an invigorating gust of heath and damp anoraks.

'Where's Mom and Ferdi?' she asked. 'I think they are getting milk or something,' her brother Aaron said shrugging off his coat. 'I fell off my motorbike three times!' the younger Jordan called from the door, while Jonathan, my son-in-law, tried to dislodge him from muddy galoshes. 'Come see what I drew, Dad,' Mia coaxed and they came to view her sketches.

My wife and daughter returned with a few groceries and flowers. In the hubbub of milling kids, pancake batter being prepared and the table set, a *déja vu* reached me on the centrally-heated air. Freesias! The hybrids, flown in from any part of the world, are much more potent and I took the kids over to show them.

I gave each a chance to press their nose to the flowers and they accommodatingly 'Ooh-ed' and 'Aah-ed'. 'Grampa-them used to pick these when they were little,' Mia informed her brothers with a conspiratorial nod of having set a secret free. It did not have much effect, but when she added, 'They had competitions to see who could pick the most flowers...' they became a little more interested.

'And who would find the very, very first flower,' I added to the bait.

'What did you call them again, Grampa?' she asked. 'Aand-blomme,' I enunciated. Jordan wanted to commandeer the bunch my wife had put in a vase and the older two brought him to order with some firm reprimands.

'So Dad, are you going to write something about your Colesberg days and the family, sometime?' Gita asked, ladling

314